IMAGES
of America

YONKERS

On the Cover: The Yonkers downtown waterfront was visited by Henry Hudson on his first voyage of discovery in 1609. Trade and industry were centered around this prosperous confluence. Soon, buildings and businesses crowded the once agricultural acreage formerly dedicated to orchards and gardens. The cover photograph was taken of this industrialized waterfront around 1910. Few of these original buildings remain and the ones that do have been adaptively reused. The Yonkers Pier, the last remaining Victorian steel pier on the Hudson River, houses a gourmet restaurant on the second floor that was once used to board passengers onto huge dayliners that plied the Hudson from Manhattan to Albany. The Trolley Barn is now apartments, office space, and commercial storefronts. The Metro-North train line still carries passengers from upstate New York to Midtown Manhattan, much as it did when it was built in the 1850s. (Richard Moore.)

IMAGES
of America

YONKERS

Joan Jennings and Luis Perelman

ARCADIA
PUBLISHING

ISBN 978-0-7385-9789-8

Published by Arcadia Publishing
Charleston, South Carolina

Printed in the United States of America

Library of Congress Control Number: 2012942433

For all general information, please contact Arcadia Publishing:
Telephone 843-853-2070
Fax 843-853-0044
E-mail sales@arcadiapublishing.com
For customer service and orders:
Toll-Free 1-888-313-2665

Visit us on the Internet at www.arcadiapublishing.com

This book is dedicated to our families and friends and those wonderful citizens who strive to keep Yonkers history alive.

Contents

ACKNOWLEDGMENTS

The authors wish to acknowledge the Friends of Philipse Manor Hall, the Yonkers Historical Society, Blue Door Art Gallery, City of Yonkers Planning Department (Mario Caruso), the Yonkers Fire and Police Departments (especially Yonkers Police Department historian George Rutledge), Otis Elevator, the Hudson River Museum, Flynn Funeral Home, and Yonkers residents who contributed their personal images and support. Unless otherwise noted, all images in this book come from the Yonkers Historical Society (YHS), Friends of Philipse Manor Hall (FPMH), City of Yonkers Planning Department (COY Planning), Yonkers Fire Department Museum (YFD), Yonkers Police Department Museum (YPD), Hudson River Museum (HRM), Flynn Funeral Home (Flynn), and Blue Door Art Gallery (BD).

INTRODUCTION

Yonkers, a blue-collar industrial town located about 20 miles north of Midtown Manhattan, grew up around its waterfront along the historic Hudson River. Over the centuries, the waterfront has grown—from a bay that was filled in with stone from these palisades on the eastern shore, to a railroad bed, to an elevator and carpet industry, to upscale housing with dramatic views. Henry Hudson would not recognize the estuary where he dropped anchor over 400 years ago. Follow the story of the rivers and the downtown that grew up around them in the saga that is Yonkers, New York.

Henry Hudson, an English explorer working for the Dutch East India Company, in his ship the *Half Moon*, navigated and documented a large bay on September 11, 1609. After trading with the natives on Mannahatta, he continued his journey north in search of the Northwest Passage, which was to remain elusive for centuries. On September 13, according to the ship's log kept by Robert Jouet, Hudson dropped anchor in a small bay created by the confluence of the Shatemuc and Nepakamack Rivers in what was to become Yonkers.

Adriaen van der Donck, the first lawyer in the Dutch colony that followed, was given a patroonship just north of New Amsterdam. His book, *A Description of New Netherland*, chronicles the Dutch way of life, as well as native flora and fauna. Van der Donck built a sawmill here that gave a local river one of its two names—the Nepperhan (an old Indian appellation) and the Saw Mill River. Because of his efforts in brokering a peace treaty with the local native tribe, the Lenape, he was referred to as the "Jonkheer" (young gentleman), a name that was to become Yonkers.

After his death, the land was sold to an enterprising couple, Frederick Philipse and Margaret Hardenbroeck, who built their Manor Hall (around 1682) where the Saw Mill River ran into the Hudson, on a bay that was large enough for sloops to put in. Margaret, in the Dutch tradition, was considered a "she-merchant" who was an equal to a man in the marketplace or the courtroom. Through their industry, Frederick and Margaret built their fortunes to the extent that they became one of the wealthiest couples in the colony. They built their Manor House at the confluence of the Nepperhan and Hudson Rivers and their working farm (the "upper mills") in what was to become Tarrytown. Their fleet of ships sailed from the port of New Amsterdam, up the river north to New Orange, present-day Albany, for beaver pelts; to the Caribbean for sugar, rum, and slaves; and across the Atlantic to the Netherlands. As their ships returned from Europe, they carried linens, furniture, and other household goods for the settlers.

Their heir, Frederick Philipse III, donated money in 1753 for the construction of an Episcopal chapel, St. John's, for an existing congregation begun in 1693. "Freddy 3" had become enamored of the English lifestyle and he signed a so-called Declaration of Dependence pledging his loyalty to the British crown during the American Revolution. When the rebellious Americans won, the Philipse lands, by then comprising almost 52,000 acres, were confiscated by the new republic and the family was exiled to England. St. John's functioned as a hospital for wounded soldiers during the Revolution. Now a thriving parish, a grand new edifice, designed by famous architect Edward Tuckerman Potter, was built alongside the original chapel in 1858. Many contemporary architects consider St. John's the most interesting 19th-century church in the United States.

Philipse Manor Hall was sold by the new republic and an idealized painting of it called the *Stauffer View* was distributed to advertise it. Now in private hands, the hall passed through several private owners, including Judge Woodworth, after whom an adjacent street is named, before finally becoming Yonkers Village Hall in 1858. The Gothic Chamber was the site of municipal council meetings.

Given its ideal location on the Hudson River, the proximity to the bustling port of New York, and water and rail accessibility for trade and passengers, Yonkers began to thrive and grow. Inventions by Yonkers residents gave rise to manufacturing that employed residents; immigrants flocked there for work.

There were many firsts in Yonkers. One of its many creative inventors, Elisha Graves Otis, a machinist, was intrigued by the potential of the elevator. The elevator had existed in one form or another since the days of ancient Egypt, but Otis invented a locking cog device that prevented the cabin of the elevator from falling, thus inventing the first safety elevator. He dramatically demonstrated his invention at New York's Crystal Palace in 1854, theatrically severing the cable that held the carriage with a saber. Orders flowed in. His safety device allowed buildings to soar to new heights and led to the building of the first skyscrapers in New York City. Otis Elevator became so successful that it moved from its original location at the foot of Vark Street to a huge factory just north of the main train station. Rudolph Eickemeyer modified electric engines. His employee, the brilliant Charles Steinmetz, discovered a usable form of alternating current. Halcyon Skinner invented the Axminster and Moquette looms to make patterned carpeting in the Alexander Smith Carpet Mills. John Masefield, who would become poet laureate of the United Kingdom (1930–1967), actually worked in the carpet mills for two years and wrote *In the Mill* about his experiences there.

Leo Baekeland, working in a laboratory adjacent to his house on North Broadway, would invent Bakelite plastic. Charles Harvey developed an elevated train. And we listen to FM radio because of the pioneering work of Edwin Armstrong; the tower he built on the Palisades across from Yonkers still stands and is visible from most locations in Yonkers. Boyce Thompson worked with plant genetics, and he located the Boyce Thompson Institute in northwest Yonkers, close to his palatial mansion Alder Manor on North Broadway. The home has a second-story indoor pool with Tiffany windows, which were unfortunately vandalized. There are sweeping staircases and an idyllic garden with a gazebo that makes filmmakers drool. Many movies, like *A Beautiful Mind* and *Mona Lisa Smile*, were filmed there. The building functions as an Irish cultural center and is known as Tara Circle. An old German social club, Teutonia Hall, had an enormous ballroom; while its facade is being preserved, the building is being demolished to develop LEED-certified housing, with plans to have a hydroponic garden on its roof.

The train, whose tracks ran along the banks of the Hudson, would spur increased industry and commerce but was originally considered a risky business. Travel north and south along the Hudson was made by steamship, and competition for passengers was cutthroat. Engaged in a race with another steamship in 1852, the *Henry Clay* caught fire, killing scores of people including members of prominent families. When the steamship *Chrystenah* became fogbound in Yonkers in the 1860s, impatient passengers took to the train to get to New York City. They discovered it was a comfortable, safe, reliable form of transportation and never went back.

The original New York Central Railroad Station was built when the tracks were installed; a new, grander station, designed by Warren and Wetmore, the architects who designed Grand Central Station in New York City, opened in 1911. The station was totally renovated by Metro-North in 2004; it also serves as an Amtrak station.

The river and the ponds it created along its banks provided hydroelectric power used to power factories that made a material in high demand. No man was considered well-dressed unless he wore a hat; hats were made of felt. Yonkers felting factories provided that material, and hat manufacturing became a major industry.

Combined, Otis Elevator, the Alexander Smith Carpet Mills, and hat manufacturers like Waring would become the largest employers in Yonkers. Yonkers downtown's Getty Square (named for local mogul Robert Parkhill Getty) became a thriving shopping area for the residents. The abundance of work attracted the immigrants who were pouring into the United States from Europe. These new arrivals, primarily from Italy, Poland, Germany, the Ukraine, and Ireland, settled into distinct neighborhoods in Yonkers and built churches where they could worship in their native tongues: St. Casimir's (where Polish masses are still said), Mount Carmel (Italian), and the Ukrainian Orthodox churches in The Hollow are but a few examples of the many houses of worship begun by immigrants. New Irish citizens in America not only supported the building of a Roman Catholic church, but Irish carpenters and stoneworkers actually built St. Mary's/ Immaculate Conception themselves. Attached to these churches were parochial grammar and high schools. Reflecting the desire to make their children assets to the workforce, the Yonkers High School of Commerce was established. Yonkers was truly a melting pot.

In the late 19th century, Yonkers became a country haven for the very rich, who built enormous mansions overlooking the "lordly Hudson" and Palisades on its western banks. These granite pillars, some rising up to 300 feet above the river, gave millionaires an unparalleled view as the rising sun hit the rocks in the morning and set behind them in the evening. Staggered construction along Warburton Avenue and North Broadway optimized viewpoints. However, their very grandeur contributed to the homes' destruction. As the original wealthy owners died off or relocated, there were no new owners who were capable of supporting the structures and sumptuous surrounding grounds and gardens.

Many edifices burned; land was divided up and sold for apartments, development tracts, and shopping areas. A few, like Glenview Mansion, remained, and it became the original home of the Hudson River Museum. The magnificent castle-like home built by presidential candidate Tilden, later owned by Samuel Untermyer, was lost but its amazing gardens remained. Designed by Welles Bosworth, the gardens were modeled on a classic Persian design using high walls to create a sanctuary, entered through a large ornate gate. At the northern end were high columns topped by gryphons. A Greek-style temple has a center mosaic of Medusa, and stairs lead west to a now unfortunately deteriorated pool with mosaic sea life. The gardens were used for years as a free performance venue sponsored by the Untermyer Performing Arts Council (UPAC) and are currently being restored to their former splendor by the Untermyer Parks Conservancy.

A retail innovation built on the east side of Yonkers would spark a national trend but, in an ironic twist, would negatively impact Getty Square. Cross County Shopping Center is generally considered one of the first shopping malls in the United States. Postwar America had begun its love affair with the car, and prosperity allowed most Americans to own one. The appeal of driving to Cross County to shop was a powerful lure, and soon customers left the square to buy from large department stores like Gimbel's and Wanamaker's, located at each end of the mall. Built on a swamp, the center was originally level, but because of the porous nature of the ground beneath it, the parking areas sank significantly. Many Yonkers baby boomers can remember Adventurer's Inn on Central Avenue where Gimbel's was originally located, and many have scars from the mosquito bites inflicted by bugs living in the swampy water.

Yonkers's reputation was compromised in the 1970s when a desegregation lawsuit split both the residents and the court of public opinion. The suit resulted in civil fines that had a severe negative financial and public relations impact on Yonkers. The 1980s saw continued economic deterioration. Most of the remaining mansions along the Hudson were demolished for tract housing and developments. The projects, extensive housing complexes originally built for blue-collar workers, fell into disrepair and were hotbeds of crime and the drug trade.

At the dawn of the 21st century, Yonkers shook itself off and began to rebuild what had been its original core—the downtown waterfront, culminating in the daylighting of the Saw Mill River. In the late 19th century, the Saw Mill River was used as an open sewer and fears of cholera prompted the "Tearing Down the Dams" event in 1892 to get the water dammed for hydroelectric power to move more freely. In the 1920s, the United States Army Corps of Engineers covered the river with a concrete flume; for decades, many Yonkersites had no idea that a river ran through it, under the old Victorian-era buildings on New Main Street, North Broadway, and Manor House

Square. Covered by Larkin Park due east of the train station, the river's primary use was as a parking lot. Now a beautiful ecologically informed site, downtown Yonkers has come full circle to Van der Donck Park.

As Henry Hudson had looked from his ship the *Half Moon* on the river to what became Yonkers, Yonkers now looked to the river. The Beczak Environmental Education Center, the baby of self-proclaimed Hudson water rat Bob Walters, had its start in an old Quonset hut. Outgrowing the hut, Beczak moved a few hundred feet to the north and made the old Habirshaw social club its new headquarters. There is a stuffed sturgeon and an Indian war canoe on display, as well as numerous tanks containing creatures from the river, like blue crabs.

Groundwork Hudson Valley acquired an innovative solar-powered vessel, the Science Barge, and towed it from its original home in Brooklyn to the banks of the Hudson. Herbs, tomatoes, and other plants are raised on the barge, which is totally self-sustaining. Classes in this type of farming are held onboard.

With Philipse Manor Hall anchoring the area's history, these three locations create an ideal educational triangle where student tours to visit them all can be done on a short walk. Recently, another cultural tourist attraction added even more appeal for families and cultural tourists. An initiative inspired by remarks by then New York governor George Pataki, who said that his personal dream was to see the river again open to the air and sky, spurred interest in daylighting the river. Begun by the City of Yonkers Office of Downtown and Waterfront Development under the guidance of Jim Pinto and engineered by P&S, the project started taking shape in 2008. Ecological expertise was provided by Ann-Marie Mitroff and Rick Magder of Groundwork Hudson Valley. Two signature local species—the alewife and the American eel—will now be able to spawn and thrive, using an amazing fish ladder to help them climb up an incline at the western end of the river. Rough parts of the river called riffles were engineered to automatically aerate the flowing water. Netting chambers will catch debris and trash that would otherwise flow into the Hudson River. The park will be used to teach the public about the environment and Yonkers history particular to that area. There will be an American Eel Outdoor Classroom and camps and classes will be provided by visiting three nearby institutions: Beczak, the Science Barge, and Philipse Manor Hall. The adjacent Riverfront Library will bring children to the park for story hours. The project took a total of 10 years, and the ribbon-cutting to officially open the park took place in December 2012.

Yonkers today is truly of mixture of a revitalized waterfront, historic structures, and new construction, densely populated urban neighborhoods, ethnic enclaves for new immigrants, private homes, and spacious mansions, as the photographs in this book will illustrate.

One

Discovery

On September 11, 1609, Henry Hudson, an English explorer working for the Dutch East India Company, dropped anchor in the river he hoped would be the elusive route to the Orient, the fabled Northwest Passage. Ringed by stone Palisades, the bay was the outflow of the Neppakamack ("Nepperhan") River, whose source is in modern-day Chappaqua. The bay was deep enough for anchorage for small boats, a fact not lost on subsequent settlers. Prominent among them was Adriaen Van der Donck, whose 1646 land grant called the patroonship "Colen Donck" would extend through much of what is now modern Westchester County. He built mills on a waterfall that would give name to the feeder river—the Saw Mill River. Because of his efforts to trade with the peaceful resident Lenape Indians, he was called the "Jonkheer" (young gentleman), an appellation that would give Yonkers its name.

After his death, the lands were purchased by Dutch carpenter Frederick Philipse and his she-merchant wife, Margaret Hardenbroeck. Their trading empire extended from the Netherlands to the Caribbean, north from New Amsterdam to New Orange, present-day Albany. In 1682, they built their Manor Hall in Yonkers, which today is a New York State museum of history and art. Its rococo papier-mâché ceiling installed by Frederick Philipse III is one of three extant examples in the United States and is unique because it contains the likenesses of Sir Isaac Newton and Alexander Pope. "Freddy 3" sided with the English crown during the American Revolution, signing the Declaration of Dependence. When the Americans won the Revolution, the Philipse lands were forfeit and the family exiled to England. In 1784, the lands were advertised for sale in an early real estate advertisement painting now called the *Stauffer View*. The Manor Hall passed through private hands including ownership by Judge William Woodworth, after whom a street west of the Manor Hall is named, until becoming Yonkers Village Hall in 1868.

Growing prosperity created a larger population and Yonkers attained the status of a city in the 1880s. This prompted city fathers to built a new Yonkers City Hall. When the municipal offices moved, the now empty Manor Hall was scheduled for demolition. In 1910, through the efforts of philanthropist Eva Smith Cochran, who purchased it and subsequently donated it to remain a museum, Philipse Manor Hall still proudly stands on the corner of Warburton Avenue and Dock Street. The once vast Philipse holdings of 52,000 acres were now reduced to a small plot of land in a heavily urban setting.

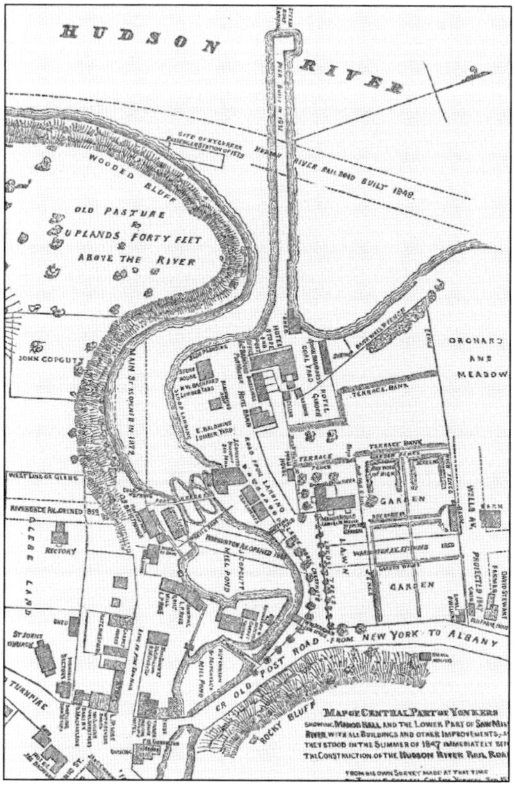

MAP OF YONKERS, 1847. This is a map of Yonkers showing the bay and south banks palisades. The proposed railroad would be built in 1849. These palisades provided the stone for the landfill that ultimately filled in the bay to facilitate the laying of the rail bed. The path of the Saw Mill River continued to be encroached upon by building, and in the early 1920s was covered over by a flume. (COY Planning.)

STAUFFER VIEW. This illustration was used as a real estate advertisement when the Manor Hall was confiscated by the new American republic after the Revolutionary War. This idealized view of the Manor Hall shows the mills and waterfalls. The perspective is from the bluffs whose stone was used to fill in the bay. (FPMH.)

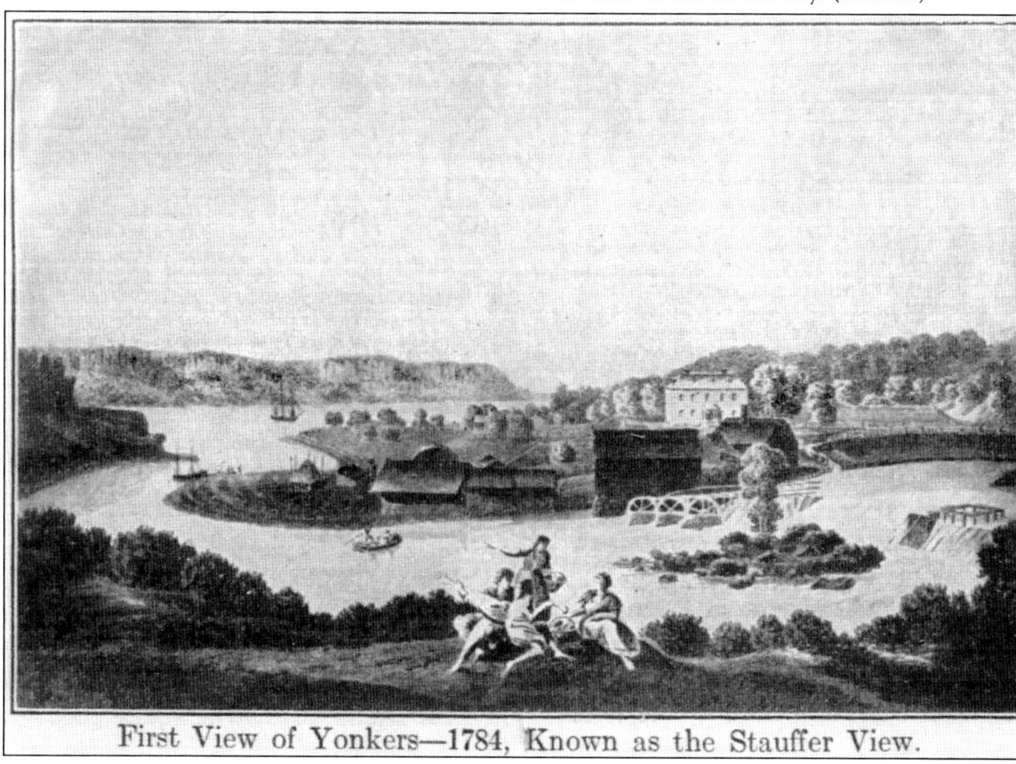

First View of Yonkers—1784, Known as the Stauffer View.

Two

The Dutch and the English

While the first European settlers in New Amsterdam and Yonkers were from the Netherlands, their ascendancy did not last very long. However, their traditions and influences did. When the Dutch surrendered to the British, their customs were already well ingrained. Prosperity was the primary motivator that informed early Dutch settlers and wealth was the yardstick by which one was measured. British colonization negated the equality women had enjoyed under the Dutch, which was not restored until the 20th century.

The Dutch architectural styles were ubiquitous in lower Manhattan, and examples of some classic Dutch design can still be seen in Yonkers. However, Philipse Manor Hall, did not reflect the Dutch influence. Wealthy scion Frederick Philipse III became enamored of all things English and, in 1750, installed a rococo papier-mâché ceiling in the parlor. "Freddy 3" also donated funds to build St. John's Church to house the congregation started in 1693. A larger edifice, designed by Edward Tuckerman Potter, was built alongside the original chapel in 1872.

An addition to the original manor house in the 1860s incorporated a Gothic chamber where official meetings were held. Other city offices occupied what had been living areas. When Yonkers attained the status of a city in 1872, a new Beaux-Arts edifice was built in Washington Park at 40 South Broadway; it was completed in 1911. The then empty Manor Hall was to be demolished until philanthropist Eva Smith Cochran purchased and donated it to New York State to be used as a museum of history and art. Her husband acquired a collection of presidential portraits, which were to be displayed there. In 1891, patriotic citizens raised funds to erect a Civil War Soldiers and Sailors Monument, which was installed on the front lawn. The statue incorporates depictions of an infantryman, sailor, marine, and cavalryman with a color-bearer holding an American flag standing atop a granite column. Quotations from Abraham Lincoln and others are inscribed around the base. The site displays a letter from President Lincoln, thanking Yonkers citizens' Sanitary Committee for their support of the Union during the Civil War.

Philipse Manor Hall, one of the oldest structures in the region, continues to house the Cochran Collection of Presidential Portraits and presents culturally and historically significant multimedia displays. For its significance to local and national history, First Lady Laura Bush designated it as a Save America's Treasures site.

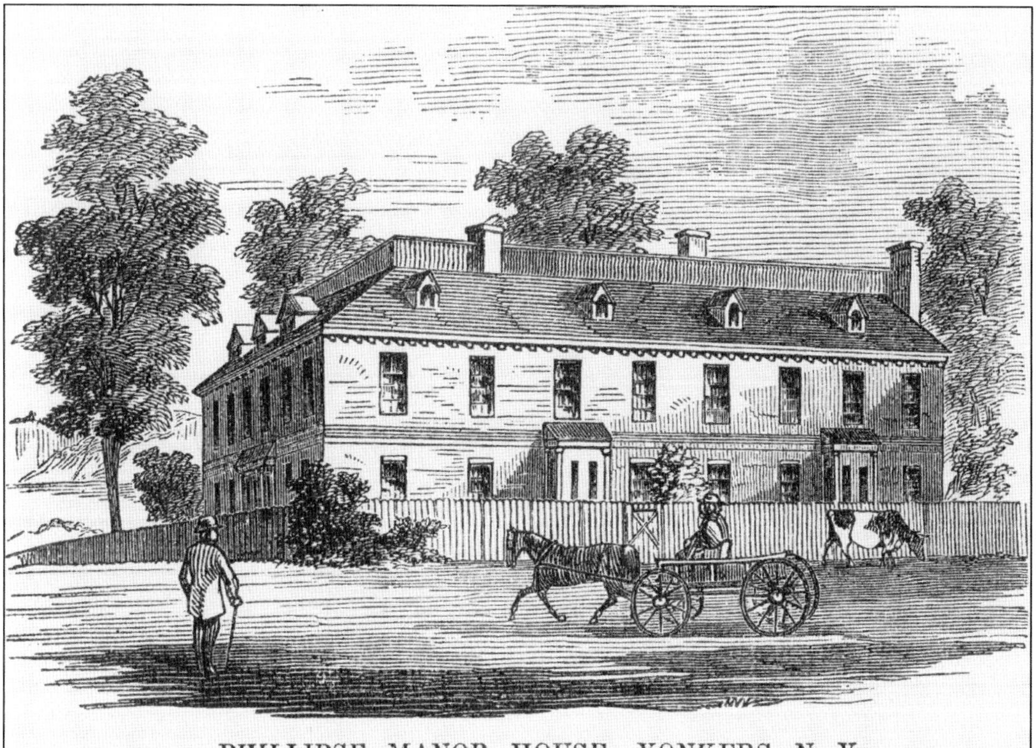

PHILLIPSE MANOR HOUSE, YONKERS, N. Y.

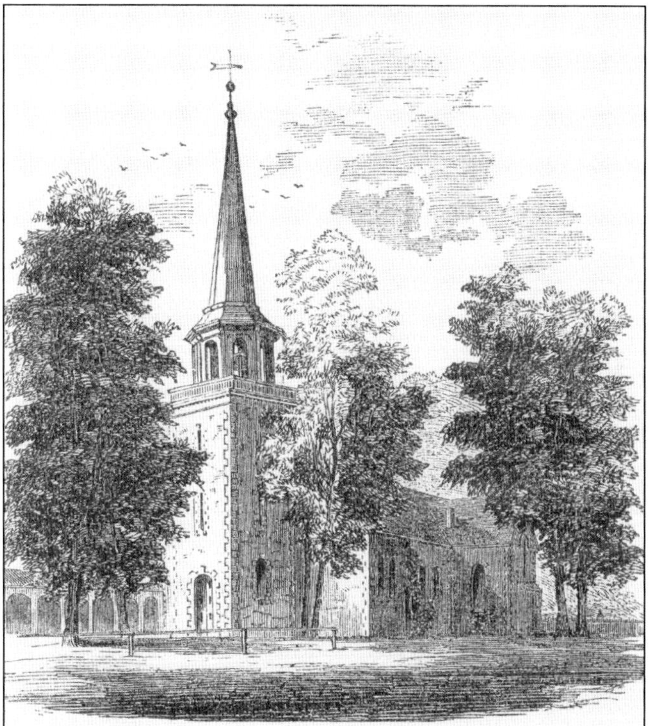

ST. JOHN'S CHURCH, YONKERS, N. Y.

ENGRAVINGS OF PHILIPSE MANOR HALL AND ST. JOHN'S CHURCH, 1885. These illustrations of Philipse Manor Hall and St. John's Church accompany an article about Yonkers history in 1885 in the popular periodical *Ballou's Illustrated Newspaper.* As the two oldest structures in Yonkers, both the Manor Hall and St. John's Church (illustrated here as originally built by Frederick Philipse III) are not only of great historical and architectural significance but also provide the two reference points when one studies the growth and expansion of downtown Yonkers through the centuries. (Both, FPMH.)

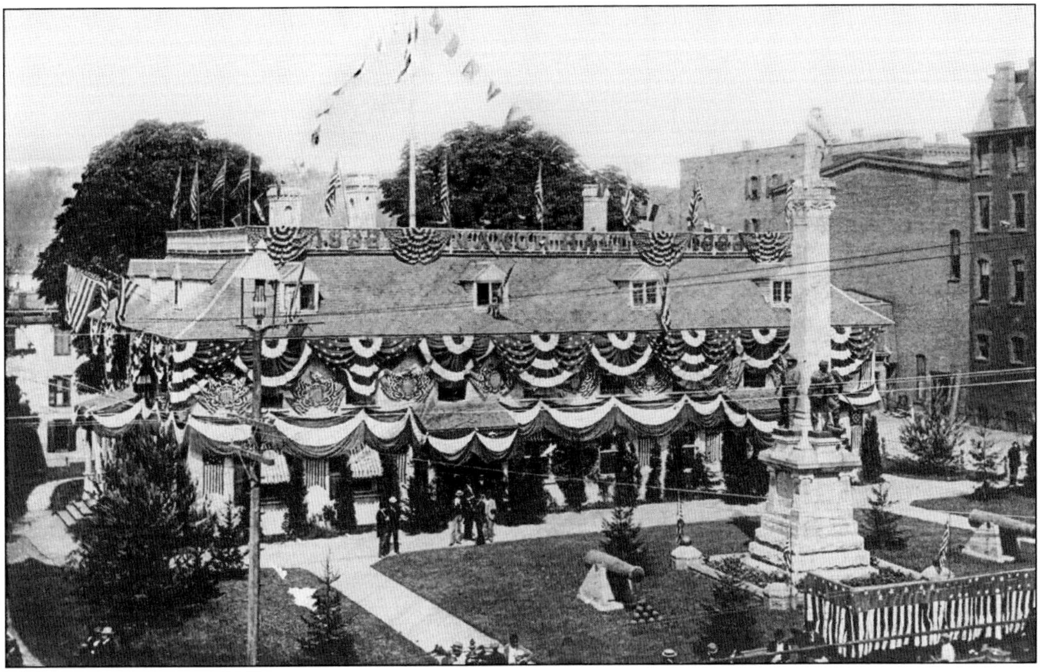

PHILIPSE MANOR HALL WITH BUNTING. In Yonkers, 1909 was a very important year, marking the 300th anniversary of the European discovery of the river by explorer Henry Hudson, who in autumn of 1609 sailed up the river that was to bear his name. Note the decorative balustrade that was erected in 1882, the 200th anniversary of the building of the Manor Hall. (FPMH.)

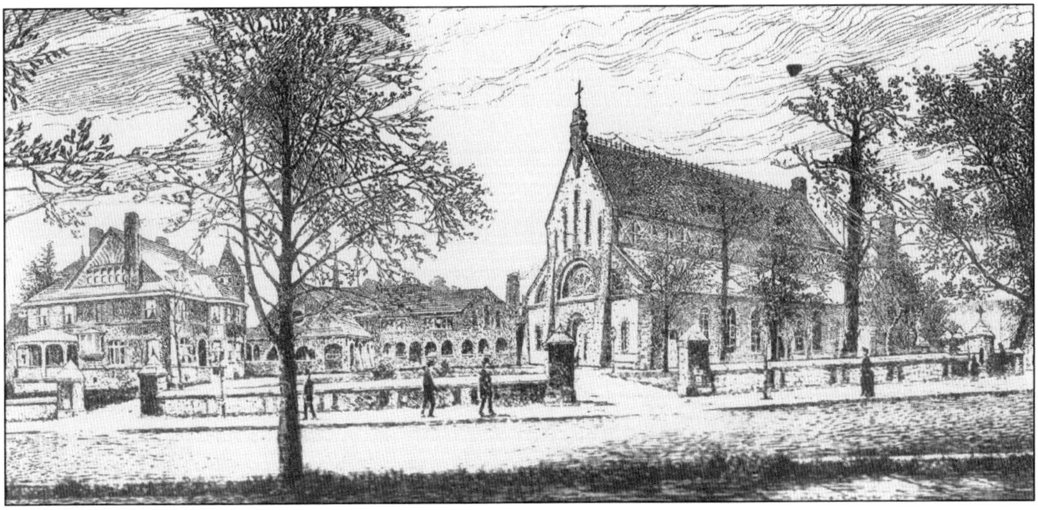

ST. JOHN'S. VICTORIAN ERA ETCHING. An illustration of St. John's Church, Getty Square shows pedestrians walking on Hudson Street, the new church, the Guild Hall (center), and the rectory (left). Note the round structure to the right that contains an ice water fountain donated by Eva Smith Cochran. Little has changed in the years since this illustration was made. (St. John's Episcopal Church.)

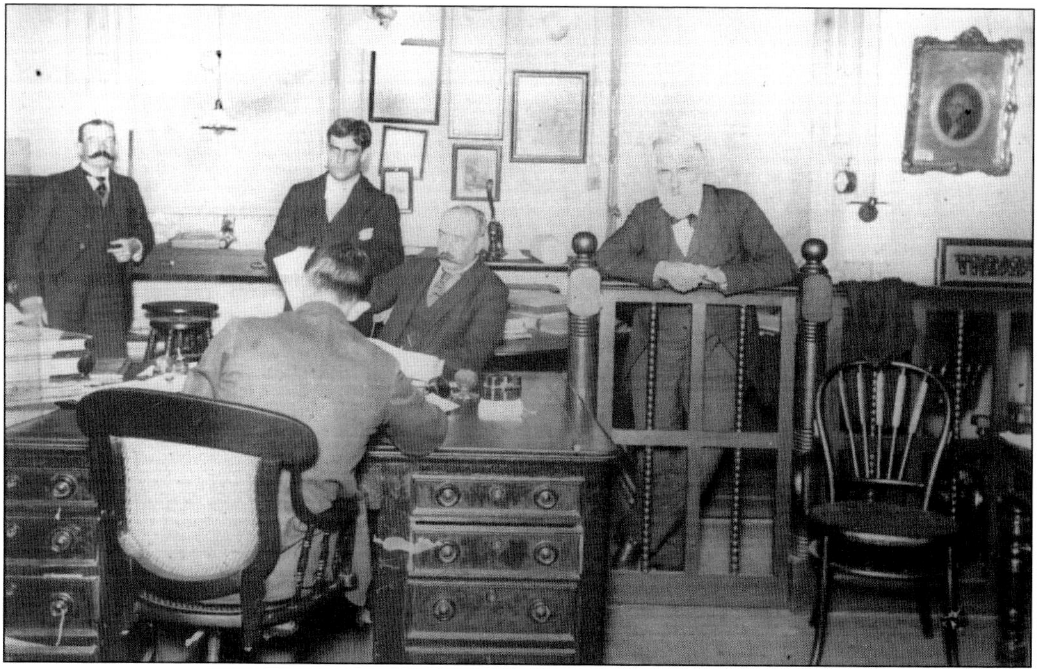

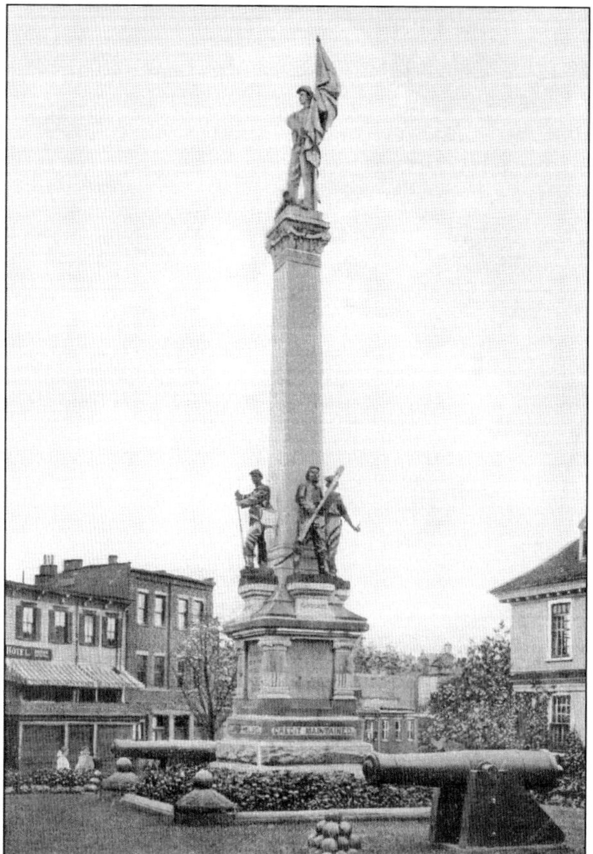

VILLAGE CLERKS AT PHILIPSE MANOR HALL, 1870S. Philipse Manor Hall was Yonkers Village Hall from the 1860s until Yonkers became a city and built a Beaux-Arts city hall on a high bluff in Washington Park at 40 South Broadway. The Yonkers municipal offices moved from the Manor Hall into city hall in 1910. (FPMH.)

CIVIL WAR SOLDIERS AND SAILORS MONUMENT. Yonkers citizens, including children who gave pennies, raised the money to erect the Civil War Soldiers and Sailors Monument on the front lawn of Philipse Manor Hall in 1891. The monument is flanked by two cannons and piles of shot, and quotations from Lincoln, among others, are engraved around the plinth. The figures represent an infantryman, marine, sailor, and cavalryman with a flag-bearer atop the granite obelisk. (Bill Tarmaz.)

Three

The Industrial Age and the Age of Invention

Yonkers has been home to people of creativity for decades. There are many Yonkers "firsts."

While elevators had been known in ancient Egypt, their tendency to drop the carriage containing the passengers, often with fatal results, limited their use. Elisha Otis, working in a machine shop on the rail line along the Hudson River at Vark Street, invented the first cog design that would stop a falling elevator after a few feet. He demonstrated his invention at the Crystal Palace in New York City and was soon deluged with orders. Otis had to build a larger factory that eventually became one of the largest employers in Yonkers. Otis's safety elevator ushered in the age of skyscrapers.

The first Gas and Light Company began in Yonkers in 1861, the same year that the first street lighting was introduced. In 1864, Towndrow and Smith published the *Yonkers Herald*, the first daily newspaper published in Westchester County. In 1867, Charles Harvey of Yonkers invented the first elevated mass transit system, which was backed by Yonkers financiers. Yonkers was the first city to be incorporated in Westchester County in 1872 and the first to establish municipal waterworks in 1873. In 1876, Samuel Tilden, a Yonkers resident and a governor of New York State, was the second presidential candidate to win the popular vote but lose the electoral vote; other presidential candidates with this distinction were Andrew Jackson (1824), Grover Cleveland (1888), and Al Gore (2000).

The Axminster and Moquette looms invented in Yonkers, in 1858 and 1877 respectively, by Halcyon Skinner revolutionized carpet manufacturing, and streets adjacent to the Alexander Smith carpet mills are named for these looms. John Reid and his "Apple Tree Gang" introduced golf to America on a nine-hole course built in northwest Yonkers; an historic plaque marks the site. Yonkers was the first city in New York to build public baths in 1896; the only remaining one on Yonkers Avenue is a local historic landmark. Synthetic plastic was invented by Yonkers resident Leo H. Baekeland in 1906. Called Bakelite after its inventor, the synthetic found universal uses including jewelry design. Edwin H. Armstrong invented FM (frequency modulation) radio broadcasts in 1912; the tower he erected in Alpine, New Jersey, is still visible from most locations in western Yonkers. Rudolph Eickemeyer and his associate Charles Steinmetz invented and produced the first practical alternating current (AC) motor. Yonkers, its downtown and waterfront, were thriving and this prosperity was reflected in its shops and hotels.

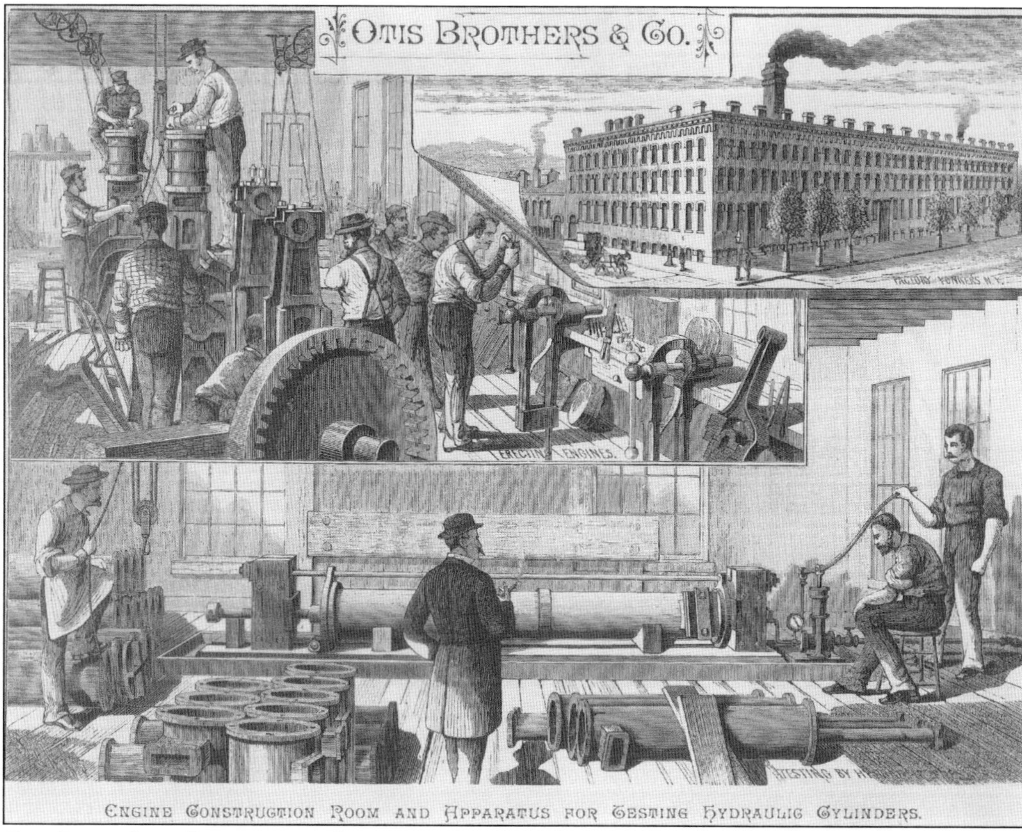

OTIS BROS. SHOP ENGRAVING. The invention of the safety elevator incorporating a cog that stopped the carriage from falling any distance revolutionized construction in the mid-19th century. This innovation made skyscrapers possible. (FPMH.)

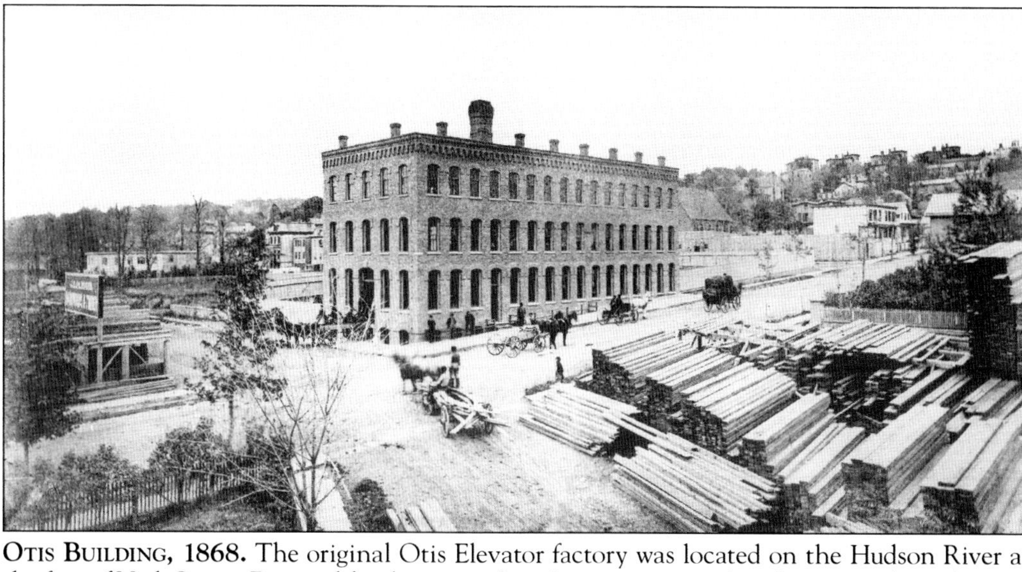

OTIS BUILDING, 1868. The original Otis Elevator factory was located on the Hudson River at the foot of Vark Street. Demand for the new safety elevator increased to the point where the Otis Brothers had to build newer and larger manufacturing facilities. (YHS.)

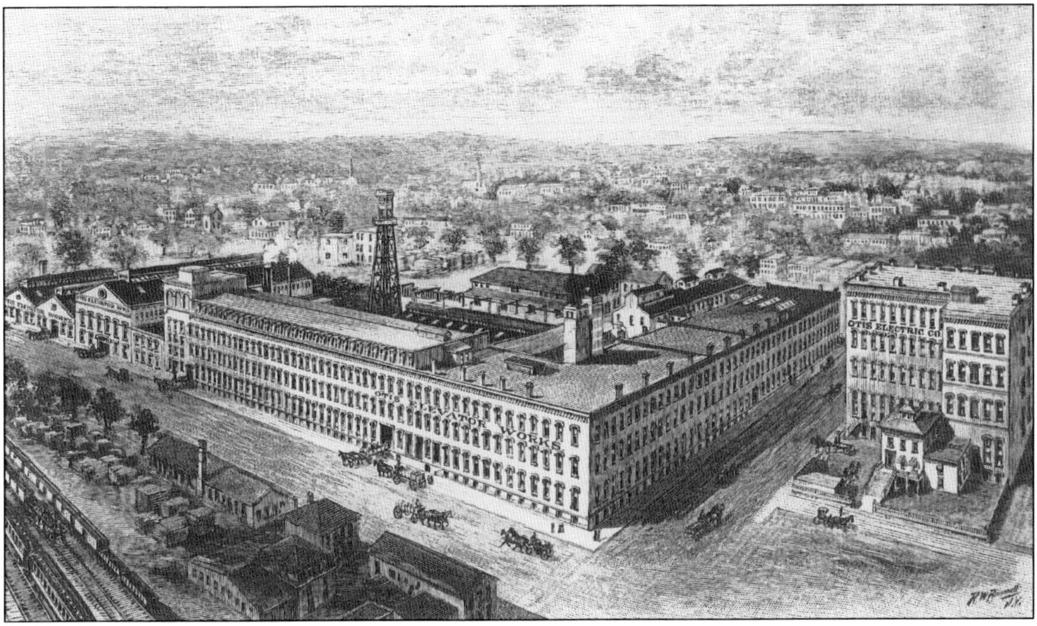

Otis Works, 1896. Otis's invention was immediately a smash hit. A huge factory complex was built on the shores of the Hudson River, with proximity to the then New York Central Railroad tracks that could carry the parts into Manhattan. (FPMH.)

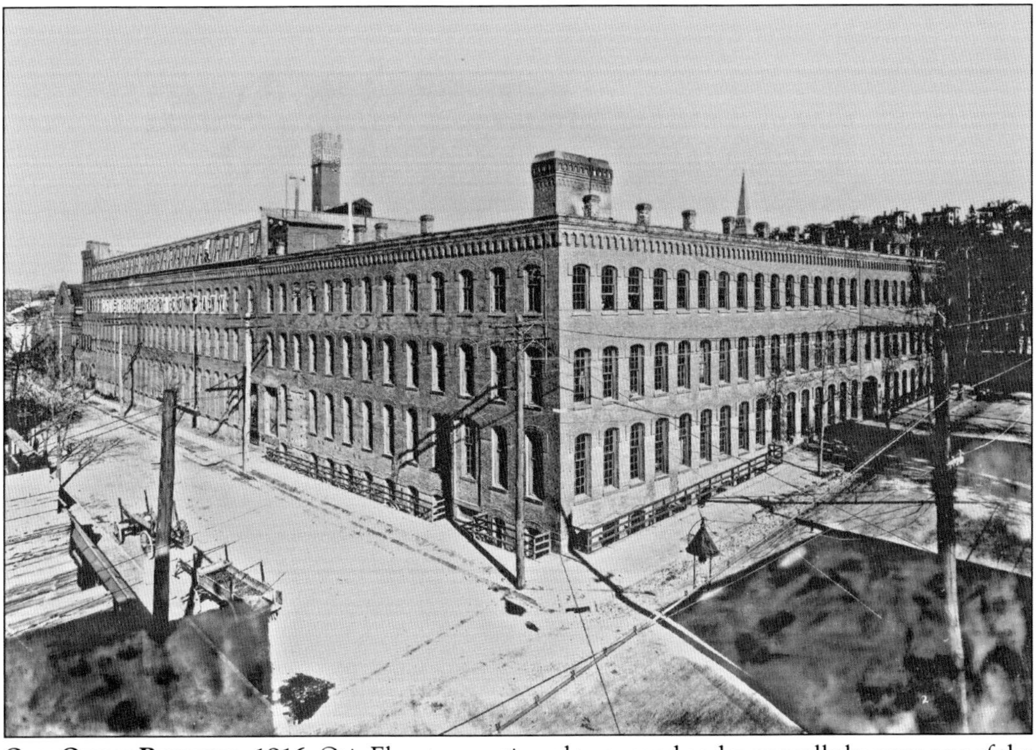

Otis Office Building, 1916. Otis Elevator continued to expand and eventually became one of the largest employers of Yonkers residents. This distinction was maintained until rising costs forced the company to close its Yonkers operation and relocate to North Carolina in the 1970s. (FPMH.)

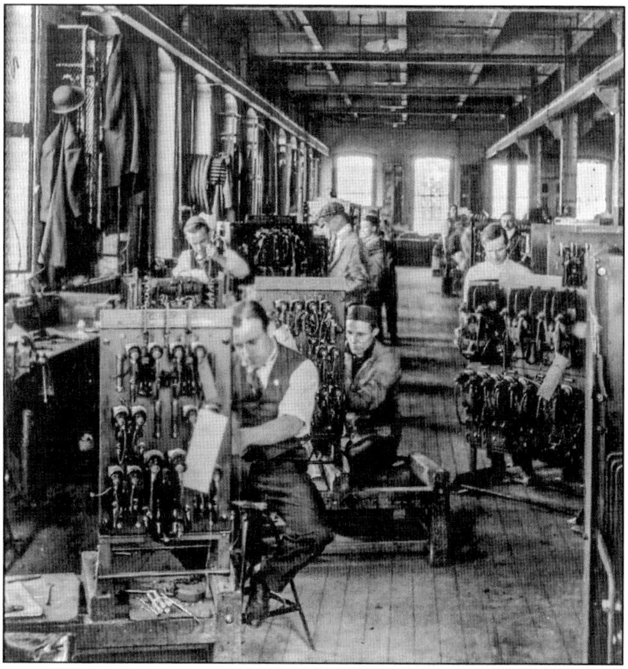

OTIS WORKERS TESTING EQUIPMENT. Since the entire success of the Otis Safety Elevator was obviously safety, all of the parts were extensively tested prior to leaving the factory. Note the high ceilings and ceiling rails used to move the elevators through the factory building. (COY Planning.)

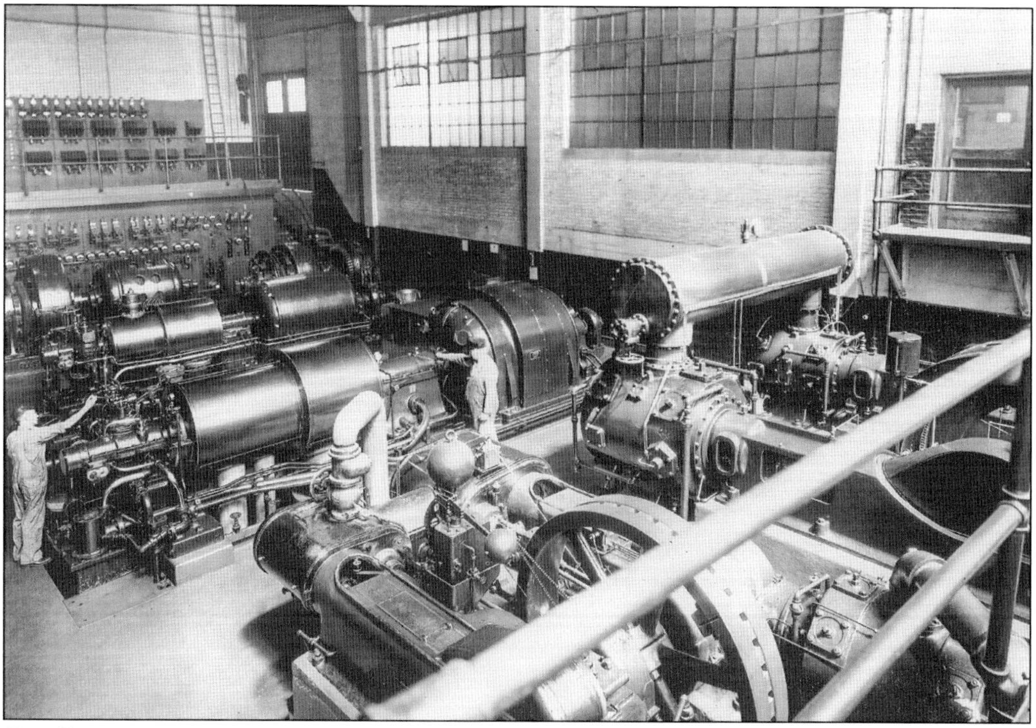

OTIS POWERHOUSE INTERIOR, 1930. Both the machinery to make the Otis safety elevators and the elevator parts themselves required strong floors and high ceilings. Made of heavy oak beams, Otis Elevator was adaptively reused. The Yonkers Riverfront Library and board of education are housed in one of the former buildings. The Kawasaki Rail Car Company, which manufactures New York City subway cars, and other businesses also occupy the former elevator factory. (COY Planning.)

TEXTILE WORKER LITHOGRAPH. The Otis safety elevator was not the only early Yonkers innovation. The Alexander Smith Carpet Mills, known to Yonkers natives as the Carpet Shop, fostered the invention of the Axminster and Moquette weaving looms. (YHS.)

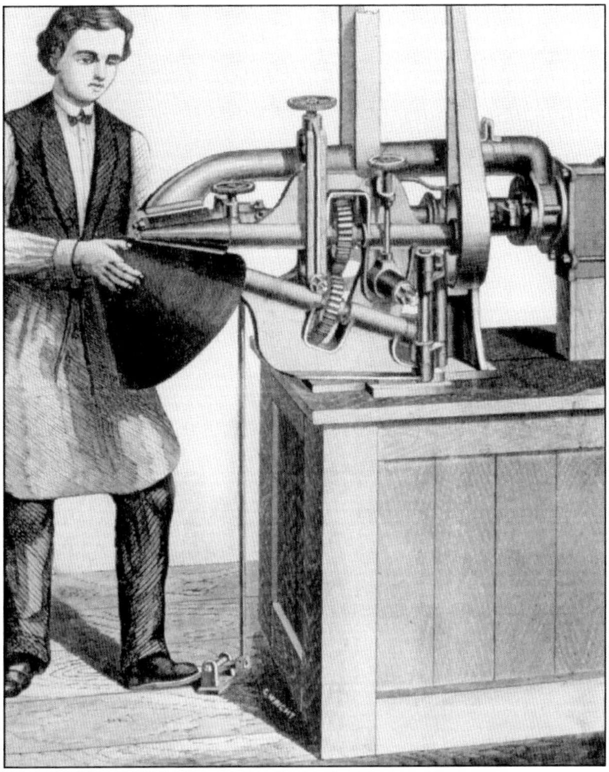

ALEXANDER SMITH CARPET MILLS. Built in the Nepperhan Valley, the sprawling Carpet Shop was built along the banks of the Saw Mill River. (COY Planning.)

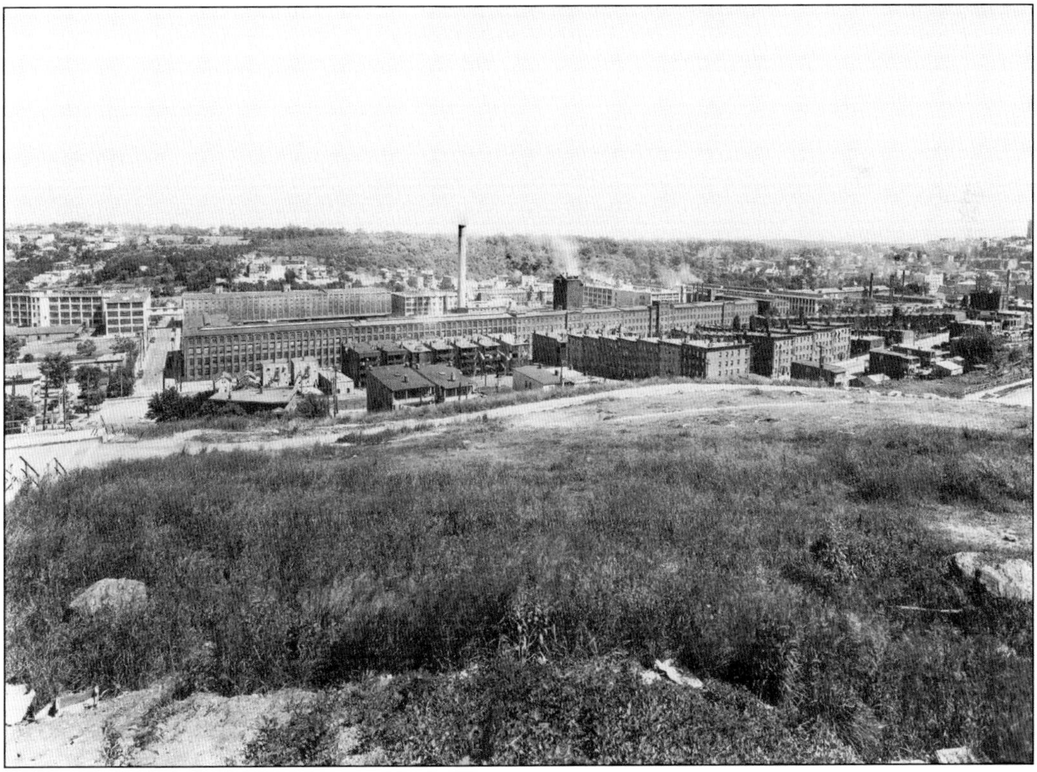

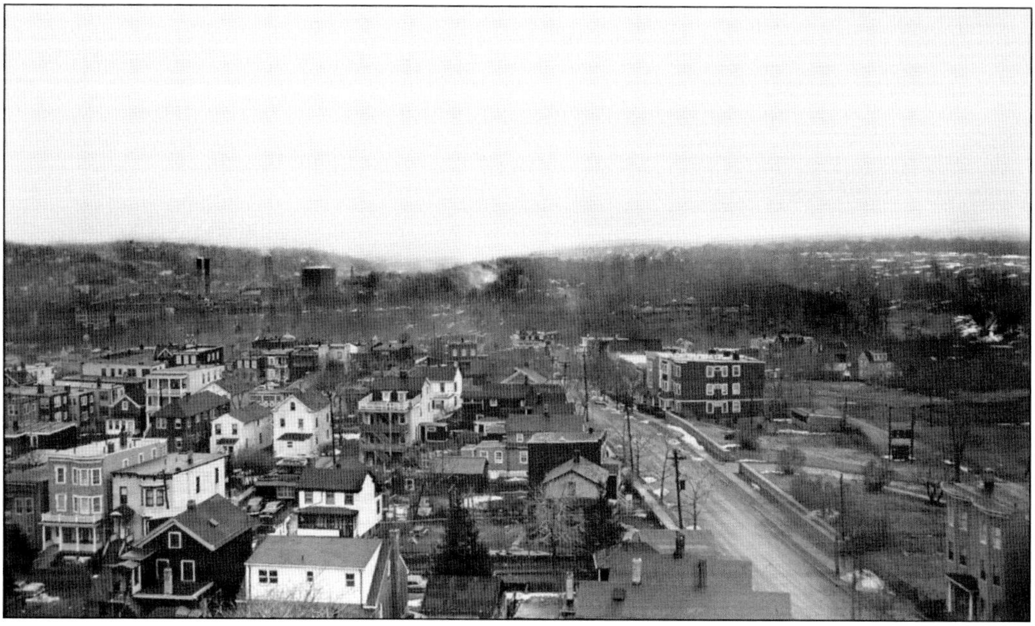

Carpet Factory Panorama. The Carpet Shop, as a major employer of Yonkers residents, spawned the construction of housing in the vicinity of the mill, making it easy for people to walk to work. A somewhat ubiquitous style of home developed, which was basically a three-floor walk-up that was long and narrow rather than squarish, with one family accommodated per floor. (COY Planning.)

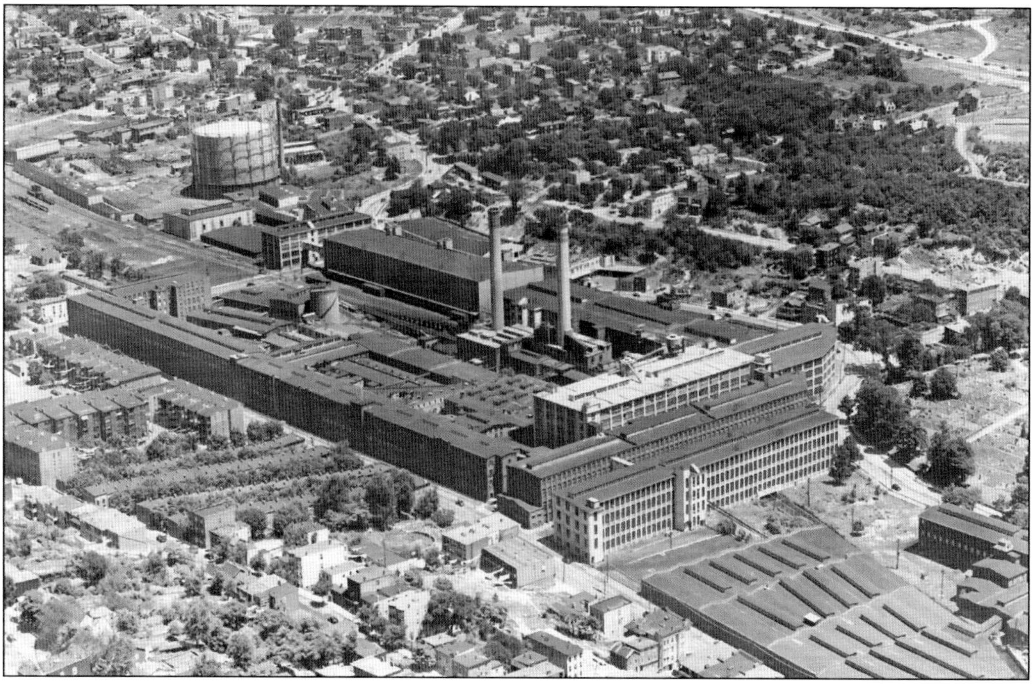

Carpet Factory Panorama Two. This panoramic shot shows the entire sprawl of the Carpet Shop, including the worker housing build around it. The land sloped up from the Saw Mill River bed. (COY Planning.)

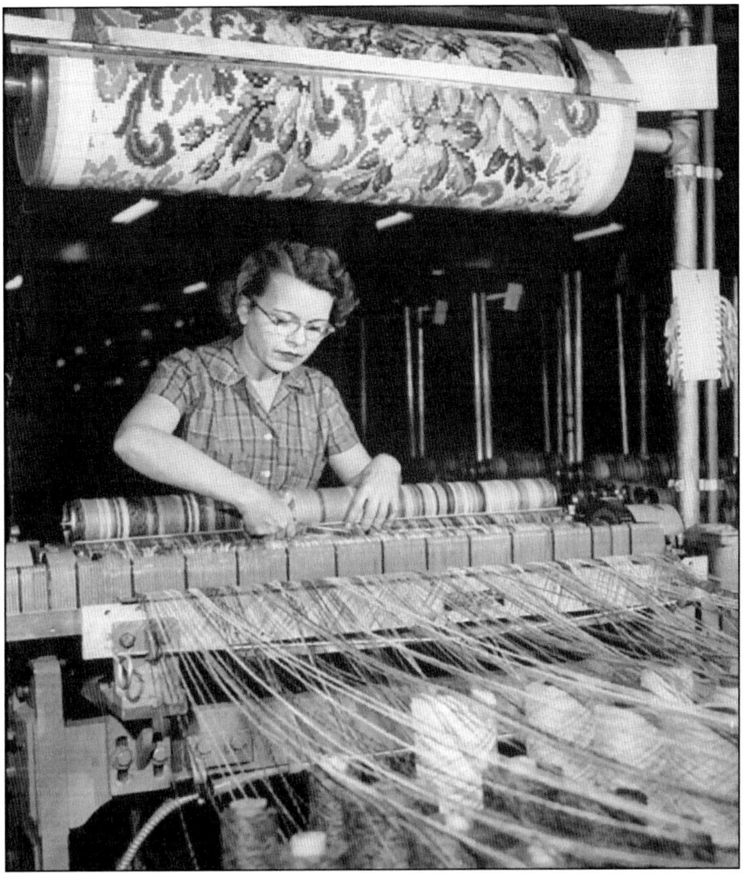

CARPET SHOP WORKER. The proprietary looms invented by the Carpet Shop engineers made weaving complex patterns possible by mechanization. In the postwar boom of the 1950s, Alexander Smith's patterned carpets were particularly popular and many new homeowners installed wall-to-wall carpeting manufactured by the company. (COY Planning.)

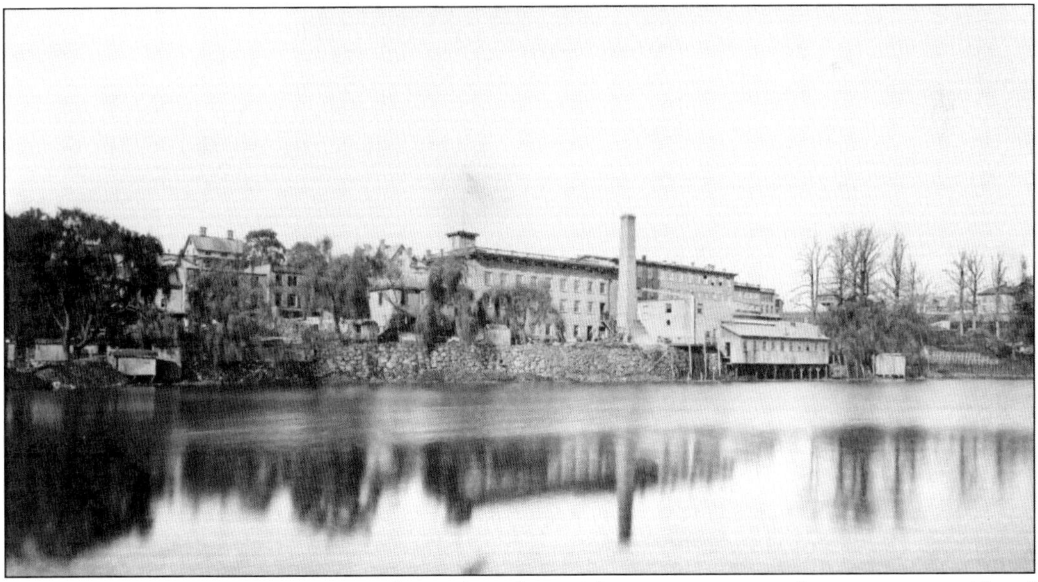

BALDWIN AND FLAGG FACTORY. In the mid- to late 19th century, no gentleman was considered dressed without a hat. Yonkers, because of the waterpower supplied by the Saw Mill River, became a prime location for the felting process required to produce the materials to make hats. (FPMH.)

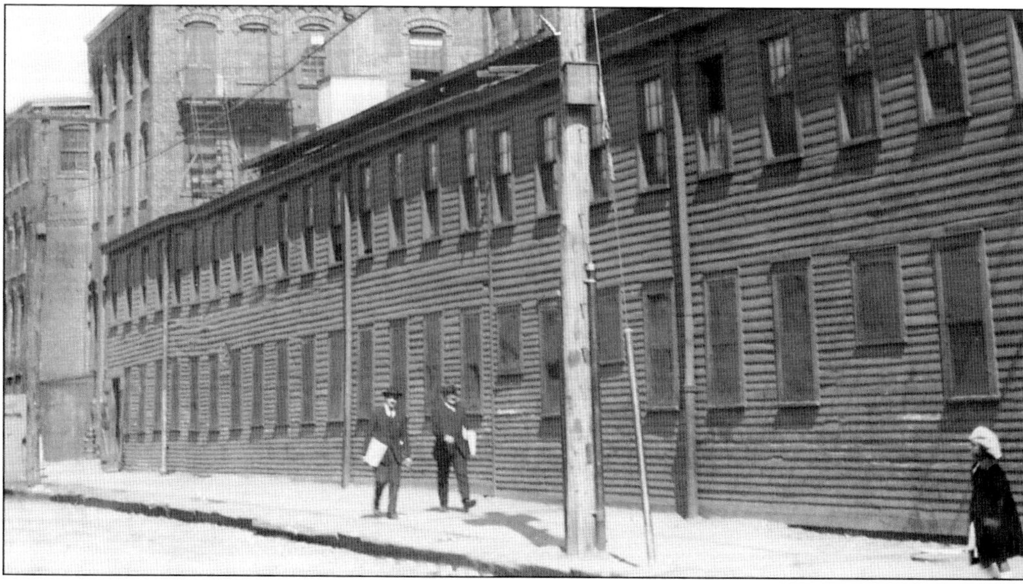

Waring Hat. Originally the site of the Starr Arms Works, a weapons manufactory, the Waring Hat Company was located on Vark Street. John Thomas Waring was a prominent early citizen of Yonkers, and his company employed around 2,000 people at one time. Like Otis and the elevator, Waring invented several new processes for hat-making. (Flynn.)

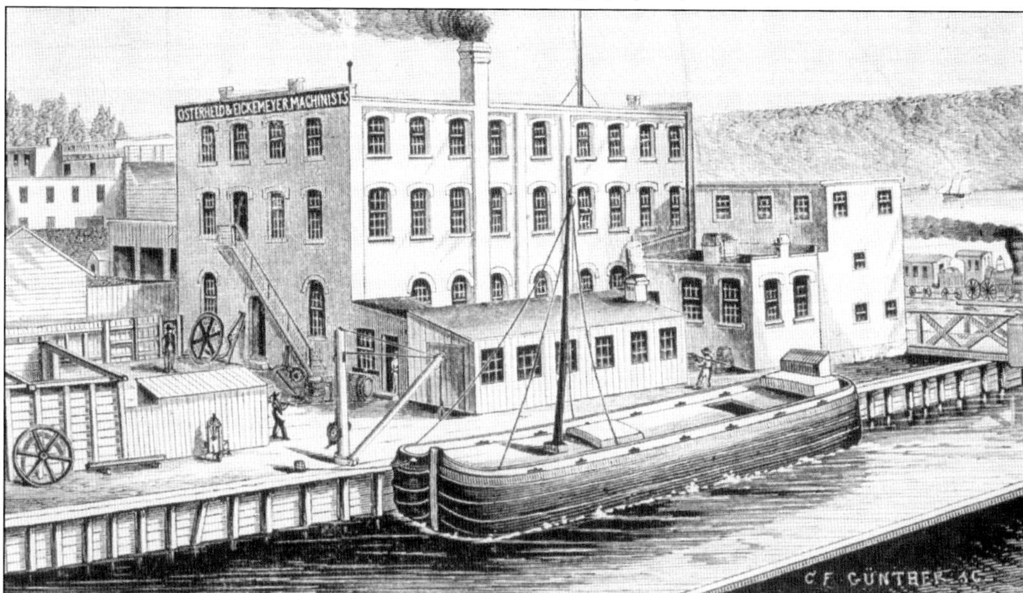

Osterheld & Eickemeyer. Osterheld & Eickemeyer were machinists whose factory was located on Chicken Island, Yonkers, and the river that created that island can be seen in this illustration. The company was an innovator and manufacturer of electric motors. In 1889, it had started to manufacture electric motors and hired Charles Steinmetz, who developed his famous law of hysteresis. General Electric bought Osterheld & Eickemeyer in 1892, and Steinmetz stayed on with the new owners. (COY Planning.)

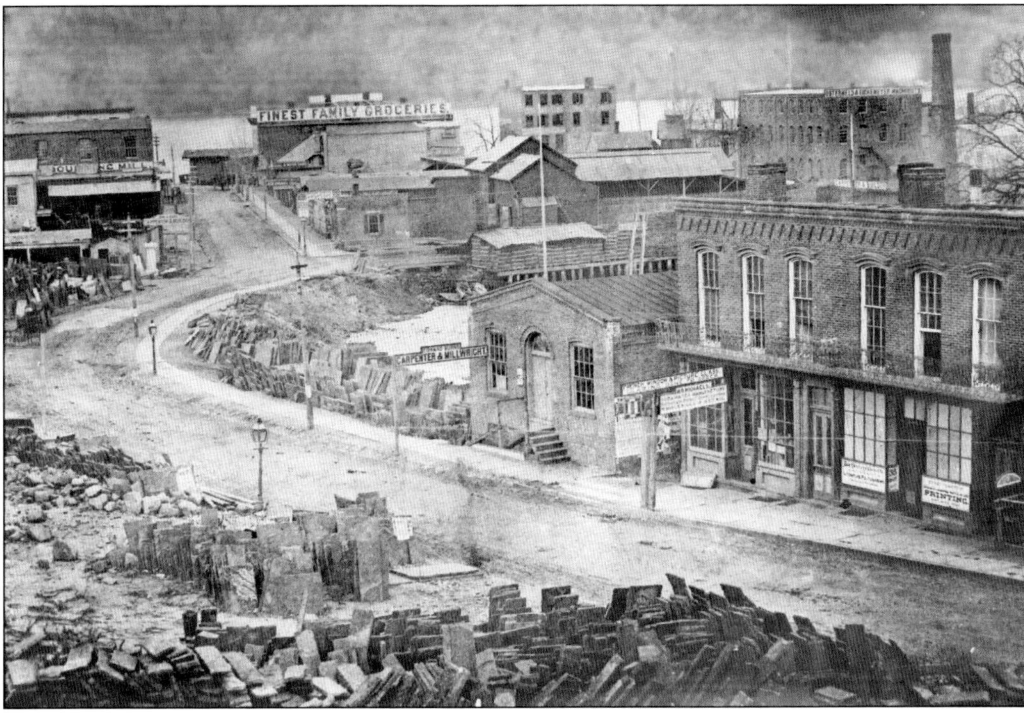

Finest Family Groceries, Main Street, 1858. This photograph represents one of the earliest taken of Yonkers. The dirt road runs to the Hudson River and the Palisades can be seen in the background. The location is roughly where Hudson and Main Streets are now located. (FPMH)

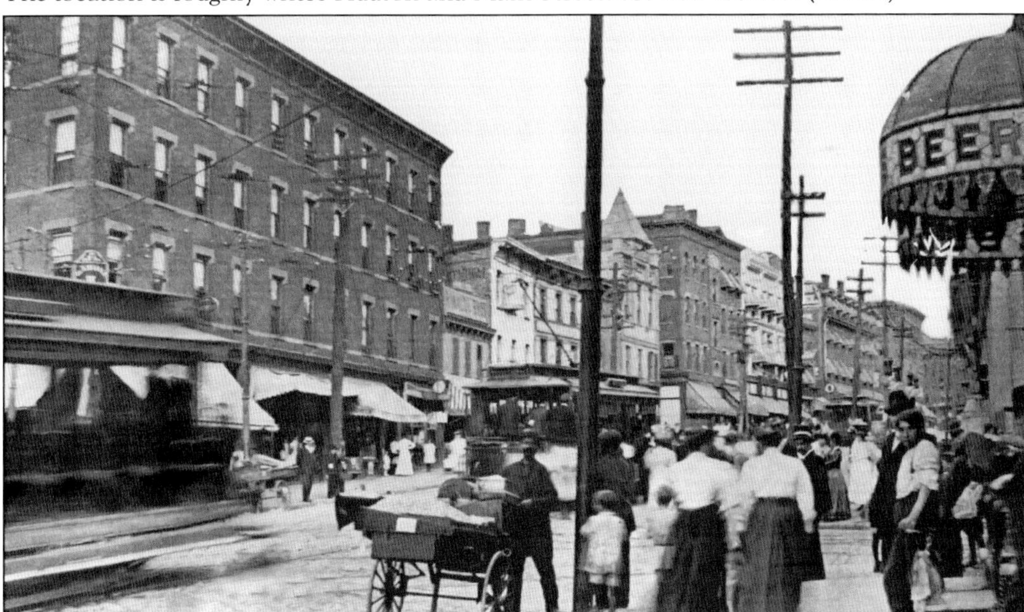

Downtown Yonkers, Main Street, 1890s. Yonkers was growing and the downtown area was rapidly becoming a center for shopping as well as manufacturing. The various large companies that were employing Yonkers residents provided wages that allowed shopping, and the area prospered. (YHS.)

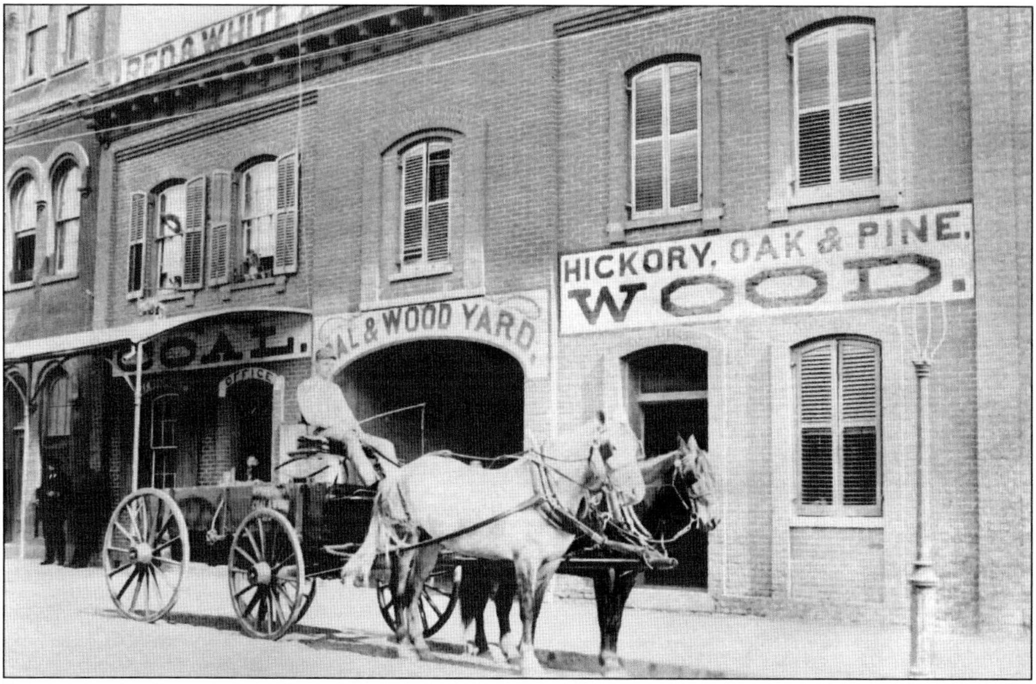

BREEVOORT'S COAL YARD, 4 DOCK STREET. Horses and wagons delivered both coal for heat and wood for building. The structures were wood-framed with a brick facade; they were attached by a party wall that did little to prevent the spread of fire from one to the other. (COY Planning.)

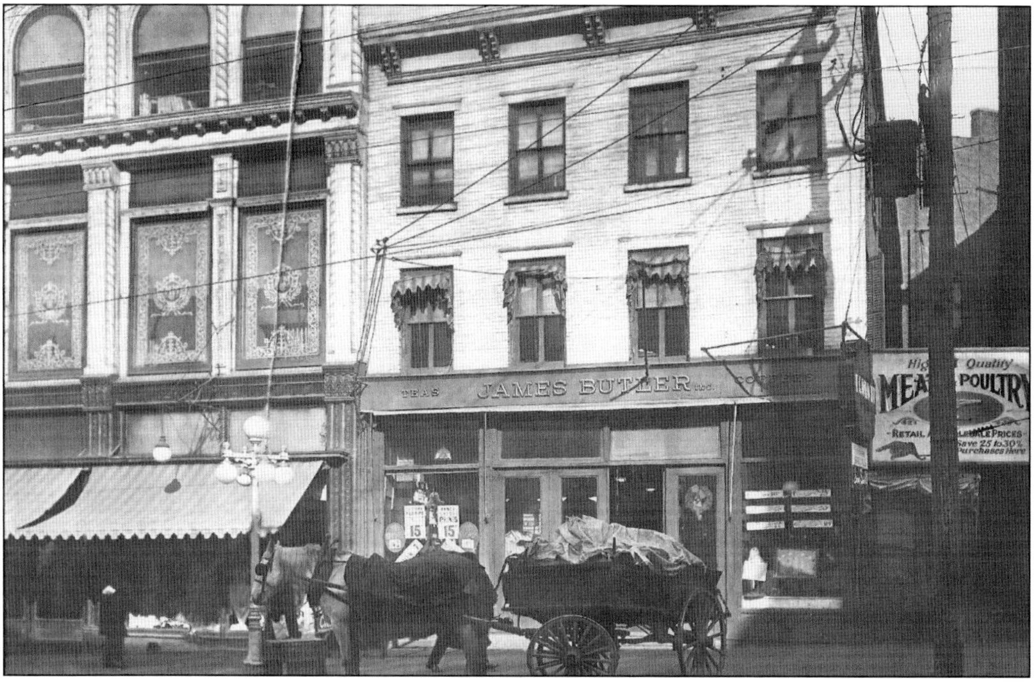

MARSHALL MATHIESON AND JAMES BUTLER STORES, MAIN STREET. A typical downtown Yonkers merchant, these stores catered to the housewives living the vicinity who walked to and from their establishments from their homes in the nearby areas, like Nodine Hill and the Glen. (YHS.)

HERALD STATESMAN (1932) AND AMELIA EARHART. The merger of two Yonkers newspapers, the *Yonkers Herald* (1899–1932) and the *Statesman* (1924–1932), created the *Herald Statesman* in 1932. It was published until 1998, when it was acquired by Gannett and renamed the *Journal News*, subsequently "LoHud" for Lower Hudson. The story about Amelia Earhart's transatlantic flight was published in the first year of the merger. (FPMH.)

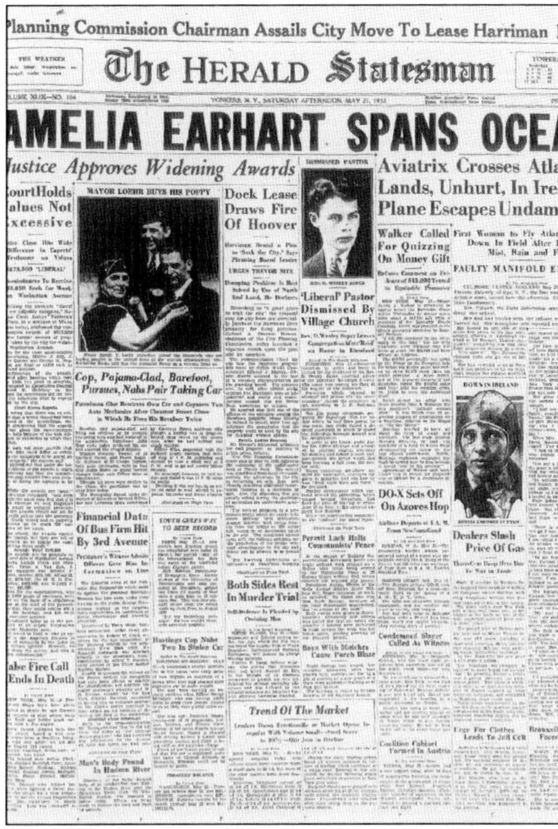

lanning Commission Chairman Assails City Move To Lease Harriman D

The HERALD Statesman

YONKERS, N.Y., SATURDAY AFTERNOON, MAY 21, 1932

AMELIA EARHART SPANS OCEA

Justice Approves Widening Awards

ourtHolds alues Not xcessive

MAYOR LOEHR BUYS HIS POPPY

Dock Lease Draws Fire Of Hoover

'Liberal' Pastor Dismissed By Village Church

Aviatrix Crosses Atla Lands, Unhurt, In Irel Plane Escapes Undama

Walker Called For Quizzing On Money Gift

FAULTY MANIFOLD EN

Cop, Pajama-Clad, Barefoot, Pursues, Nabs Pair Taking Car

Financial Data Of Bus Firm Hit By 3rd Avenue

Both Sides Rest In Murder Trial

DO-X Sets Off On Azores Hop

Dealers Slash Price Of Gas

alse Fire Call Ends In Death

Trend Of The Market

THE *YONKERS HERALD*, 10 WARBURTON AVENUE. Newsboys for the *Yonkers Herald* on Warburton Avenue are getting ready to deliver the papers. After the *Herald* and the *Statesman* merged in 1932, both newspapers' offices constructed an Art Deco building on Dock Street. (COY Planning.)

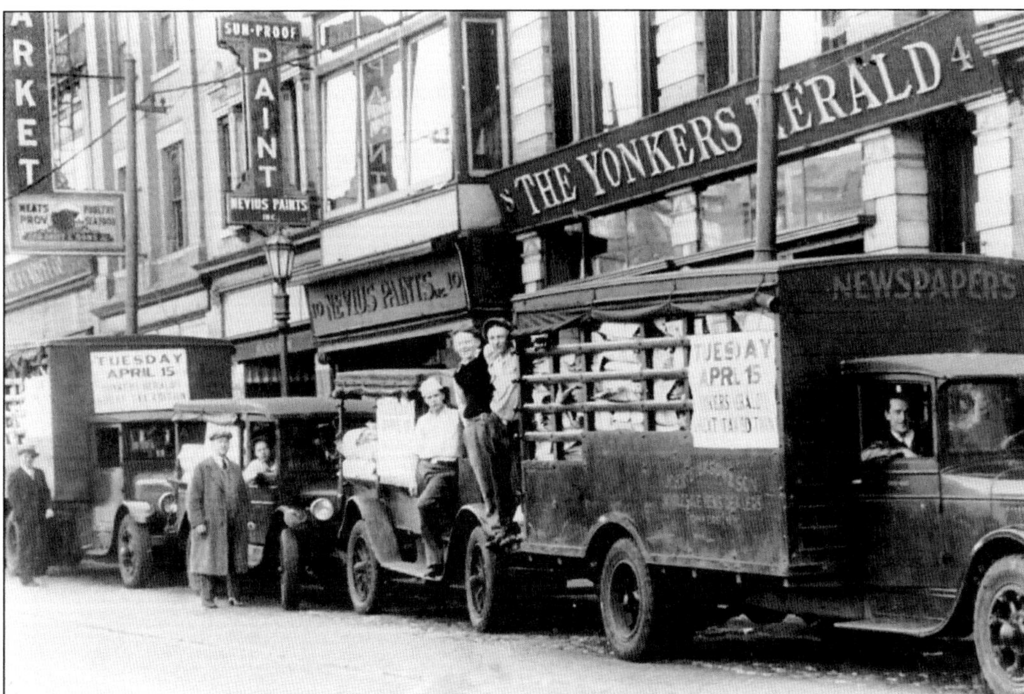

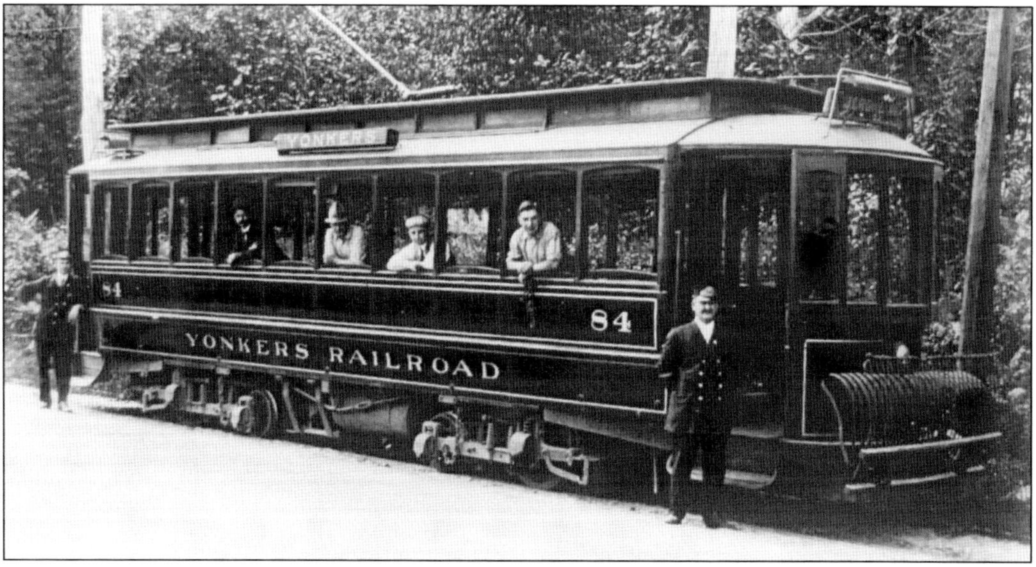

YONKERS TROLLEY, 1915. Good mass transportation is essential in a city's growth, and in Yonkers, that growth from the downtown to the residential areas was facilitated by trolleys. Running from the Trolley Barn adjacent to the Yonkers Pier and main train station, the trolleys could take people all over Yonkers and into surrounding municipalities. The trolleys ran until they were considered obsolete by the introduction of buses and were ended in 1952. (YHS.)

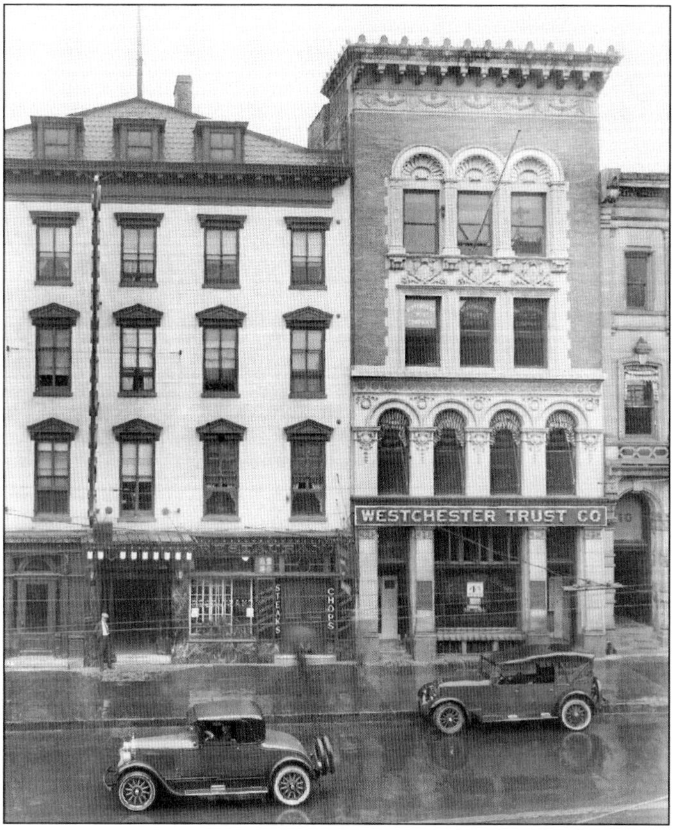

WESTCHESTER TRUST, 8–12 WARBURTON AVENUE. This distinctive Yonkers gneiss stone building still remains. Yonkers gneiss was locally quarried and has a distinctive black color and rough texture containing mica flecks. An historic plaque noting that this was the location of Van der Donck's mills is affixed to the foundation. (YHS.)

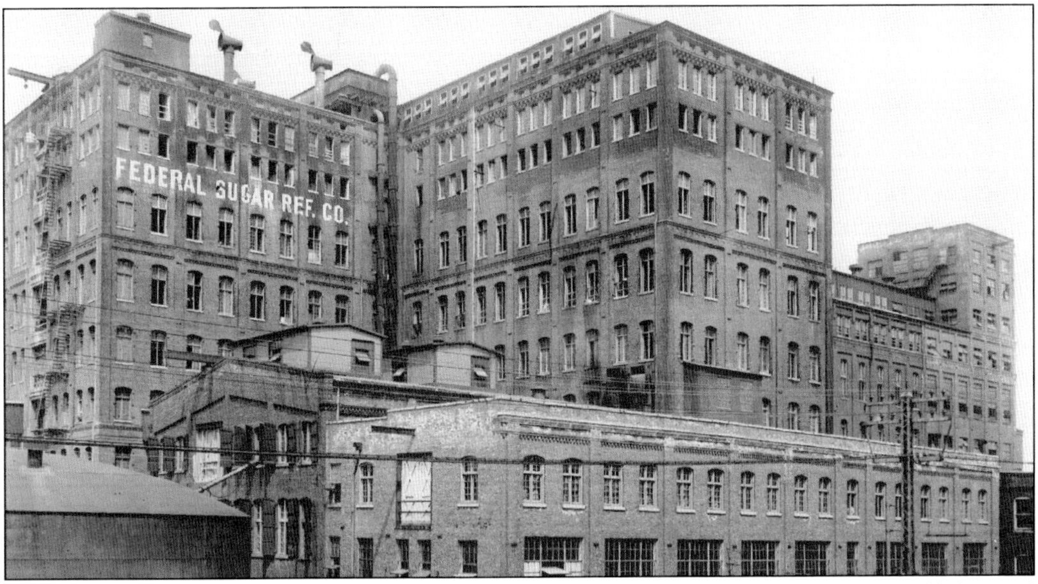

Federal Sugar Refinery. The Federal Sugar Refinery ("the Sugar House") was originally located at the foot of Main Street. There were at least two sugar refineries in Yonkers at any given time in the late 19th century until they merged to become the Federal. The huge brick building interestingly reflects elements of Dutch architecture in some roofline details of the factory. (COY Planning.)

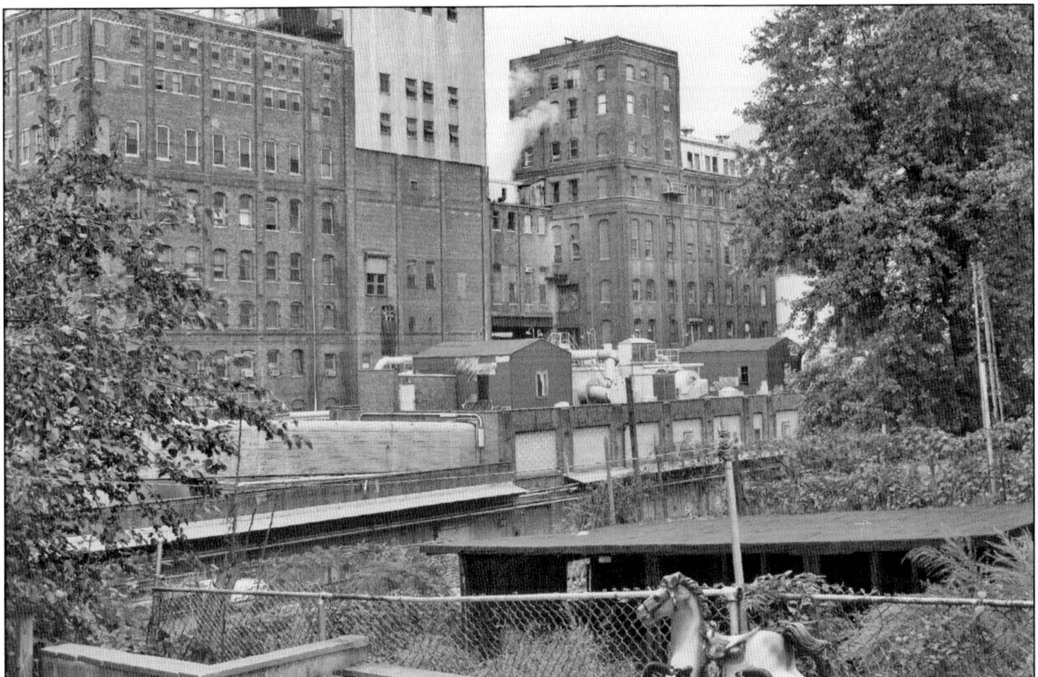

Domino Sugar. Now occupying 26 acres of Hudson River waterfront on Federal Street, this refinery still processes sugar from cane 24 hours a day, seven days a week. Receiving raw cane in huge tankers and barges that dock along the refinery, Domino is one of the last remaining water-dependant industries on the Hudson. If one picks up a bag of Domino brand sugar, it will have almost certainly come from this refinery. (Luis Perelman.)

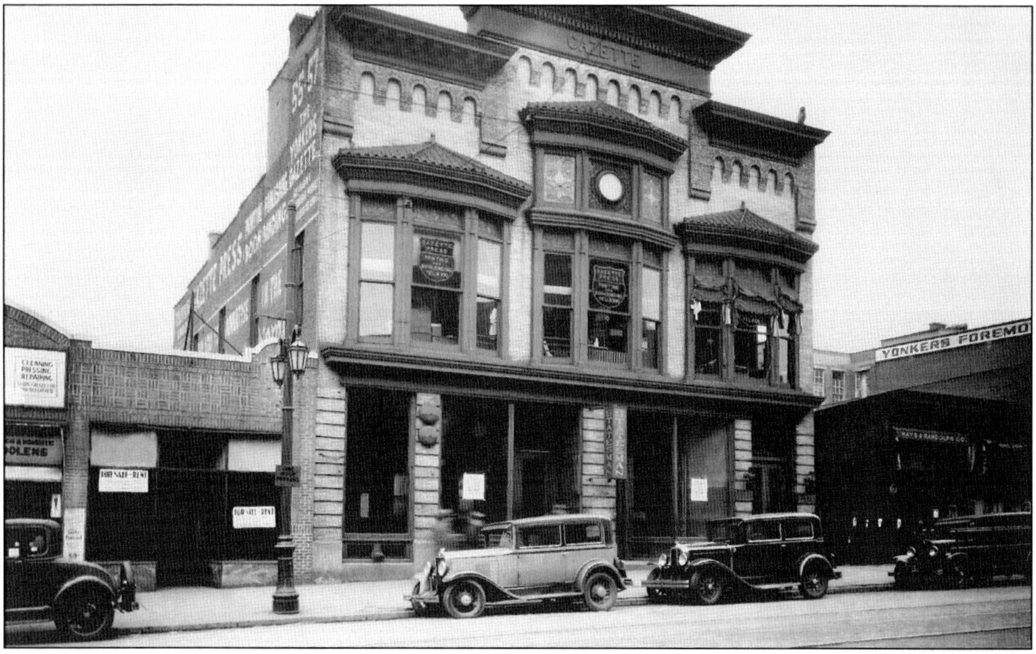

Gazette Building. Originally housing the *Yonkers Gazette*, this beautiful building was renovated and adaptively reused in the early 2000s, housing a restaurant with office space above. Through the basement of the building, where a large wine cellar is now located, runs a small tributary of the Saw Mill River. (COY Planning.)

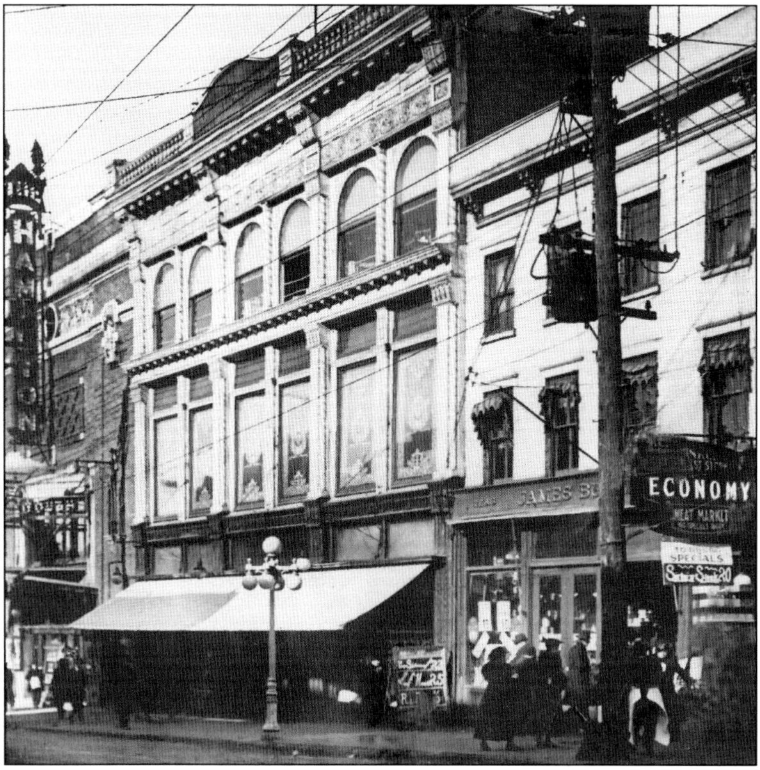

Hamilton Theatre on Main Street. Located on Main Street off Getty Square, the Hamilton Theatre was the venue for vaudeville in Yonkers. Note the distinctive light fixture along the sidewalk. In the 1970s and 1980s, several private homes with historic architectural features were saved and renovated. Each restored home was designated by placing a reproduction of these light fixtures on its front lawn. (YHS.)

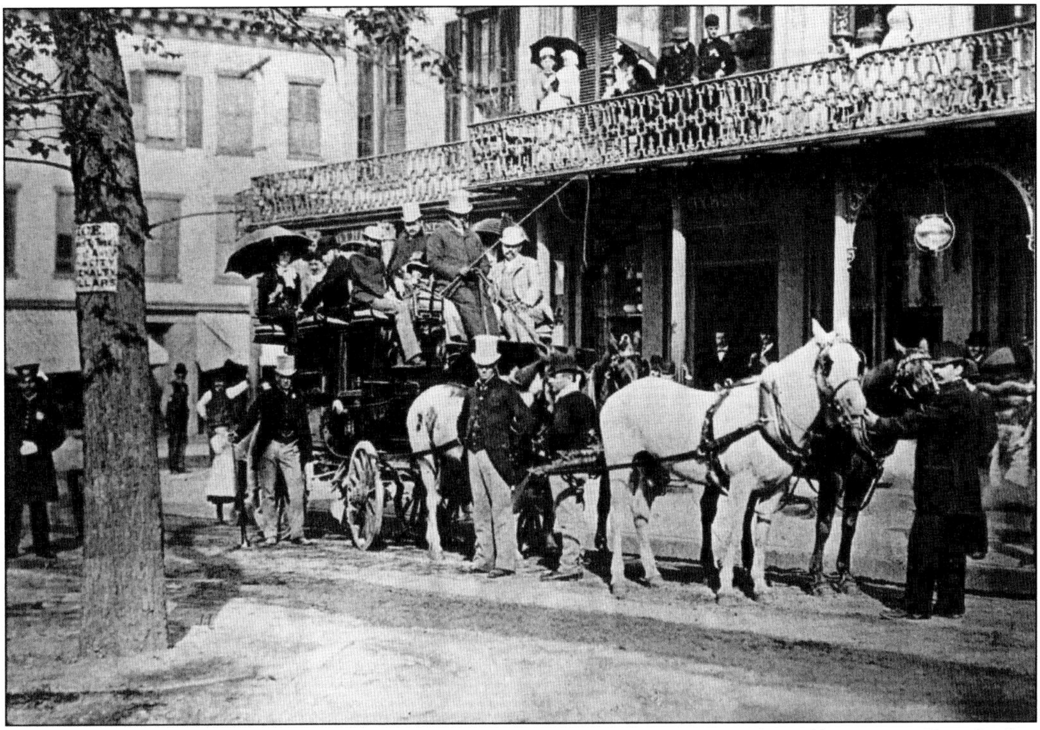

HORSE AND CARRIAGE IN FRONT OF GETTY HOTEL, GETTY SQUARE. The Albany Post Road, also known as Broadway, ran from Lower Manhattan to Albany and is still a major thoroughfare. Here, travelers use elegant horse and carriage modes of transportation. The Getty Hotel, one of the largest hotels in Westchester in the 1880s and 1890s, was a major stop on the Post Road. (YHS.)

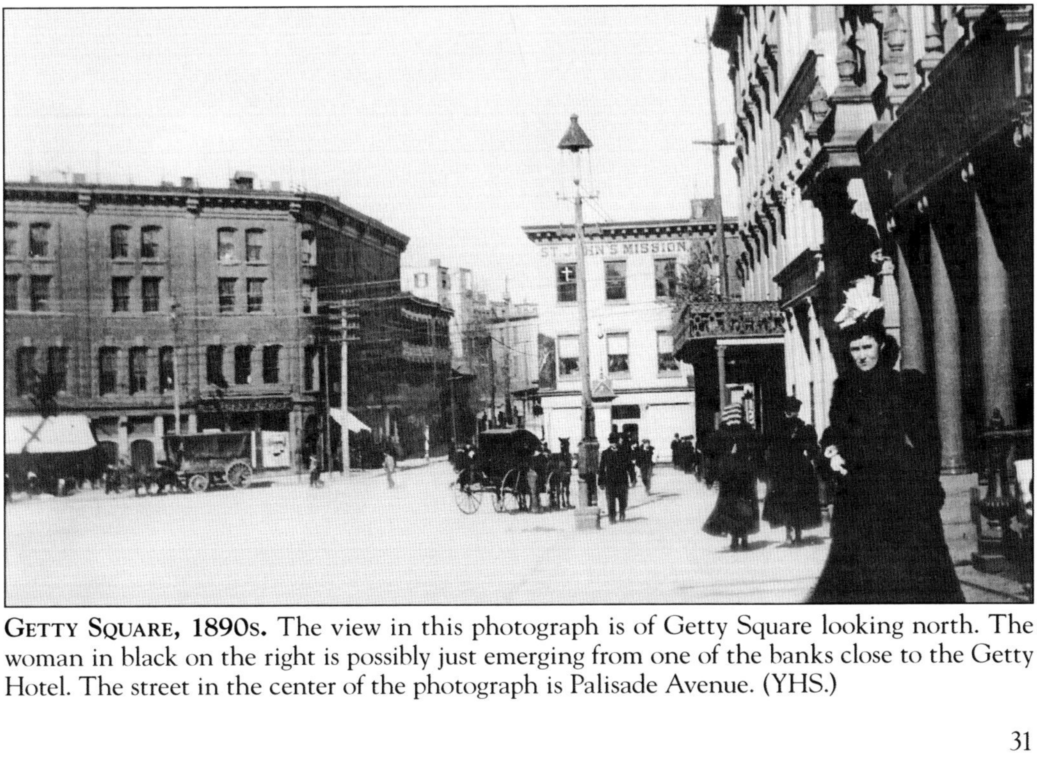

GETTY SQUARE, 1890S. The view in this photograph is of Getty Square looking north. The woman in black on the right is possibly just emerging from one of the banks close to the Getty Hotel. The street in the center of the photograph is Palisade Avenue. (YHS.)

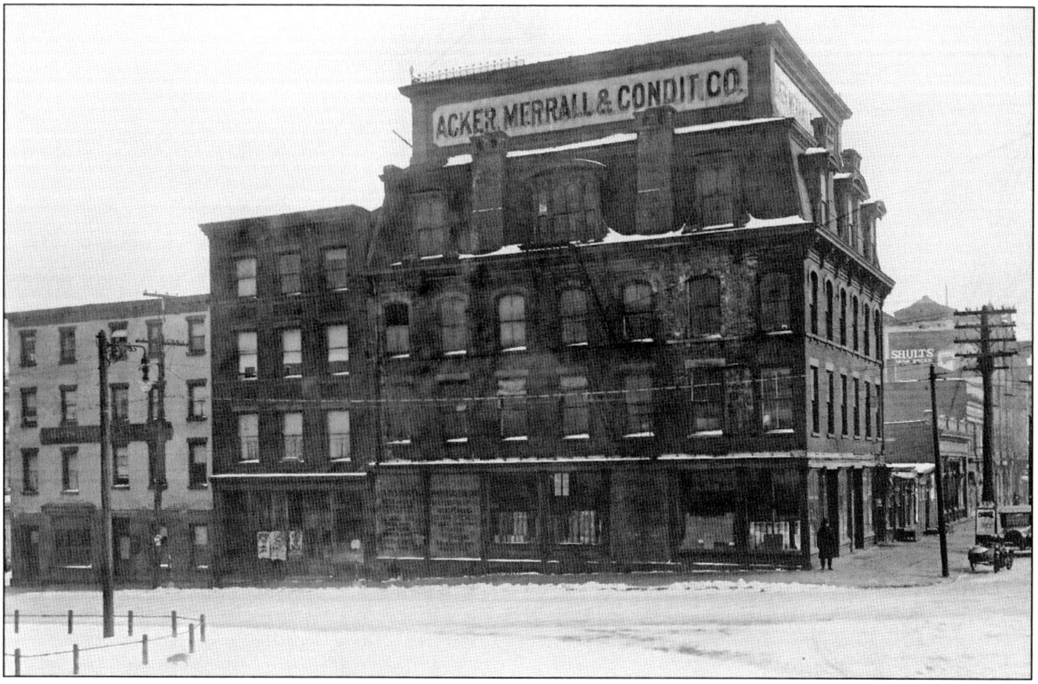

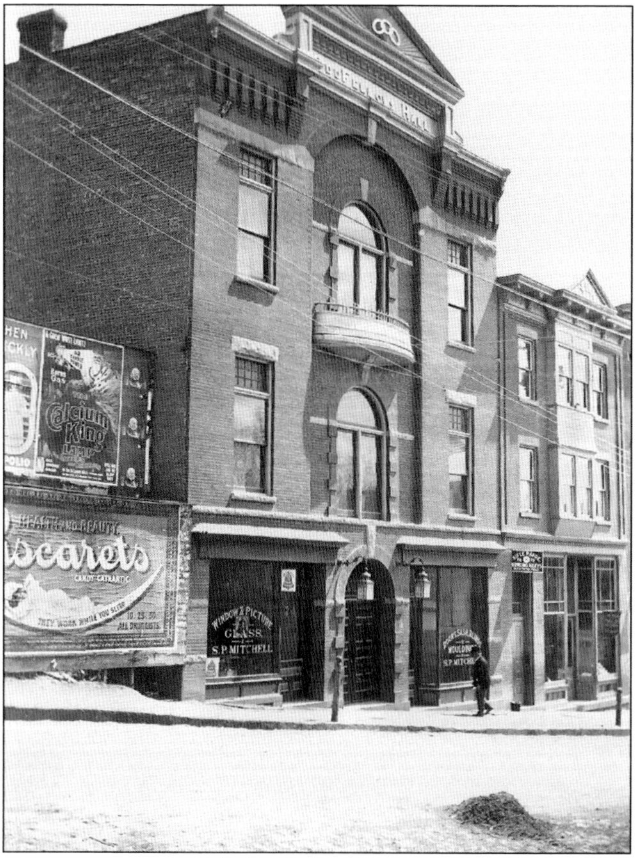

ACKER MERRALL & CONDIT. This building was located at 2 Dock Street. The company functioned much like a modern-day hardware store. Many of these beautiful old buildings on the waterfront were lost to fire or demolition. (Flynn.)

ODD FELLOWS HALL, NORTH BROADWAY. Another example of a distinctive Yonkers building, the Odd Fellows Hall was home to a fraternal organization. The building still stands, and its wonderful facade remains intact. A new middle-income housing project was recently opened directly across the street. (COY Planning.)

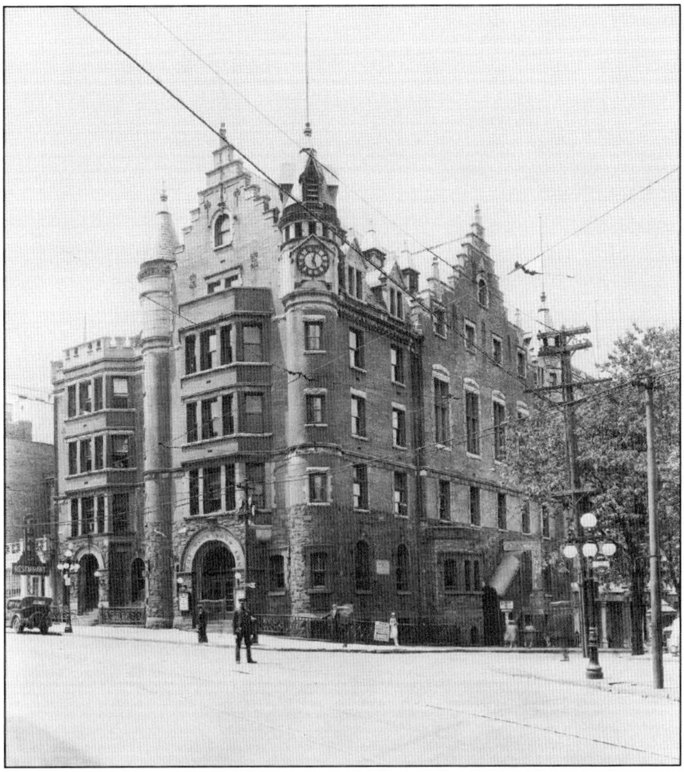

HOLLYWOOD INN. This amazingly ornate building was the product of the philanthropy of William Cochran of Carpet Shop wealth, to provide a place of peace and sober recreation for the men of Yonkers. Fueled by the Temperance Movement, it was to provide the same social and recreational opportunities as a saloon—without the alcohol. (YHS.)

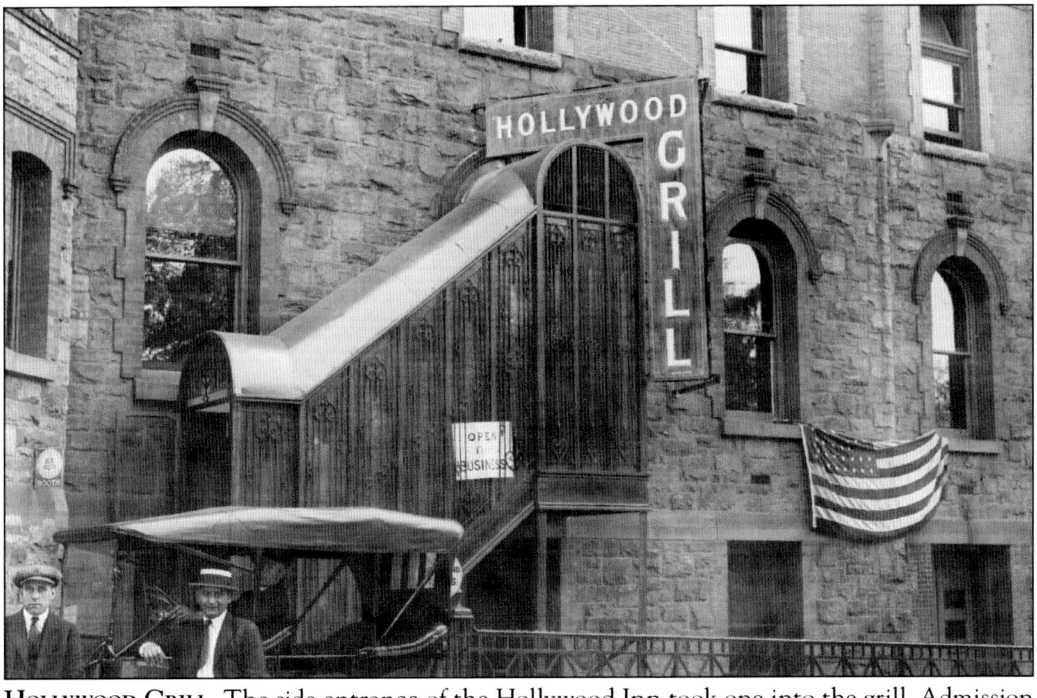

HOLLYWOOD GRILL. The side entrance of the Hollywood Inn took one into the grill. Admission was by annual membership, originally $6 per year when the inn opened in 1895 and subsequently reduced to $3 per year in 1898 to further encourage membership and use. (YHS.)

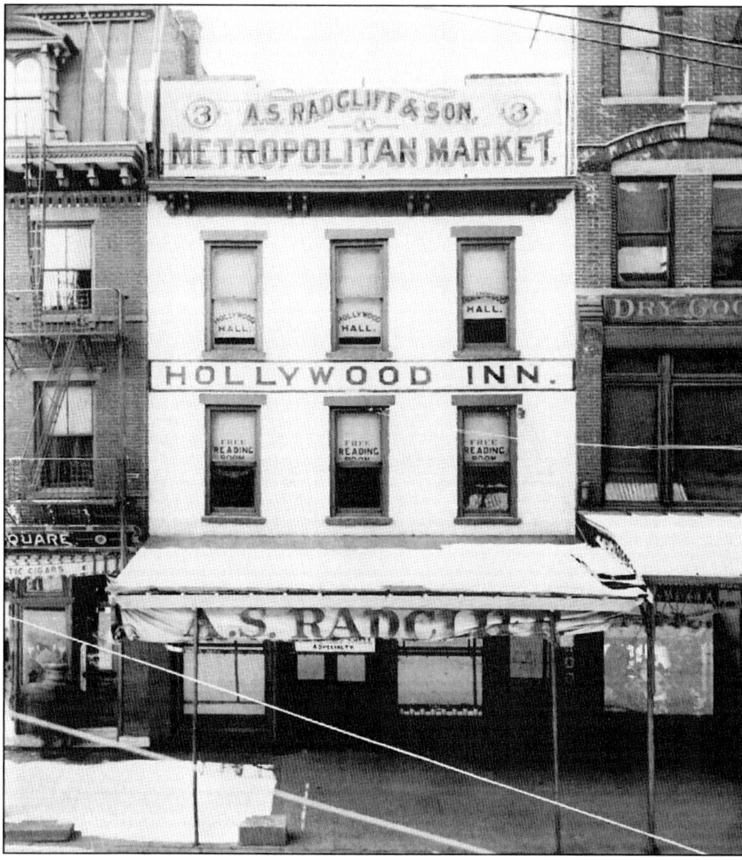

HOLLYWOOD INN. The original location of the Hollywood Inn was at 5 North Broadway in Getty Square, adjacent to the Getty House. The inn was the brainchild of Dr. James E. Freeman, rector of St. Andrew's Church and an active member of the Temperance Society. The inn also housed Radcliffe's market. This original inn soon outgrew this space, and a large new edifice on the corner of South Broadway and Hudson Street was built. (COY Planning.)

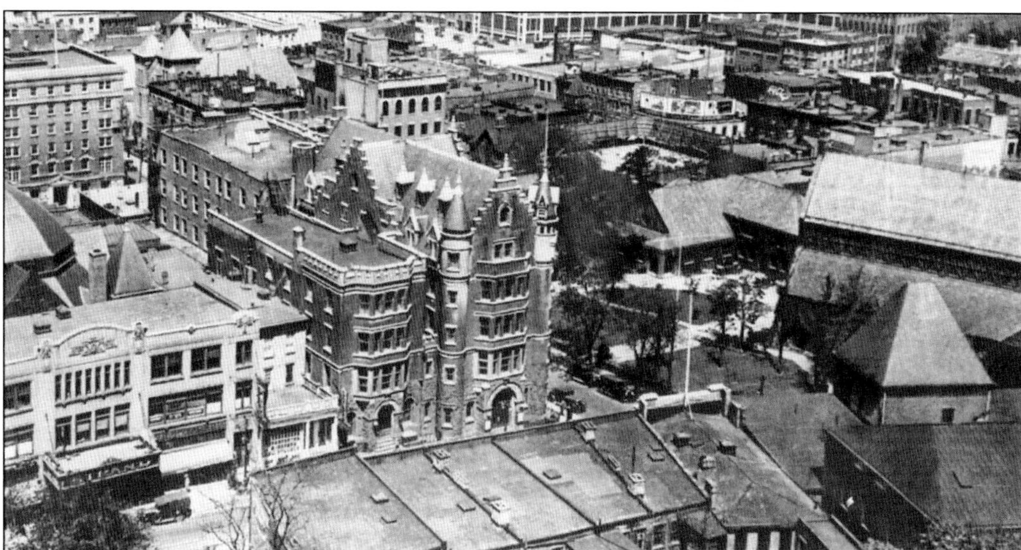

DOWNTOWN 1920S SHOWING THE HOLLYWOOD INN. The distinctive architecture of the Hollywood Inn easily stands out in this shot of downtown Yonkers looking northwest. Note St. John's Church on the right with its distinctive tiled roof. The Hollywood Inn was demolished in 1933. (COY Planning.)

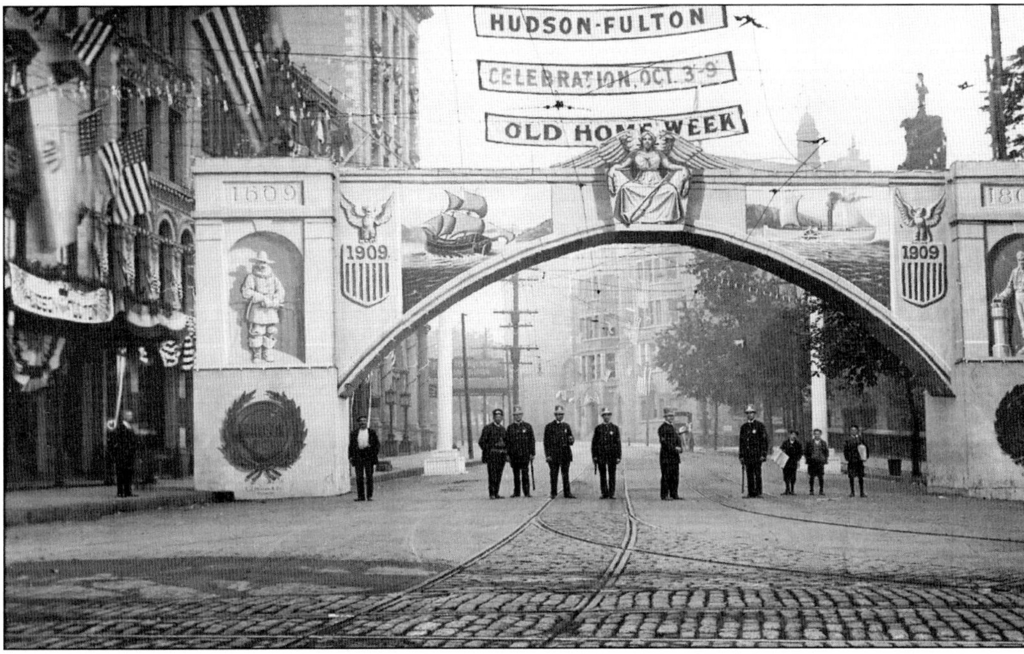

HUDSON-FULTON MEMORIAL ARCH WITH POLICEMEN, 1909. The first European discoverer to note the estuary that flows both north and south from what is now New York Harbor was Henry Hudson in the autumn of 1609. In 1909, the entire region celebrated the 300th anniversary of that discovery with parades, fancy dress balls, and other festivities. (Flynn.)

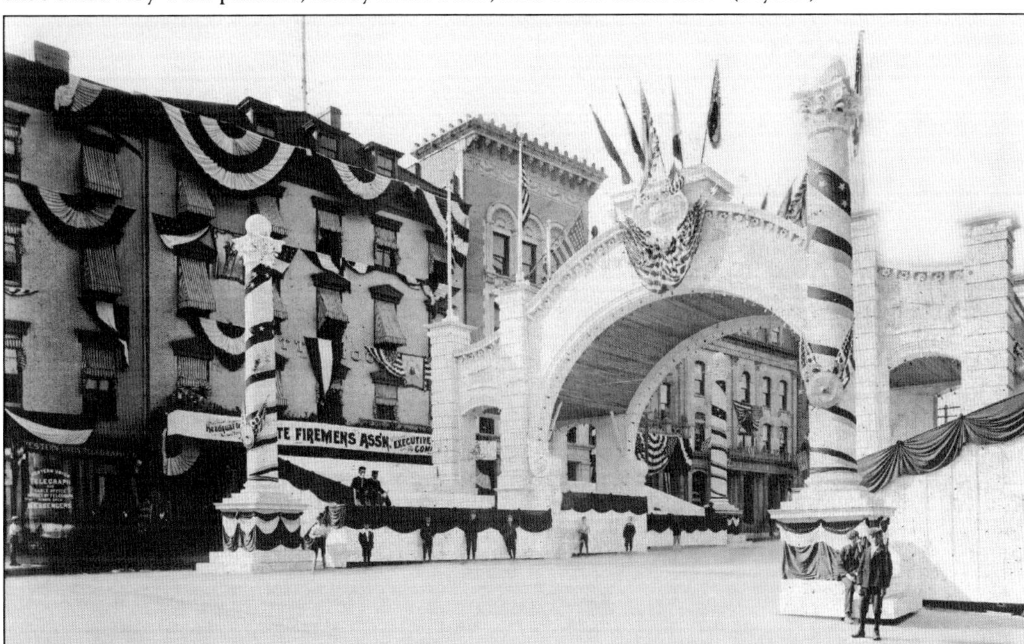

HUDSON-FULTON MEMORIAL ARCH, 1909. This arch was erected in Getty Square and a parade marched under it. The population of Yonkers swelled to 10 times its regular size with tourists who journeyed to the Hudson River Valley. A model of Philipse Manor Hall on a float was one of many features of the parade. (Flynn.)

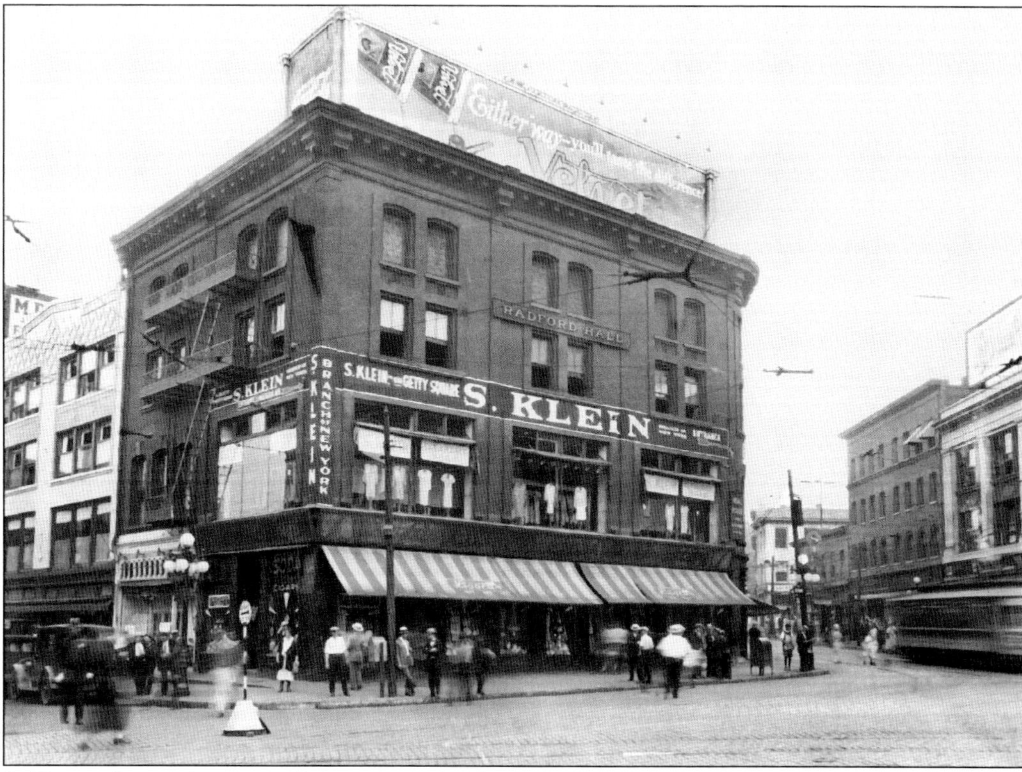

S. Klein, Getty Square. This imposing brick building formed the northern cornerstone of what was known as Getty Square. The Square, as locals call it, was named for Robert Parkhill Getty, as was an upscale planned neighborhood called Park Hill to the south. (COY Planning.)

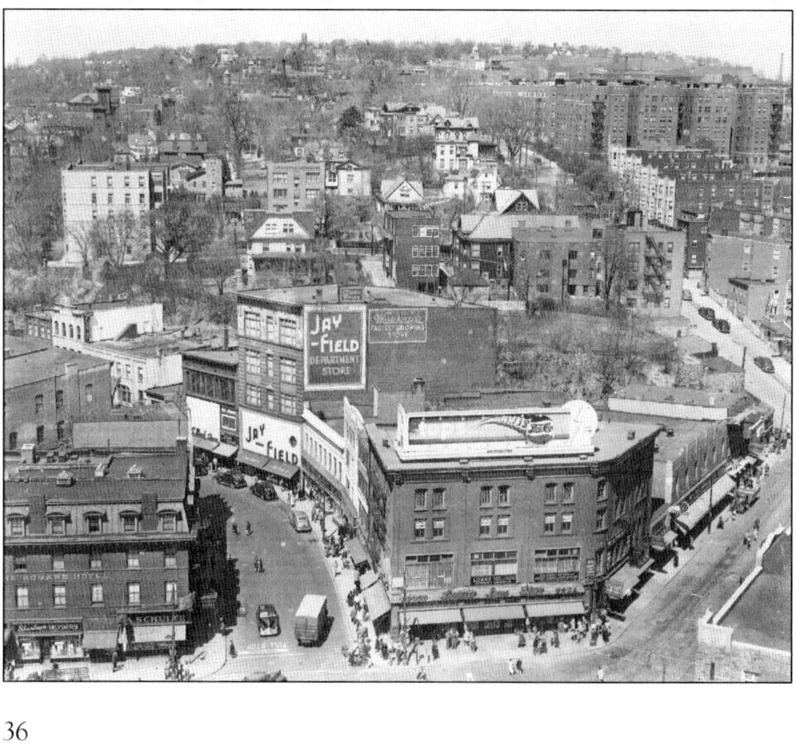

Getty Square, Looking North. This aerial view shows the Klein Building in the context of the northern-facing portion of the square. The street to the left is North Broadway or the Albany Post Road (US Route 9). The street going diagonally off to the right is Palisade Avenue. (COY Planning.)

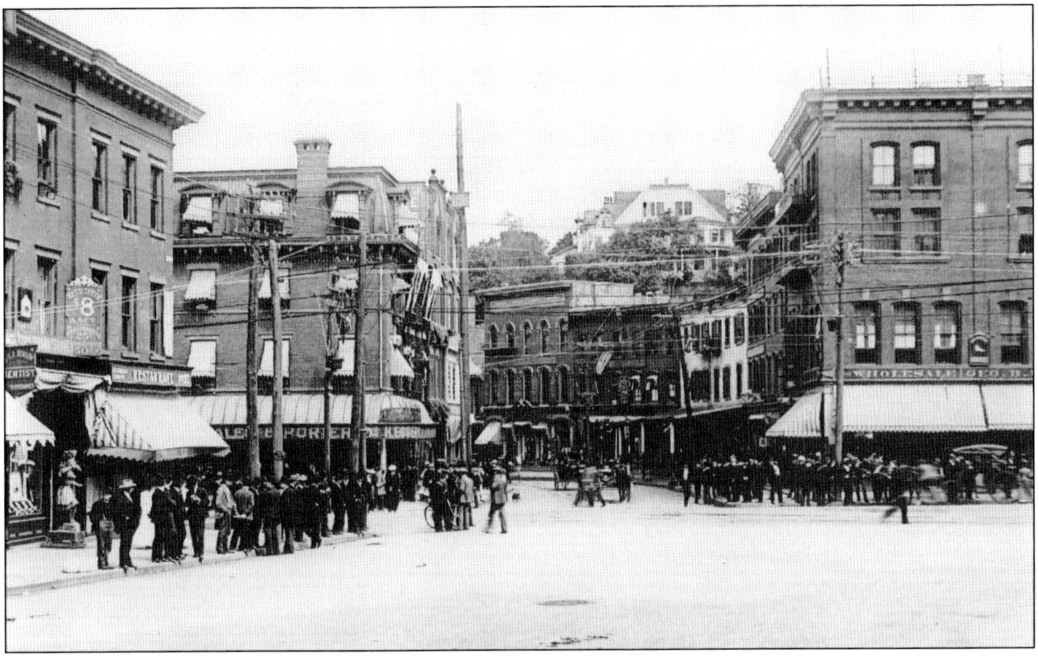

Getty Square. This view is looking north up North Broadway. In Yonkers, Broadway changes from South to North Broadway in the square. Notice that the Klein Building is lower in this image than in the opposite ones. Many buildings of the late 19th century lost their top stories to fires. (COY Planning.)

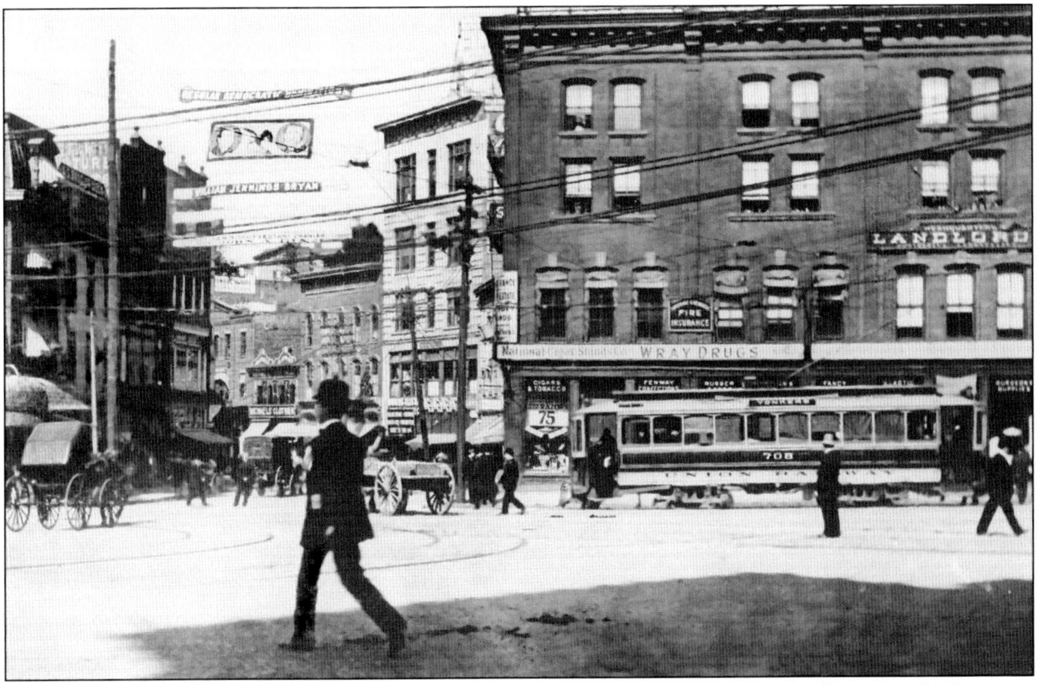

Getty Square with Banners for William Jennings Bryan. This is another view looking up North Broadway. Campaign banners for William Jennings Bryan suspended over the street date this image to 1896. (YHS.)

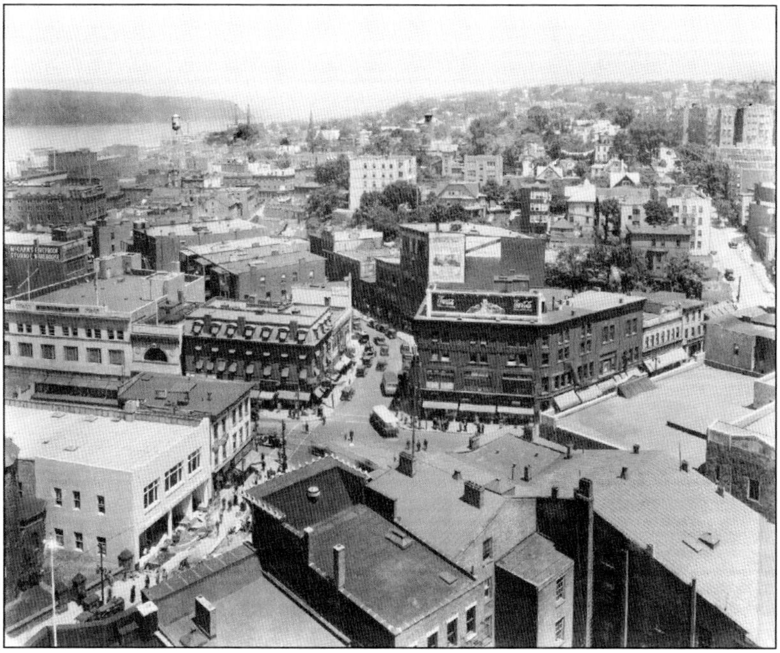

Getty Square. This aerial view of the square gives a more expansive view of the area. Note the unusual configuration of the square where a number of streets converge into an open plaza. This area was the shopping hub of lower Westchester for years, and the square and its surrounding streets were lined with mom-and-pop businesses. (COY Planning.)

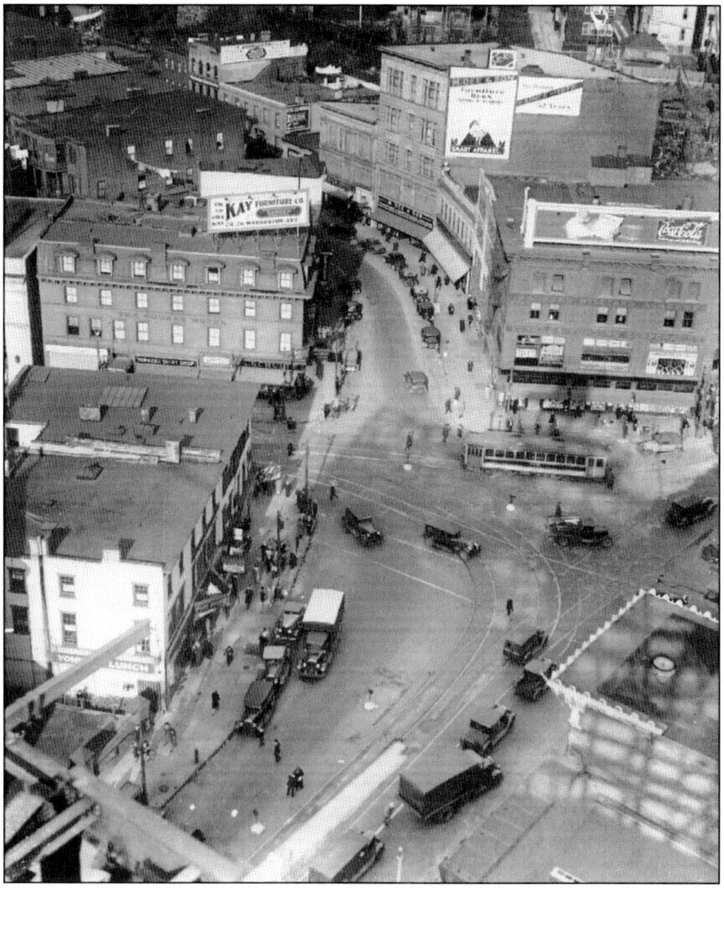

Getty Square, Looking North with Trolley. In this image showing the area in an even more open angle, the viewer can get a better feel for the square. The building at the top of the image with two billboards on its side still stands pretty much as it does in this image and was adaptively reused for ground-floor retail and upper-floor loft apartments. (Donald Kreutzberg.)

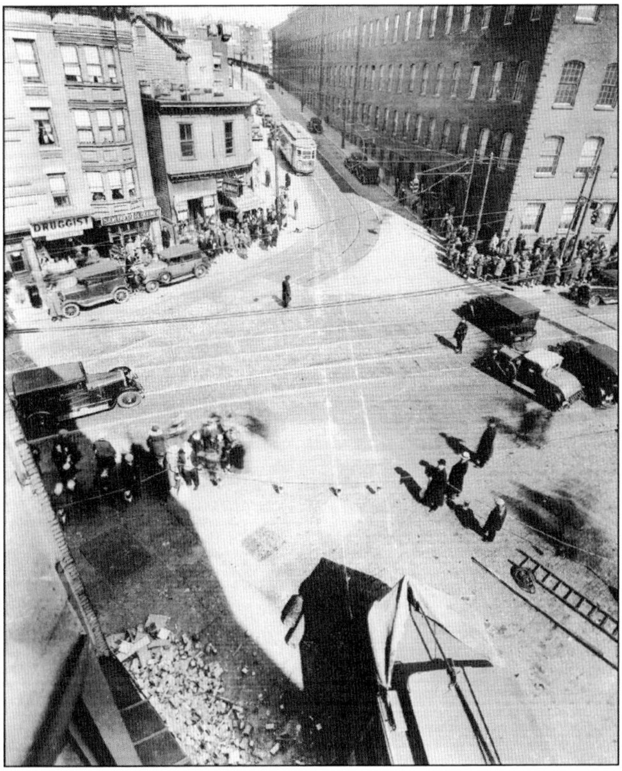

Getty Square, Looking Northeast. This aerial view is looking northeast toward Palisade Avenue, which branched off the square to Yonkers and Nepperhan Avenues, two major arterials that led out of the downtown into the more residential areas of Yonkers. Note the No. 7 trolley; the large brick building in the center was demolished. (COY Planning.)

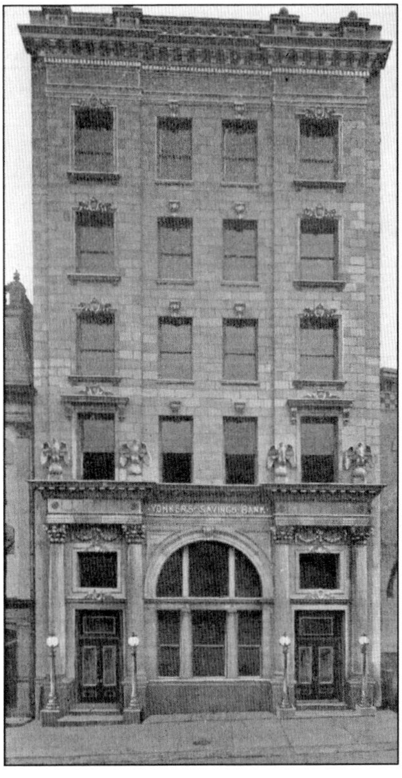

Yonkers Savings Bank, Getty Square, c. 1926. It is hard to go shopping without money. Even today, the square is home to many banks such as this one. In the early part of the 21st century, at least six major banking institutions could be found within a short walk of each other in downtown Yonkers. (YHS.)

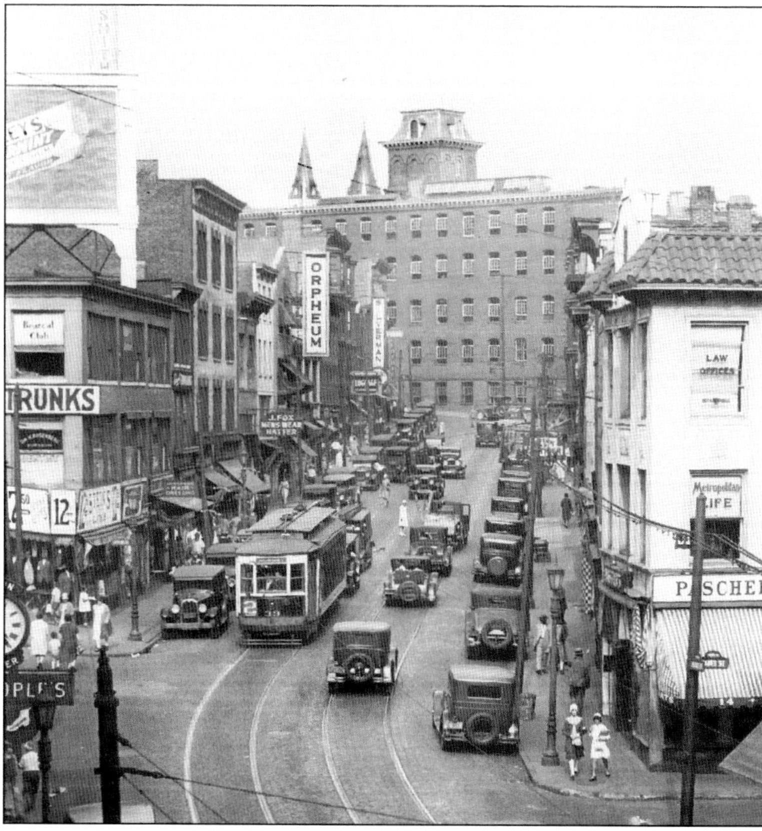

GETTY SQUARE, LOOKING EAST WITH NO. 2 TROLLEY. Another view facing northeast, this photograph shows the trolley coming down Palisade Avenue toward the square. The large building at the center of the photograph, which once housed a factory, no longer exists. The twin spires above it are St. Casimir's Church. On the lower left was a cigar store with a wooden Indian, a fond memory for Yonkers baby boomers. (HRM.)

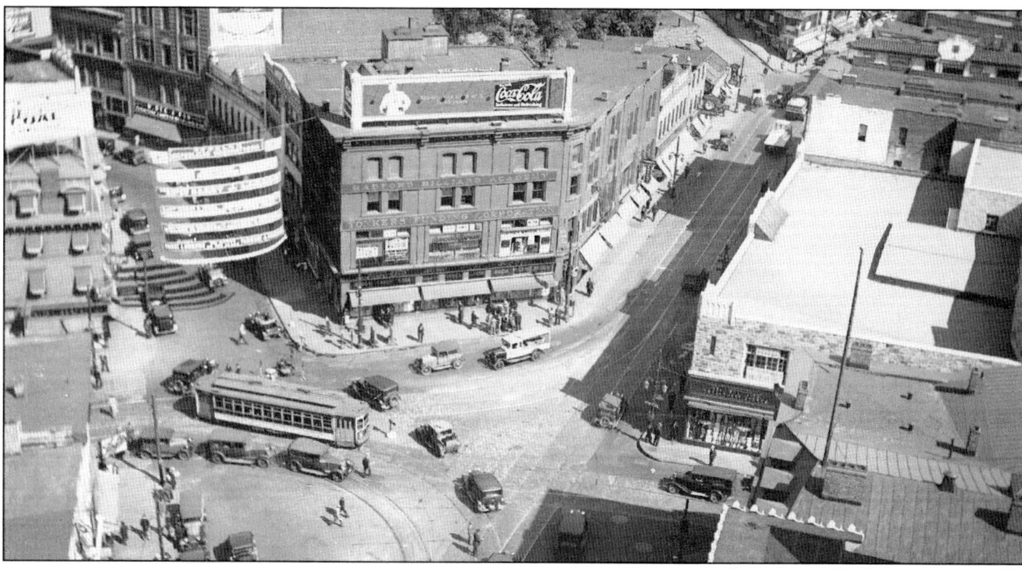

GETTY SQUARE, 1920S. Note the trolley and tracks in the square. The trolley system could carry a passenger from the Bronx line to mid-Westchester to the north and to the residential areas of eastern Yonkers. One of the hazards of the trolley tracks was to automobiles that had to navigate around and over them on narrow hard rubber tires of that era. Note the T-shaped store sign for Woodrow Jewelers (right of center), a business that only closed in 2007. (HRM.)

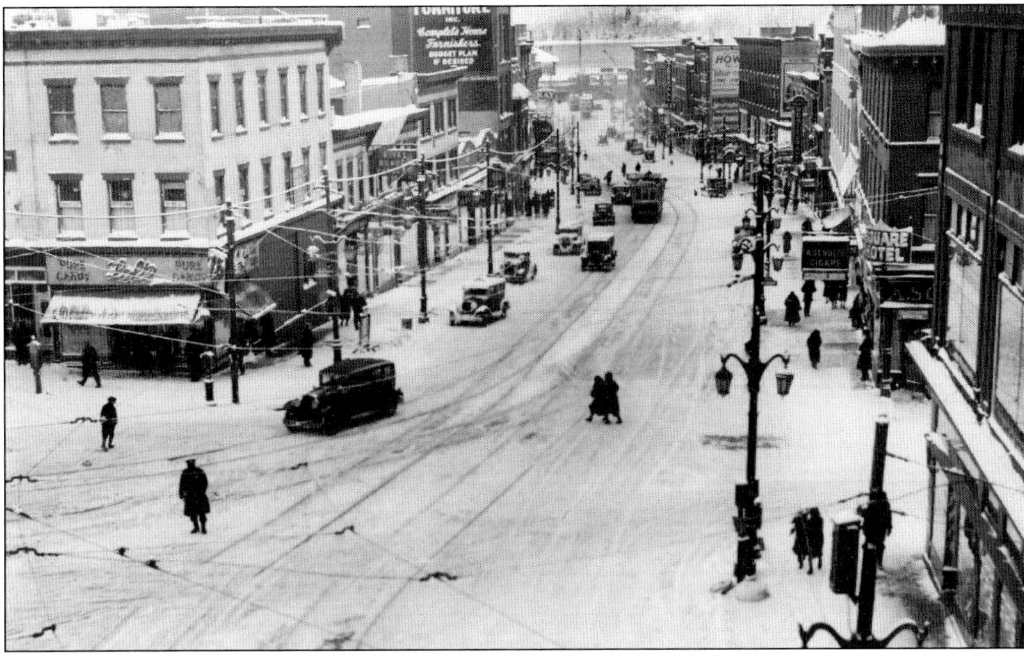

Getty Square from Roof of C.H. Martin. A wintry view of the square looking up Palisade Avenue can be seen here. The streets in the square were once two-way; increased congestion and traffic today have mandated that the streets are now one-way. Both North Broadway and Palisade Avenue are one-way going north from the square. (COY Planning.)

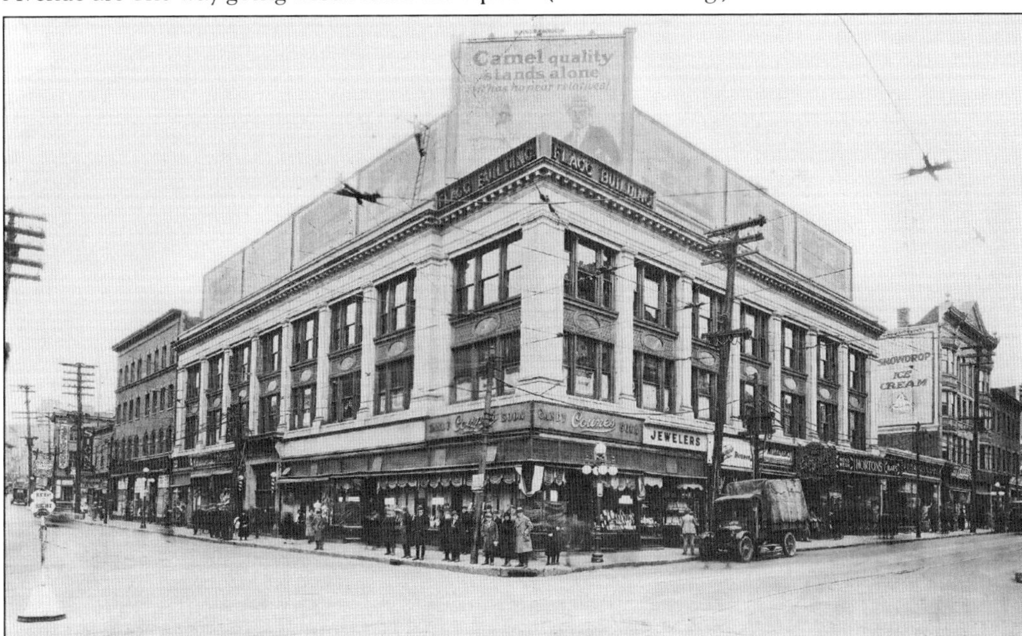

Flagg Building, C.H. Martin. Ethan Flagg was one of the major Yonkers industrialists of the late 19th century. The building he erected in Getty Square went through several manifestations, including a five-and-dime store. It is now C.H. Martin, whose owners documented its historic lineage and had it declared a landmark building. (COY Planning.)

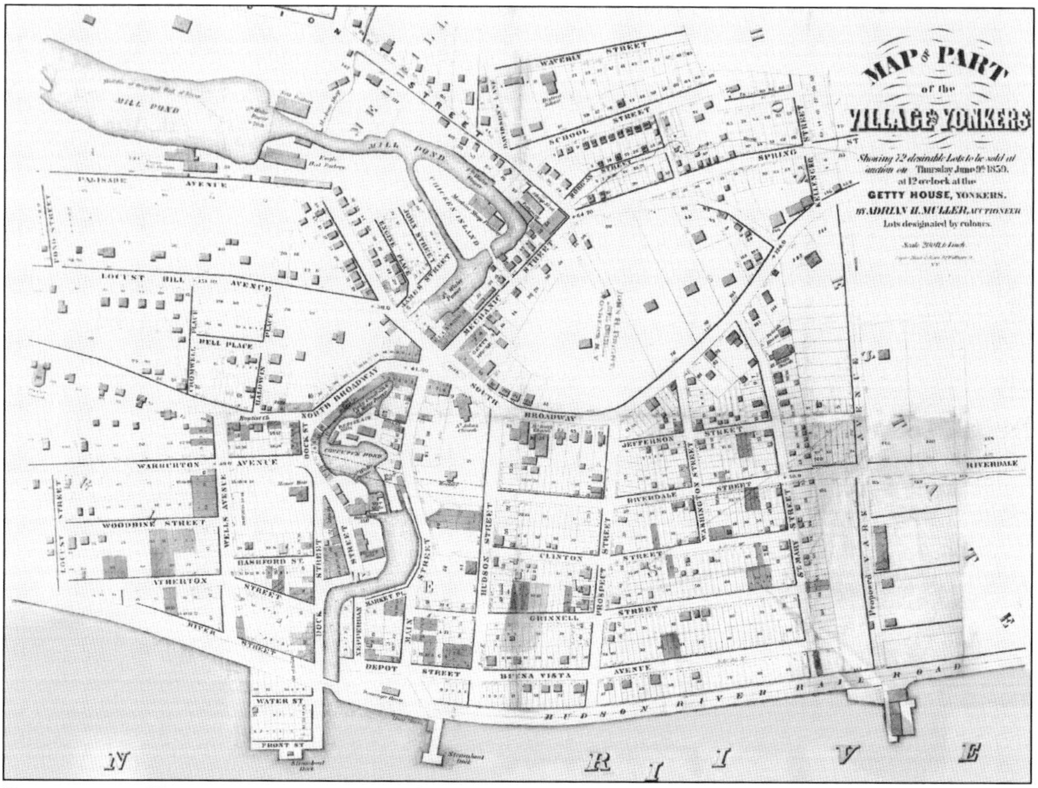

Downtown Yonkers Map, 1859. This map of Yonkers represents the configuration of the downtown not long after the building of the Hudson River Railroad tracks along the shores of the Hudson River (bottom). Note the extent of the Saw Mill River as it wends its way through the downtown towards the Hudson. As downtown developed, the Saw Mill was increasing squeezed, channeled, and covered over. (COY Planning.)

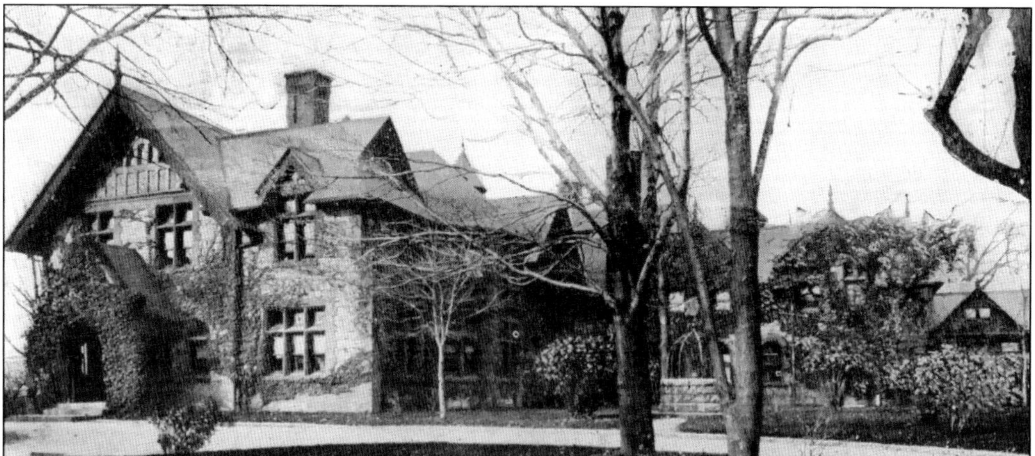

St. John's Rectory. On the grounds of St. John's Episcopal Church, the rectory is still in active use as housing for the clergy in charge, church offices, a guildhall, library, and kitchen. Much of the building remains unchanged from its origins in the 19th century. (St. John's Episcopal Church.)

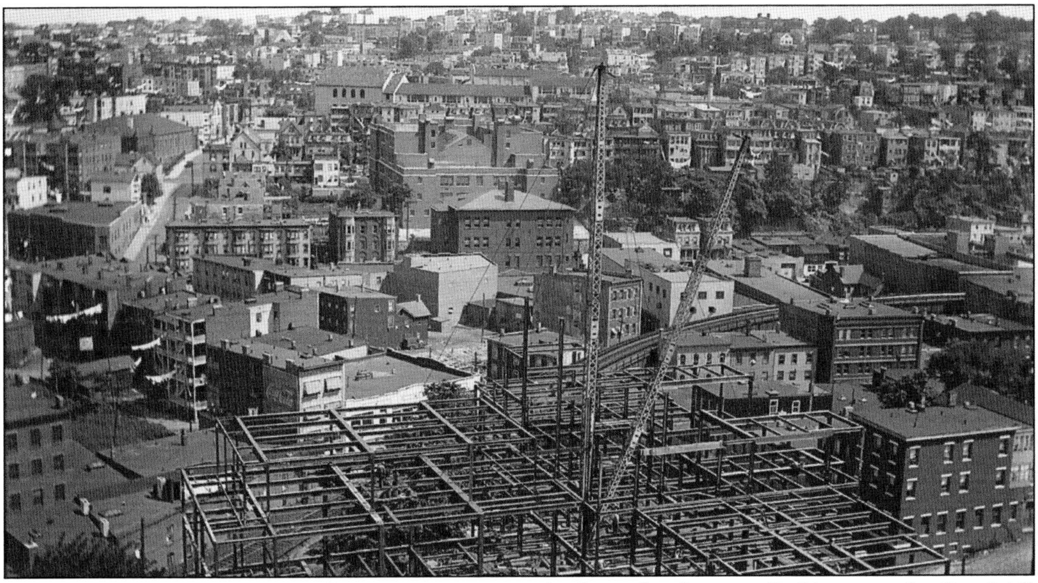

Panoramic Shot of Yonkers/Chicken Island. Chicken Island is so called because the Saw Mill River once completely surrounded this area and local residents kept their chickens there. Once this agricultural use was no longer practical, it was extensively built over. Parts of the river to the west and south were filled in, and it was an island no longer. (COY Planning.)

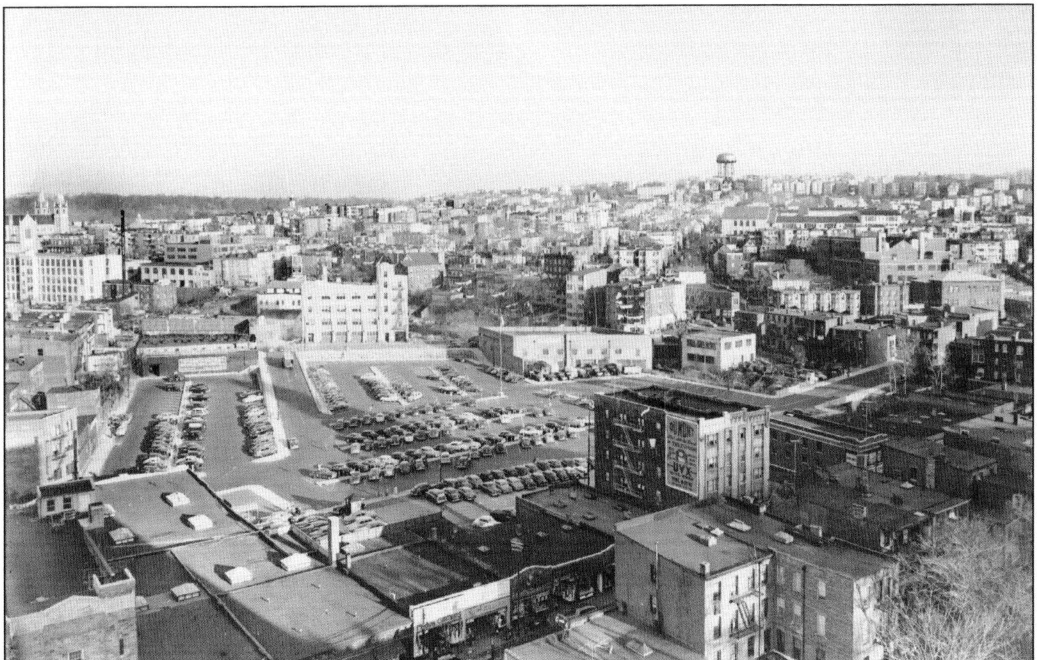

Chicken Island. This aerial view of Chicken Island shows its current use as an open parking lot. A water tower sits atop the area known as Nodine Hill. New Main Street is running diagonally across the lower part of the photograph, and the light-colored building in the center is Yonkers Fire Department Headquarters. (YHS.)

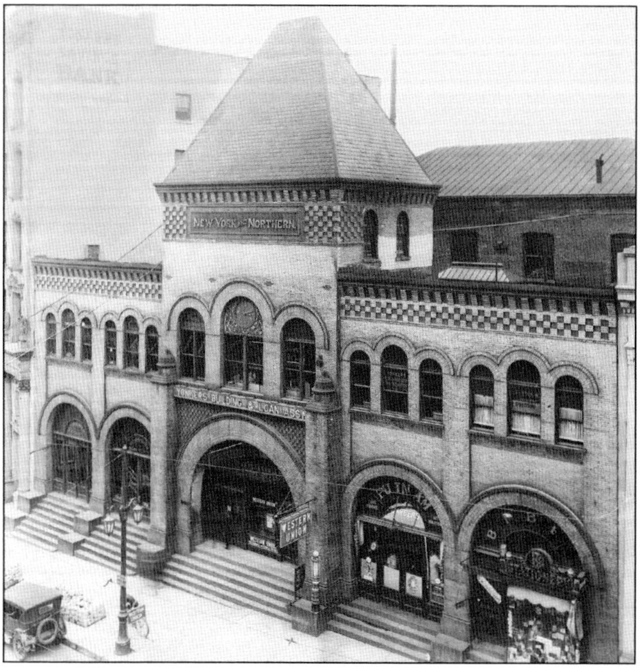

Train Station at 30 South Broadway. A branch railroad, the Putnam Division, known as the "Old Put," once ran from a station at 30 South Broadway in Getty Square through Park Hill to the Yonkers/Bronx line. The train was decommissioned in 1958, and the railbed is now used as a hiking trail. (YHS.)

Train Tracks Behind 30 South Broadway. Seen in this image taken from the rear of 30 South Broadway, these rail tracks ran alongside New Main Street into the Park Hill neighborhood, eventually taking passengers through Van Cortlandt Park in the Bronx to connect with the Broadway subway into Manhattan. (COY Planning.)

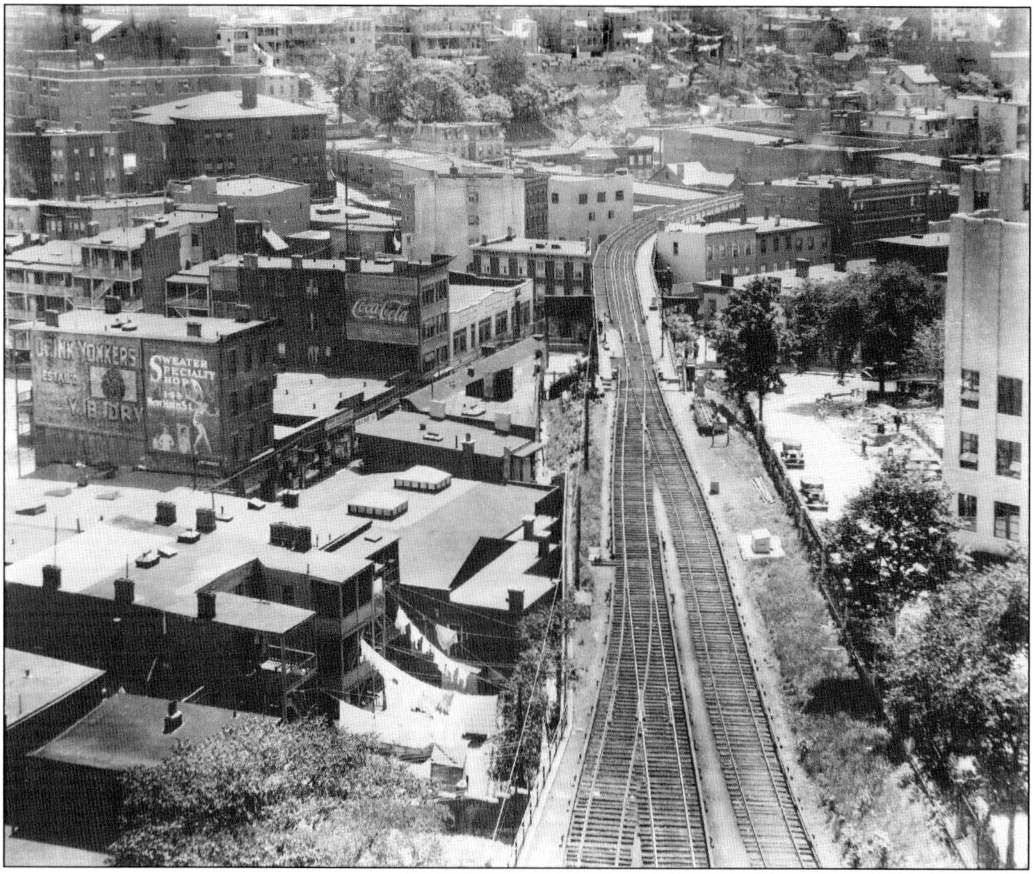

YONKERS AERIAL-TYPE MAP, 1860. This graphic map from 1860 shows how Yonkers is growing up around the downtown. Note the spiderweb configuration of the streets leading into and out of Getty Square and the new train station and pier on the Hudson. Nodine Hill is scarcely built up and Main Street was relatively new; the primary street in the downtown up to that point was Hudson Street. (COY Planning.)

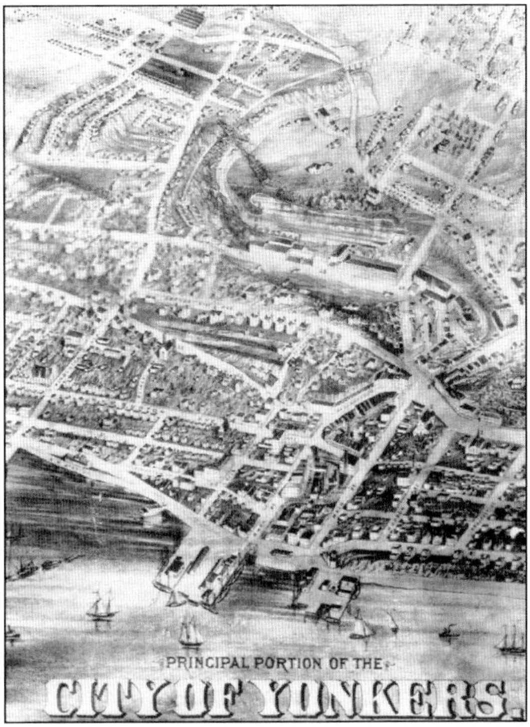

WATERFRONT. Note the outflow of the Saw Mill River into the Hudson under the now raised railroad tracks. Yonkers truly had a highly industrialized port area with the Otis Elevator Buildings in the upper right. The large boat in the foreground is the Hudson River dayliner, which took passengers to Bear Mountain on pleasure excursions. (HRM.)

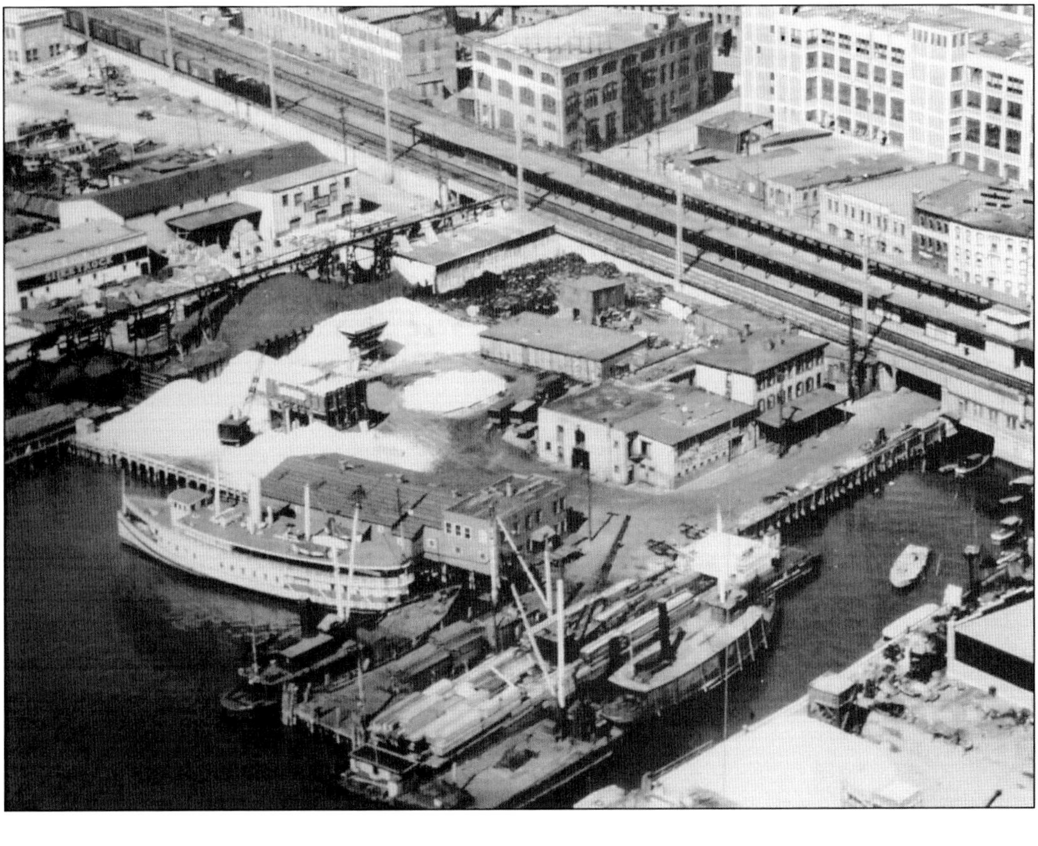

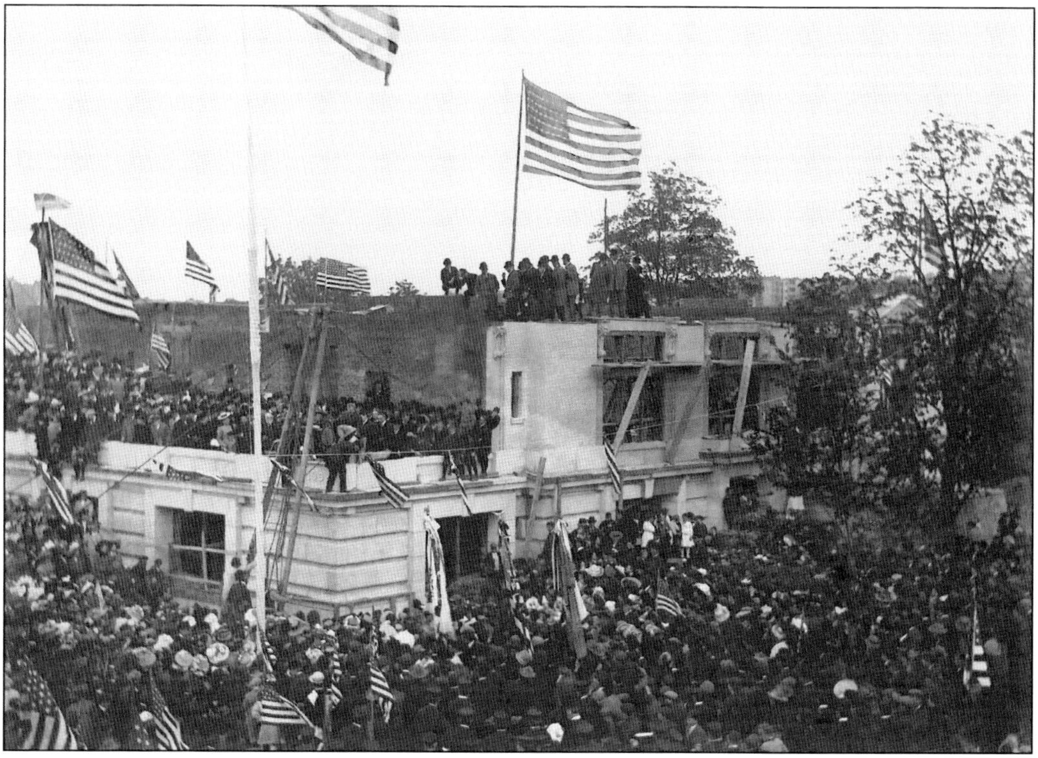

City Hall Cornerstone. As Yonkers grew, it outgrew its municipal offices housed in Philipse Manor Hall since 1868. When Yonkers attained city status in 1872, officials decided to build a stately Beaux-Arts structure on a high bluff in Washington Park, at the intersection of South Broadway and Yonkers Avenue. The cornerstone was laid with much fanfare in 1908. (YHS.)

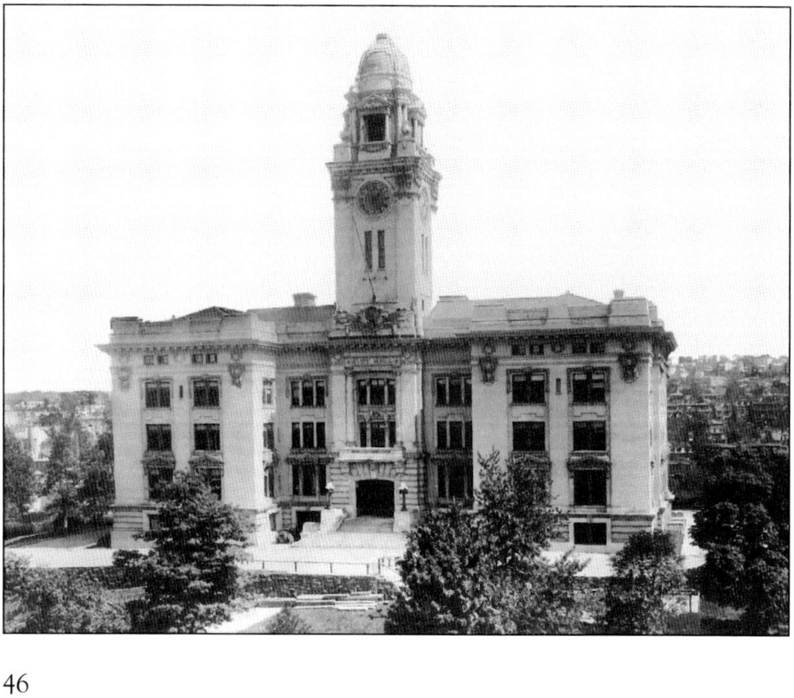

City Hall Rear View. A combination of stately architecture and imposing location make Yonkers City Hall a highly visible landmark from miles around. This view shows its western face. Stairs leading down from the base of the building go west to end at the War Memorial built in 1922. (COY Planning.)

Four

From Village to City

Yonkers has always found itself in an interesting position—literally. A location approximately 15 miles north of Midtown puts Yonkers in the "shadow of the giant." Yonkers's waterfront made it a convenient transportation hub for steamboats, starting with Robert Fulton and the *Clermont.* Some lethal steamboat accidents made passengers wary. In 1849, railroad tracks were laid across the western banks of the Hudson. When the builders encountered the bay that interrupted the straight line of the tracks, the granite palisades were torn down to use as landfill, channeling the Saw Mill River into a narrower path in the process.

Yonkers was now easily accessible from the bustle of Manhattan by two different modes—water and train. With its spectacular views from high bluffs on the eastern banks of the Hudson, the wealthy built their country homes. Samuel Tilden, one of the wealthiest men in America in the mid-19th century, actually had a private train station called Greystone. Castle-like residences were built in a staggered fashion along Warburton Avenue and North Broadway to maximize river and palisade views. Leo Baekeland, the inventor of plastic (named Bakelite in his honor), owned a large mansion in Yonkers.

As these wealthy men died off, new owners could no longer afford to maintain the enormous gardens and grounds on these estates. As properties were sold, the land was subdivided and purchased by developers who built tract homes or multiple-family dwellings. The first apartment house in Yonkers on Buena Vista Avenue is still occupied and was used in filming the Steven Spielberg–directed movie *Catch Me if You Can.*

The waterfront around the Saw Mill River, named Getty Square for wealthy resident Robert Parkhill Getty, became a major shopping area serviced by a citywide network of trolleys. The east side, now served by trolleys, became almost exclusively residential. In the 1950s, Cross County Shopping Center, which many consider the first shopping mall in the United States, was built. Postwar prosperity put a car into almost every driveway, so now shoppers could drive to Cross County. Soon, Getty Square found itself a bit of a commercial dinosaur with limited parking and traditional mom-and-pop stores that lacked the charisma and advertising clout of the large, chain department stores, like John Wanamaker's and Gimbel's.

But the population of Yonkers continued to grow and it became a city, ultimately becoming the fourth-most-populous city in New York.

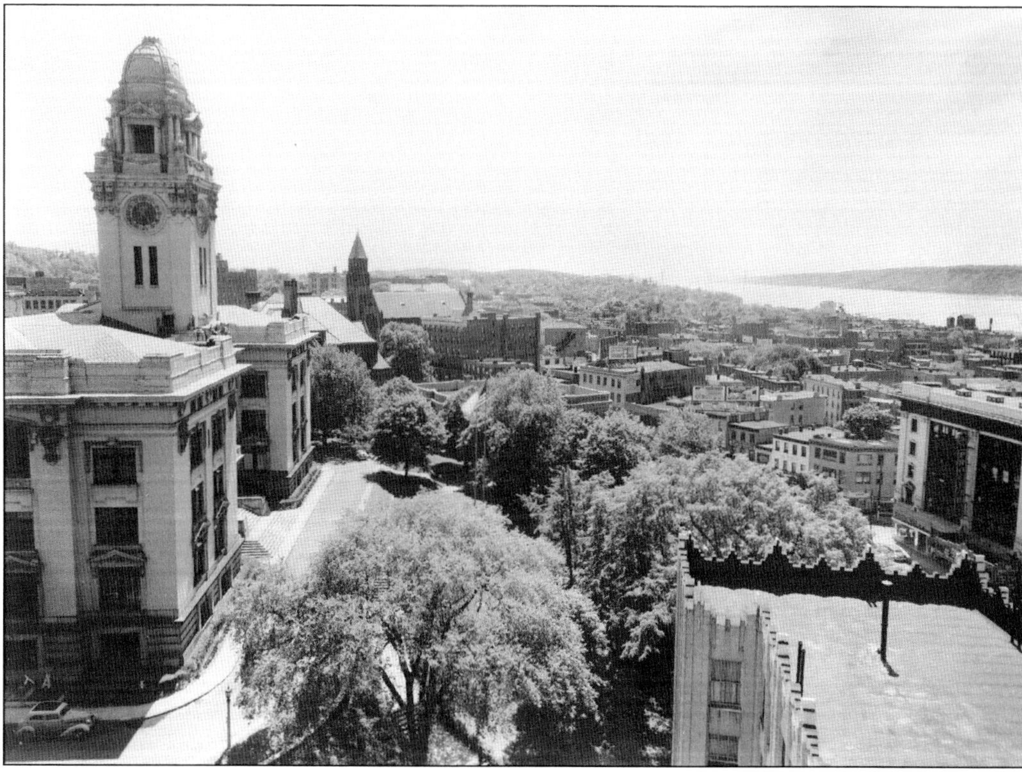

City Hall, West Facade. This aerial view of city hall shows its imposing vantage point with a view of the Hudson reaching to Manhattan in the background. The structure houses the mayor's office, the Yonkers City Council chamber and offices, and an ornate courtroom where many television scenes and movies are filmed. The spire belongs to St. Mary's Roman Catholic Church. (COY Planning.)

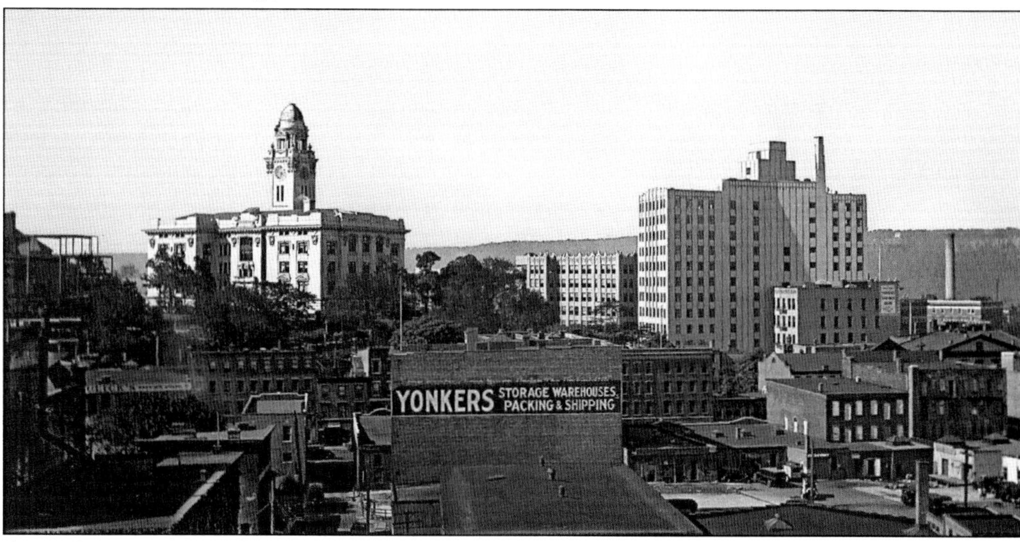

City Hall, Looking South Toward Manhattan. City hall rises above two other major office buildings on South Broadway. This shot, taken in the 1920s, shows buildings along New Main Street and in Chicken Island, which were demolished. (COY Planning.)

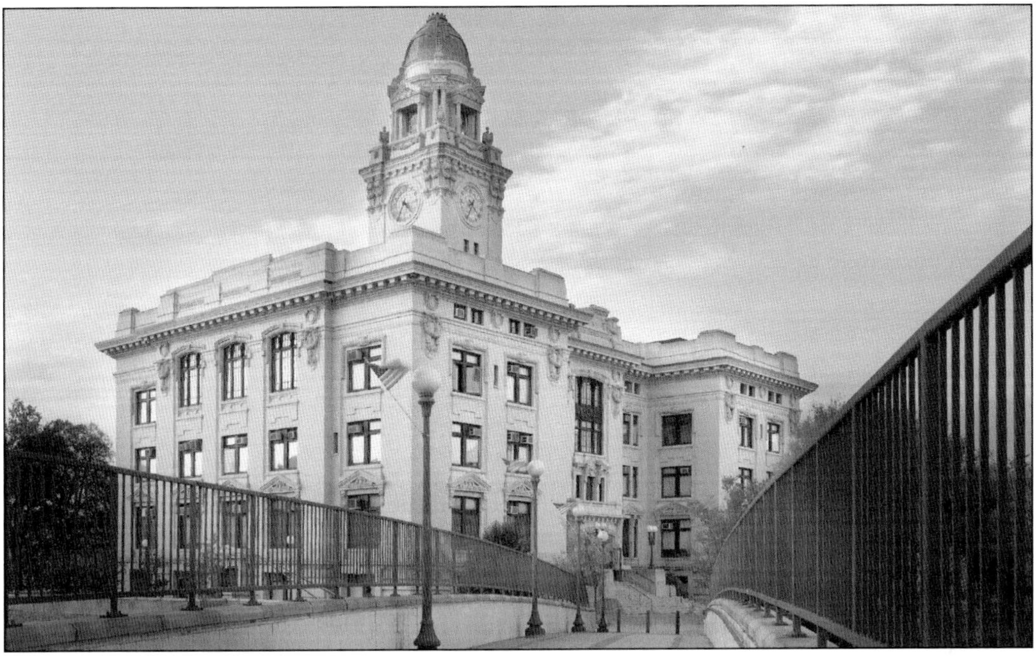

CITY HALL, EAST FACADE. This corner of the building houses the city clerk's office on the ground floor, the mayor's office on the second floor, and the Yonkers City Council chamber on the fourth floor along with the law department and other offices. The footbridge in the foreground crosses Nepperhan Avenue to the Cacace Justice Center and Yonkers Police Headquarters. (BD.)

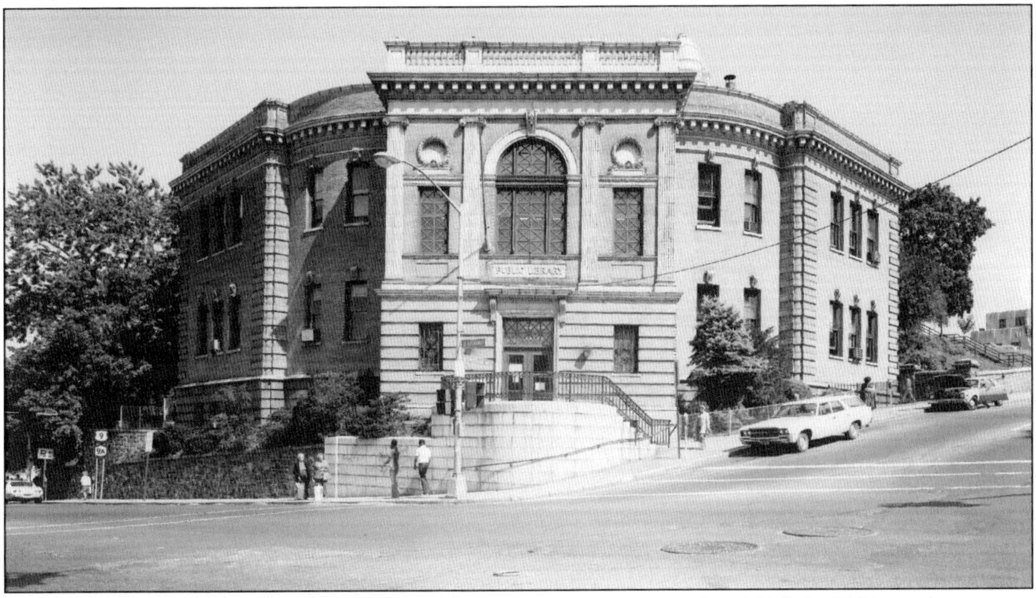

CARNEGIE LIBRARY. The Yonkers Public Library system was started in 1893. In 1901, steel magnate and philanthropist Andrew Carnegie donated $50,000 for construction of a library building. The cornerstone was laid in June 1903 for what was one of many Carnegie libraries nationwide. The library was demolished in 1982 to accommodate the widening of the Nepperhan Avenue arterial. That demolition is generally considered to be one of Yonkers's most shameful moments. (COY Planning.)

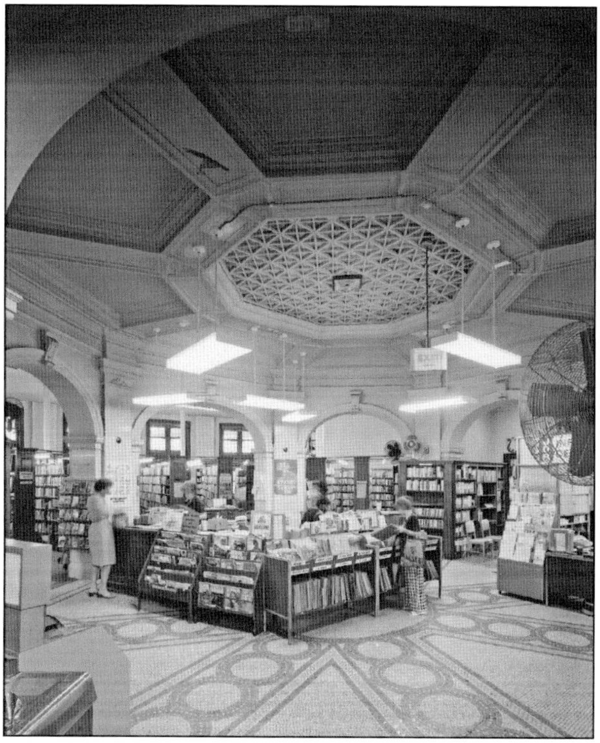

Carnegie Library Interior. The architecture of the Carnegie library was unique in many ways, as the land allotted for its construction was a hilly outcropping of Washington Park alongside city hall. The building was almost octagonal, and this is reflected in the interior themes shown in the elaborate tiling on floors and ceilings. (Library of Congress.)

Carnegie Library Interior. The second floor of the library contained lunettes, original oil paintings showing various facets of Yonkers history, including quite an elaborate arrangement of Yonkers inventors and other men of science and engineering. Fortunately, these lunettes were saved when the library was demolished, and two are housed in the Yonkers Public Library on Central Avenue. (Library of Congress.)

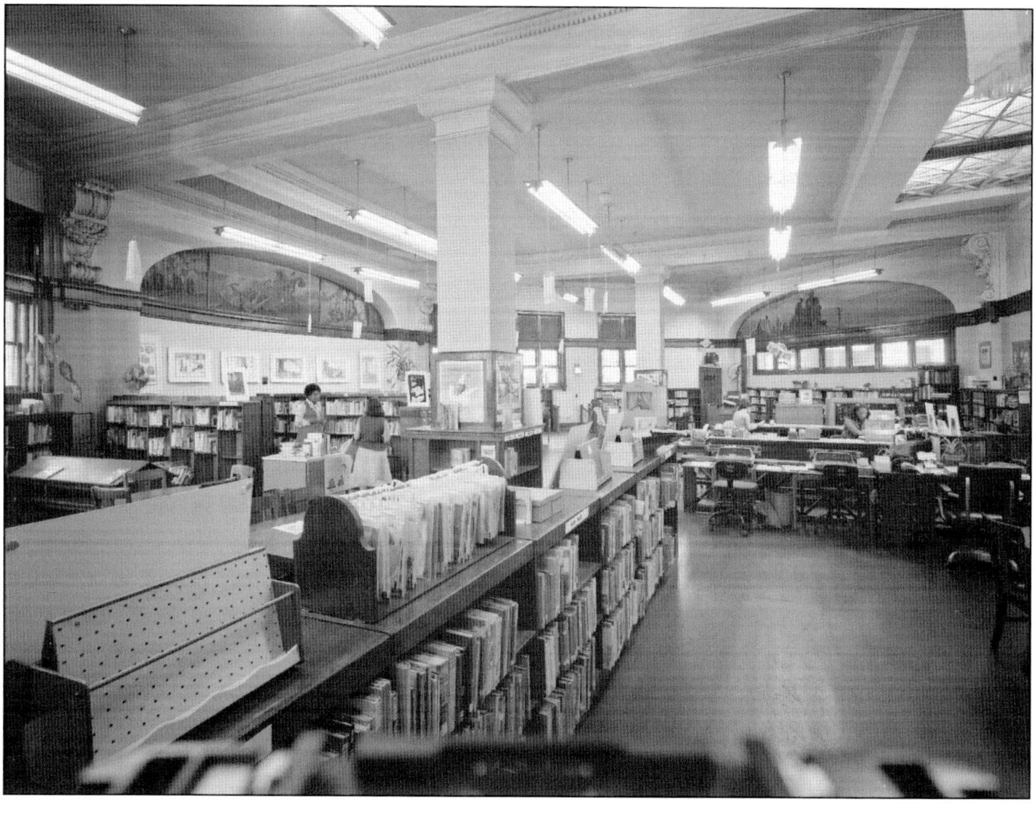

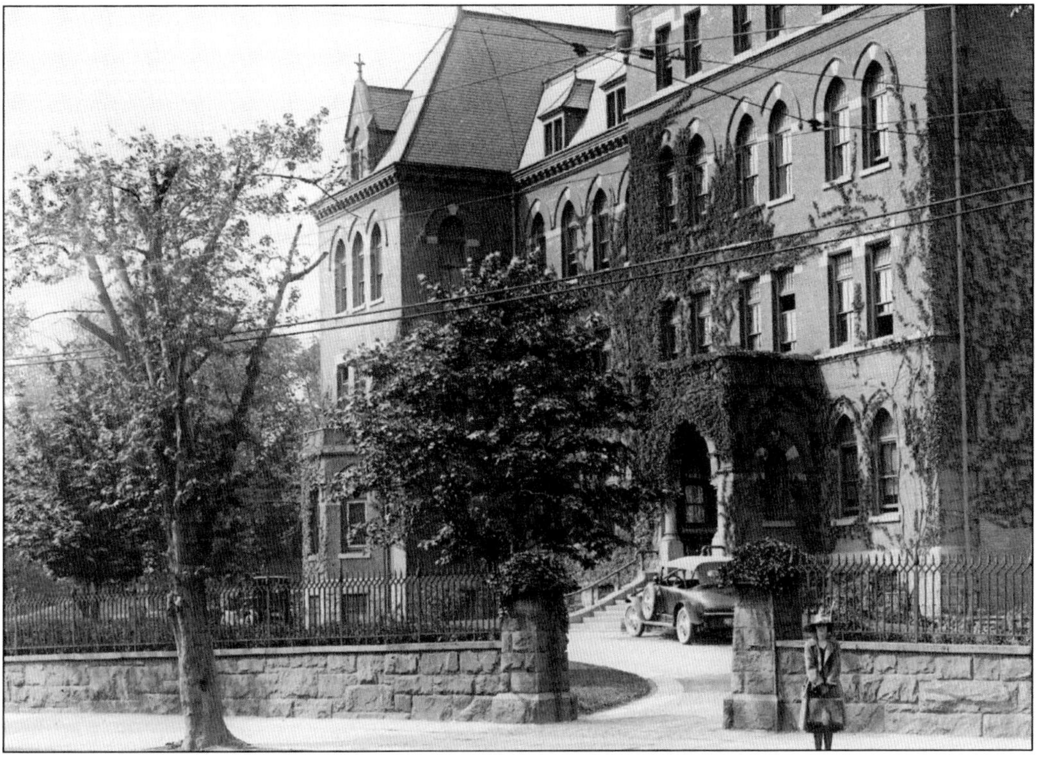

St. Joseph's Hospital. The first two major hospitals in Yonkers were founded in 1888 as part of an outreach by religious organizations. St. Joseph's Hospital at South Broadway and Vark Street was established by the Sisters of Charity of Mount St. Vincent. In 1976, it opened an adjacent nursing home, and, with its satellite branches, is now one of the largest hospitals in Westchester. (YHS.)

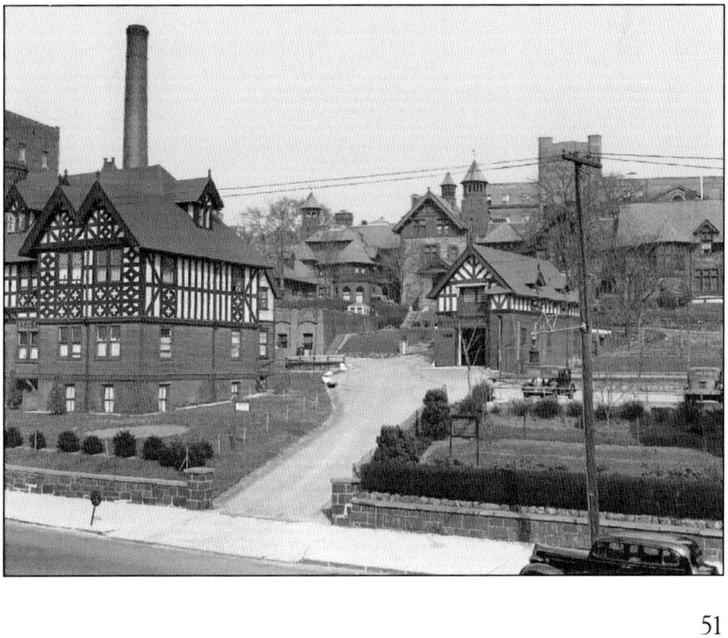

St. John's Hospital on North Broadway. Originally located at the corner of North Broadway and Ashburton Avenue, St. John's Hospital was founded by St. John's Episcopal Church, Getty Square. The buildings pictured were replaced by a large modern structure further north, and the old hospital was demolished, leaving only the smokestack, which still stands. (BD.)

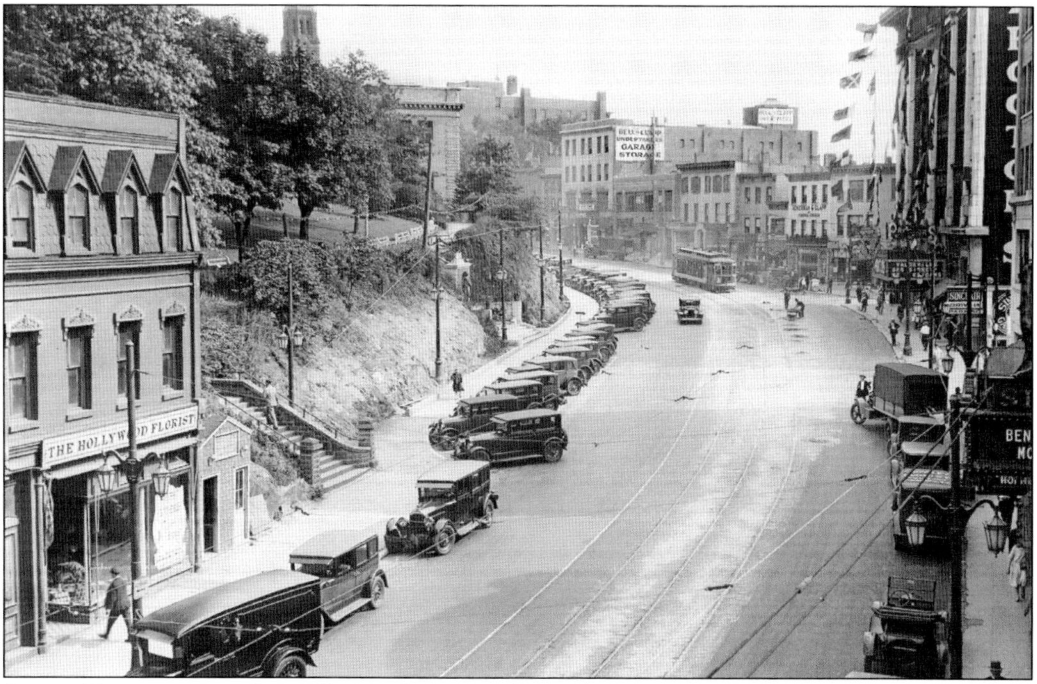

South Broadway at City Hall. This view shows the gentle curve of South Broadway as its heads south toward New York City. The tall building on the right housed the Proctor's Theatre; the painted sign for the theater can still be seen on the side of the building. (YHS.)

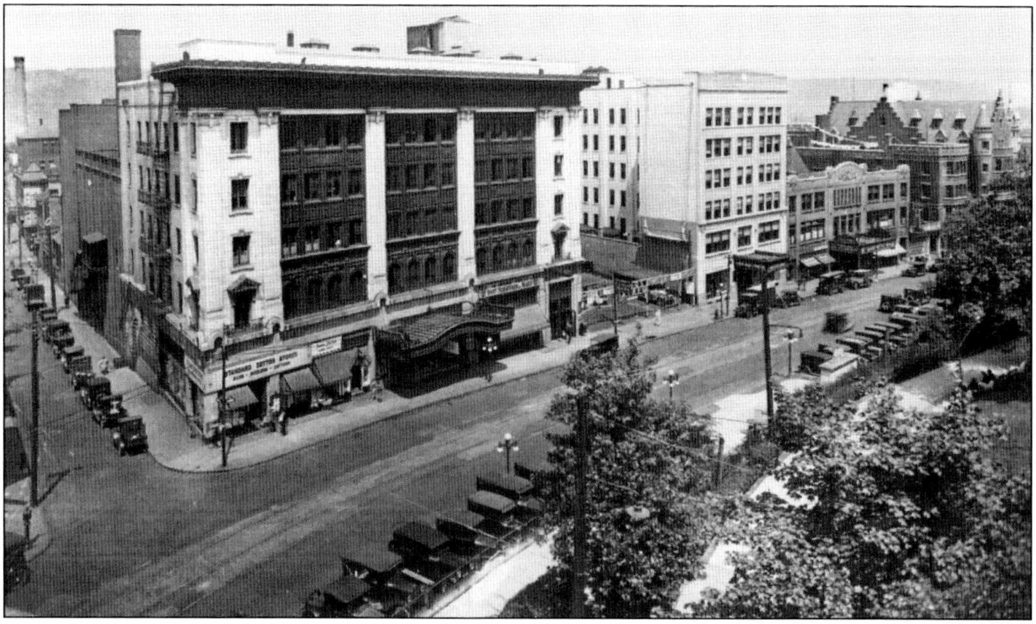

Prospect and South Broadway at City Hall. In this view looking west toward the Hudson River, 53 South Broadway at Prospect Street is the home of the Proctor's Theatre. During the 1940s and 1950s, Proctor's presented not only first-run movies but live appearances by the stars themselves. The parklike land in the foreground is Washington Park, where Yonkers City Hall is located. (COY Planning.)

Otis Elevator Building and Smokestack. This building was part of the Otis Elevator complex at the corner of Dock and River Streets. The large brick smokestack emblazoned with Otis still stands, and the building has been adaptively used for the Riverfront Library and the Yonkers Board of Education. (YHS.)

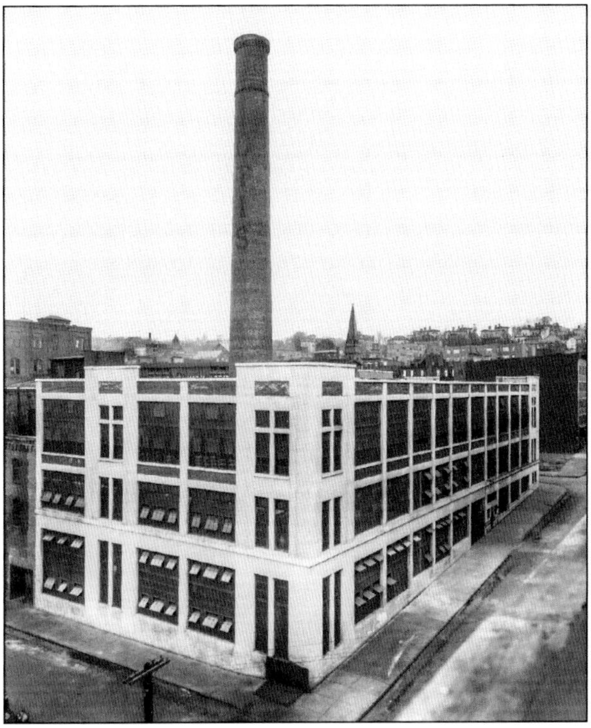

Power Plant on Alexander Street. Located on Alexander Street, this power plant is owned by Westchester County. The smokestack in the background, interestingly, is purely ornamental. When built in the early 20th century, the top was illuminated, and parties for up to 120 people were held on the top tier of the smokestack. (Westchester County Planning Department.)

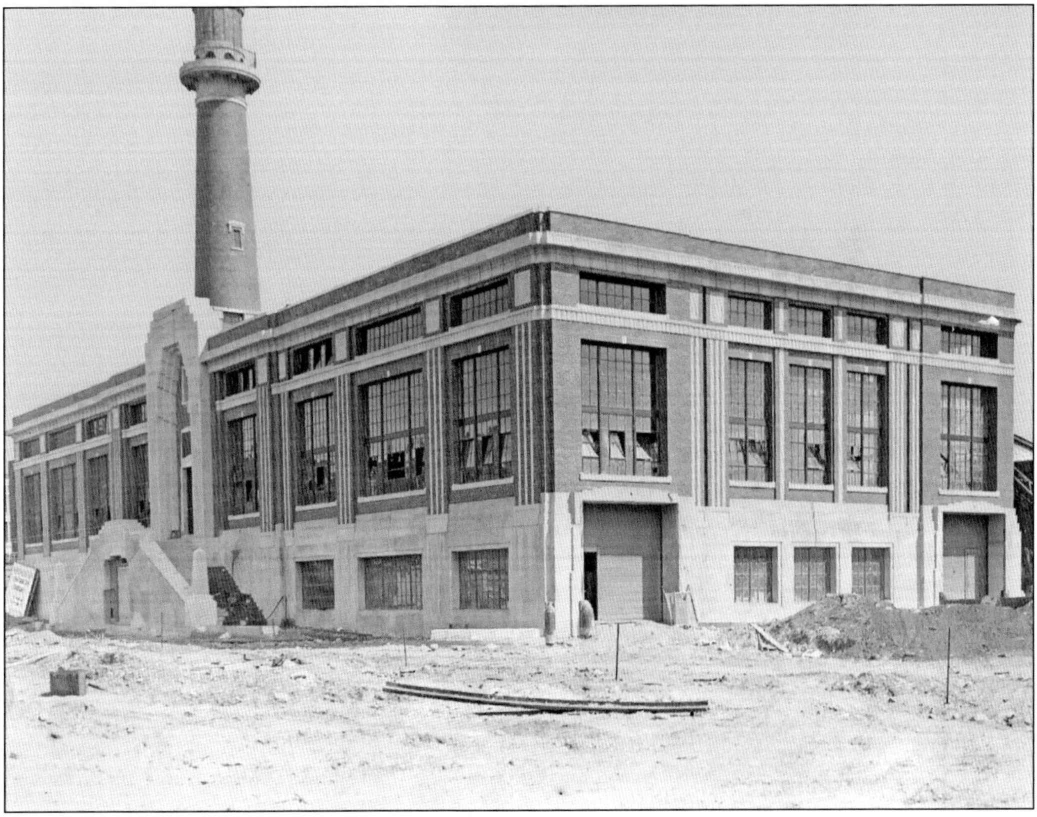

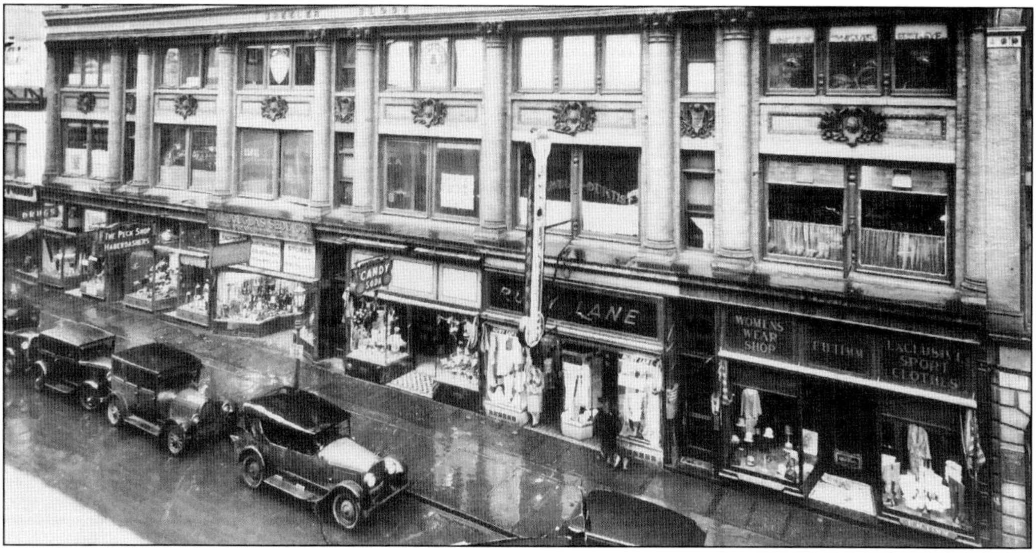

Wheeler Block Building. Located on North Broadway just north of Getty Square, the Wheeler Block Building still looks much like it did when it was built in the 1880s. Two prominent Yonkers families built the structure, and shield-like coats of armor are embedded in the facade. The ground floor is retail; the upper floors are used for storage, and some were renovated into loft apartments. (YHS.)

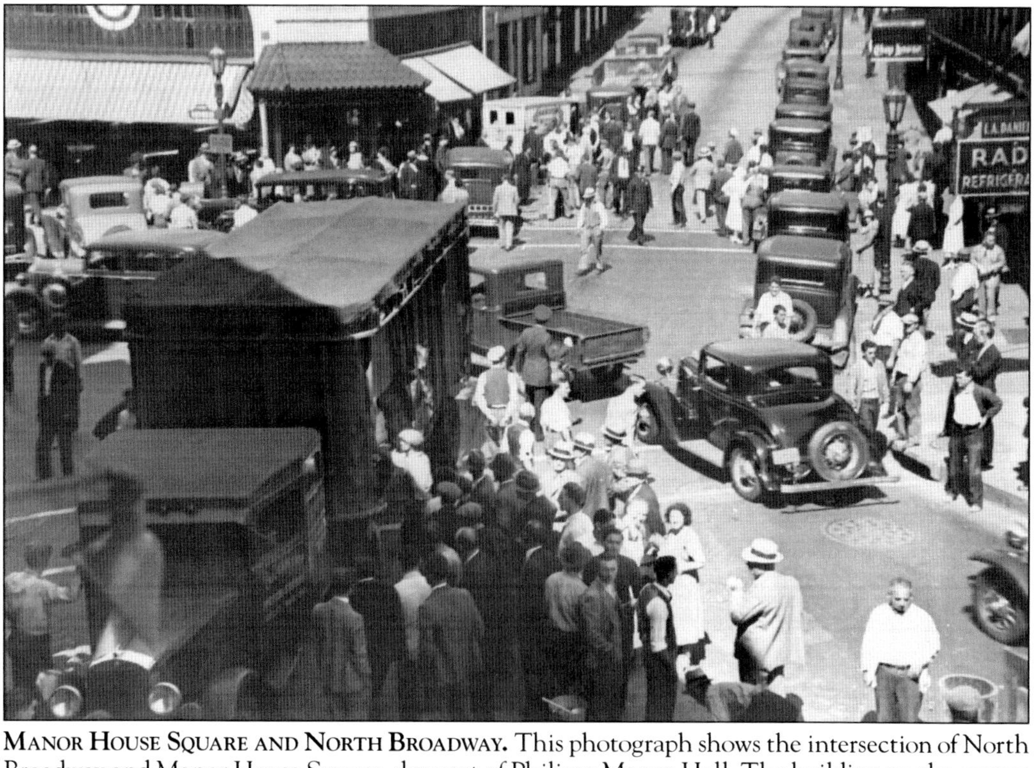

Manor House Square and North Broadway. This photograph shows the intersection of North Broadway and Manor House Square, due east of Philipse Manor Hall. The building on the corner housed a local Yonkers savings bank, which has changed hands over the years. The bank contains a large painted mural of the Stauffer View of Philipse Manor Hall. (YHS.)

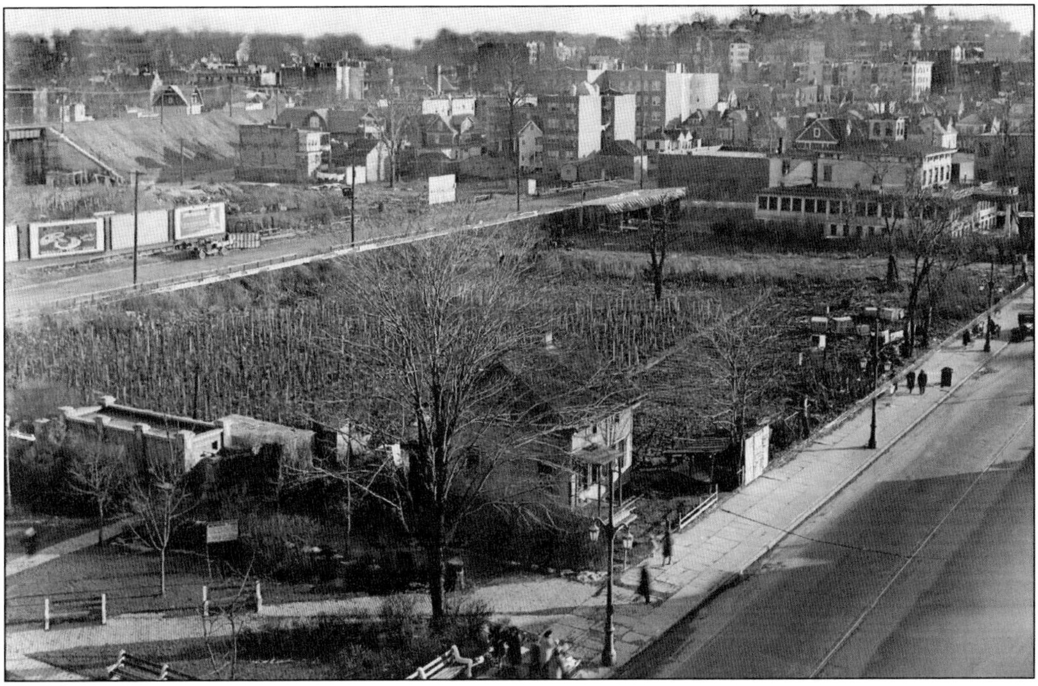

LINCOLN PARK. Shown here as an empty field, Lincoln Park, located at the corners of McLean Avenue and South Broadway, now contains a restaurant, parking lot, banks, a retail establishment, and a small plaza used for civic events. The plaza contains a standing bronze statue of Lincoln. (COY Planning.)

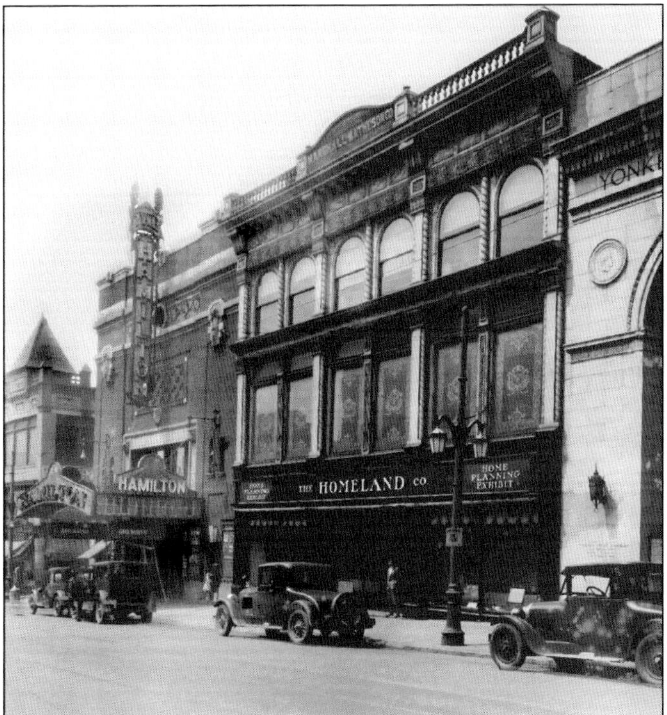

HOMELAND COMPANY, MAIN STREET. The Homeland Company on Main Street was one of the many businesses located in what was generally called Getty Square. The building had many lives, including as a large department store called Genung's and a branch of the Yonkers Public Library. Current plans call for adaptive reuse for retail, commercial, and residential tenants. (YHS.)

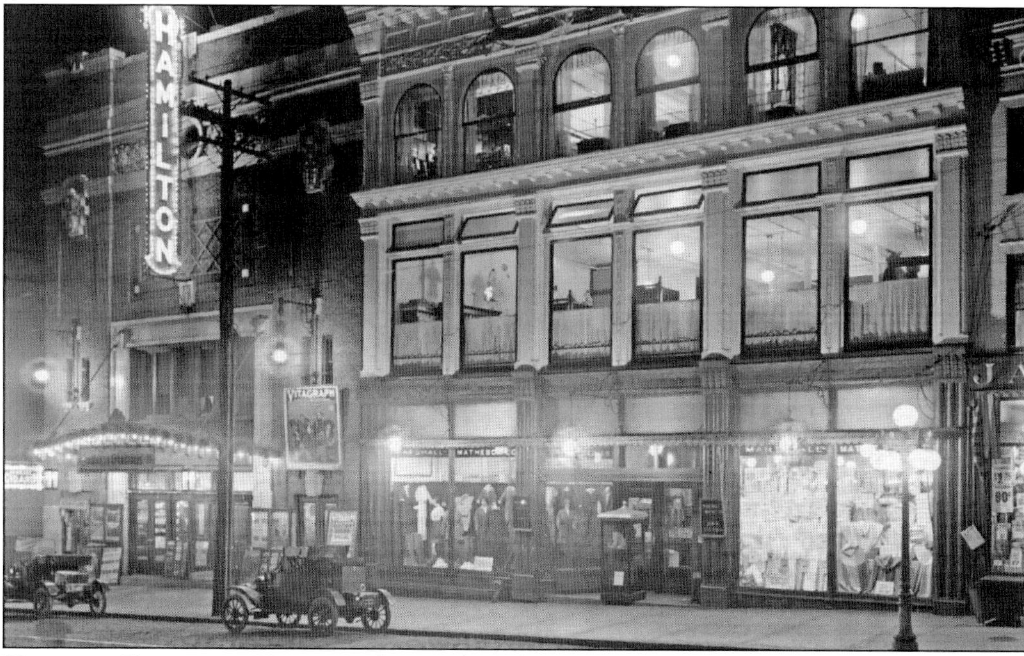

HAMILTON THEATRE AT NIGHT. Yonkersites had plenty of venues for entertainment. The Hamilton Theatre presented vaudeville and movies during its brief lifetime, which lasted from its opening in 1913 until its demolition in 1927. (YHS.)

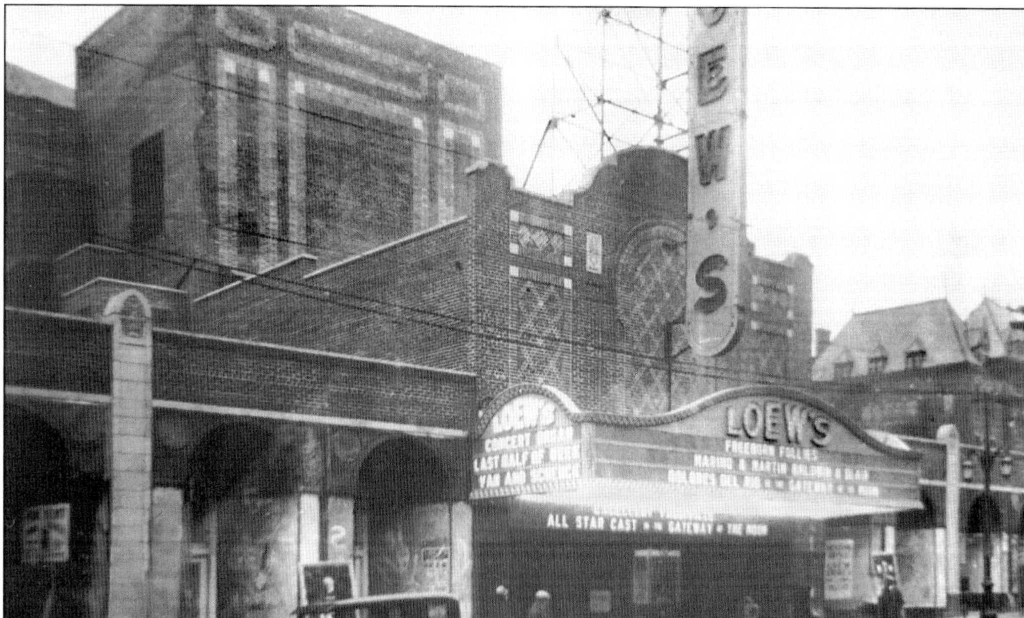

LOEW'S THEATER EXTERIOR. There were a plethora of movie theaters throughout Yonkers, primarily located in the downtown. Proctor's Palace, Loew's, and the Strand were located close to each other along South Broadway near the square. Further south was the Park Hill Theater; other Yonkers movie houses included the Warburton, Kimball, the Kent, the Lido, the Terrace (notoriously nicknamed "the Itch"), and others. (COY Planning.)

LOEW'S THEATER LOBBY. These buildings were truly movie palaces. The ornate lobby of the Loew's made going to the movies an especially moving experience. High ceilings, gilding, and elaborate chandeliers all added to the experience. (COY Planning.)

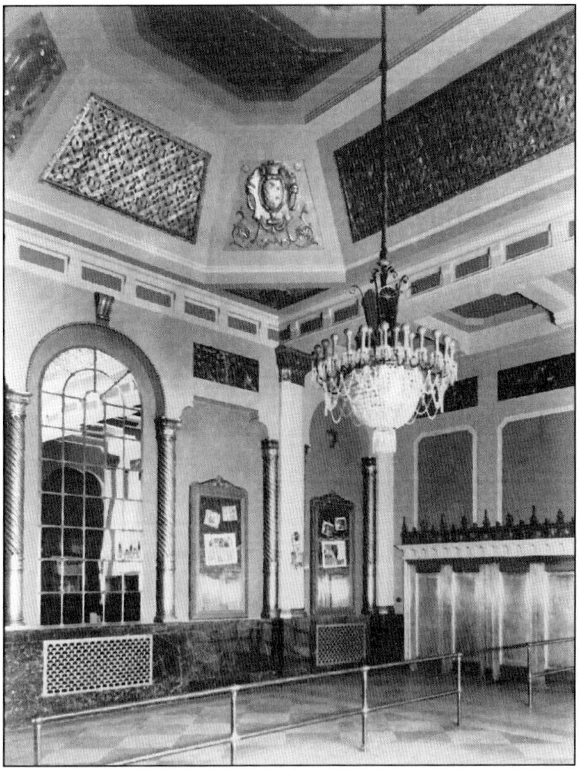

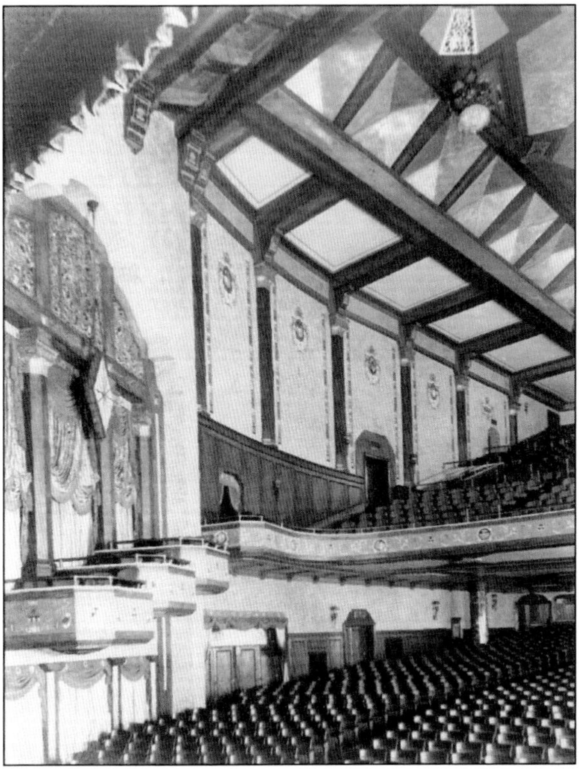

LOEW'S THEATER INTERIOR. Resembling a classic opera house, these theaters had faux boxes, sweeping balconies, and loges. Seating was usually a rich red or maroon felt with hinged seats. Interestingly, most of these amazing architectural features were not appreciated in the darkened movie houses. Loew's was renamed Brandt's in the 1950s. (COY Planning.)

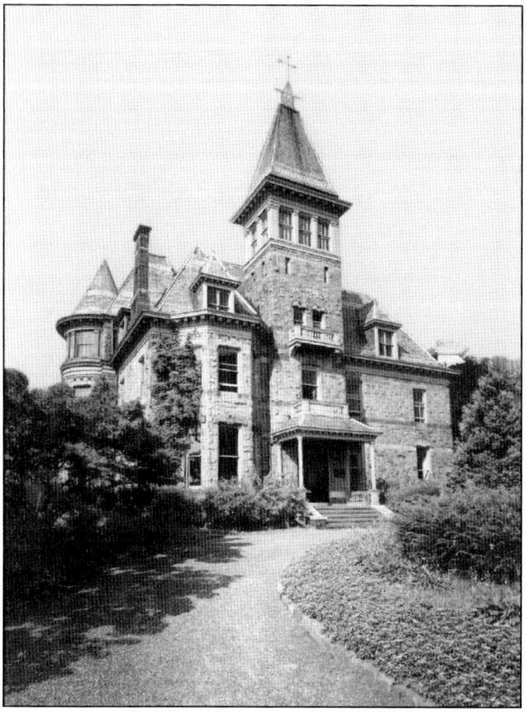

Glenview Mansion, Hudson River Museum. Glenview, the home of the Trevor family, is one of the few remaining palatial mansions built to take advantage of beautiful Hudson and Palisade views along Warburton Avenue and North Broadway. The Glenview was the original home of the Hudson River Museum, and a new building was erected alongside it. The Glenview has been kept with the furnishings and paintings reflecting the lifestyle and times of the Trevors. (HRM.)

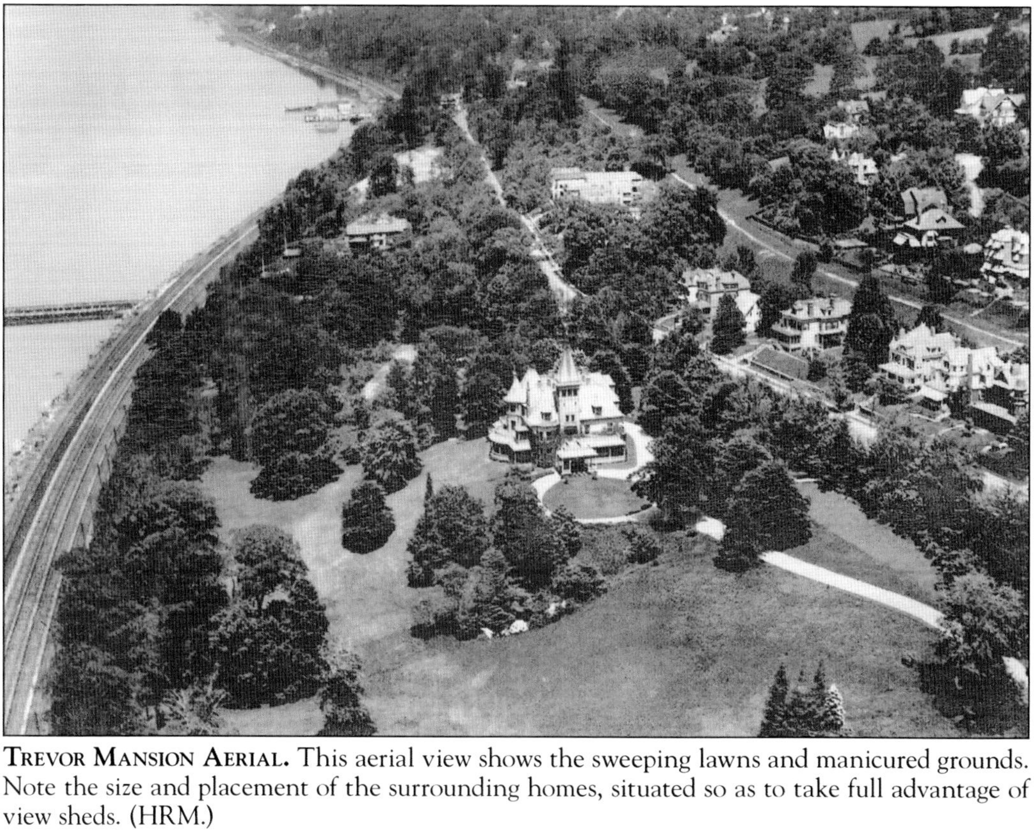

Trevor Mansion Aerial. This aerial view shows the sweeping lawns and manicured grounds. Note the size and placement of the surrounding homes, situated so as to take full advantage of view sheds. (HRM.)

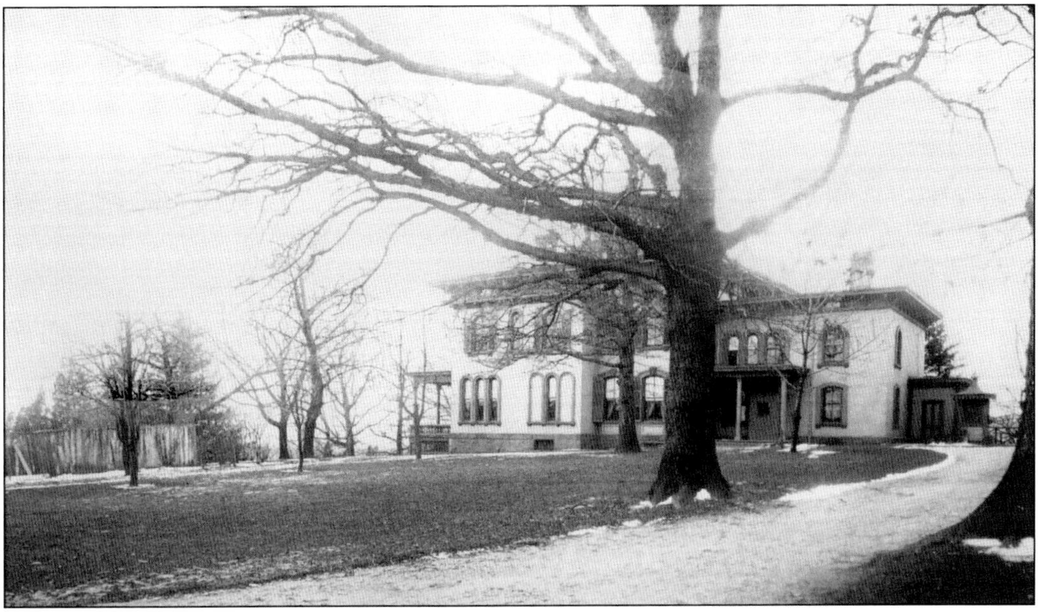

FLAGG MANSION. Ethan Flagg's home, located on Park Avenue, is also much the same as it was when built. Annexed to a cloistered order of nuns of the Blessed Sacrament who made communion hosts for Roman Catholic churches, the Flagg Mansion now houses offices of the Greyston Foundation and the former cloister provides many social services, including counseling for AIDS patients at the Maitri Center. (BD.)

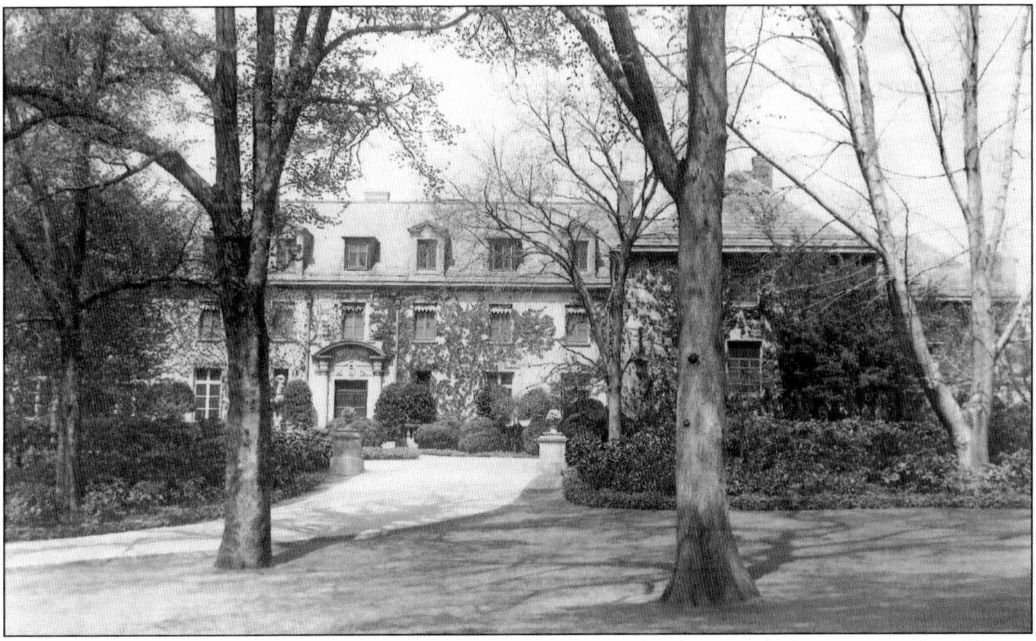

ALDER MANOR. Alder Manor on North Broadway was the home of plant researcher Boyce Thompson, whose institute was located across the street. Alder Manor was later a branch of Elizabeth Seton College, a catering hall, abandoned, and an Irish cultural center. Movies like *Mona Lisa Smile*, *A Beautiful Mind*, and others were filmed here. Both homes are in the National Register of Historic Places. (Boyce Thompson.)

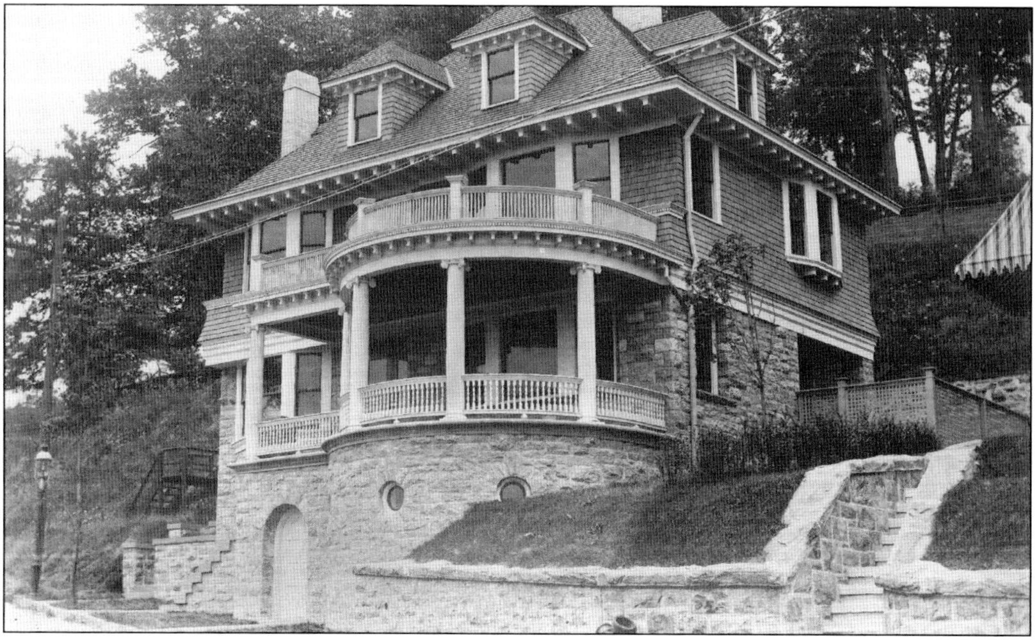

Park Hill Home. This stone home with its wraparound porch is located in the Park Hill section, an upscale development advertised to well-to-do New Yorkers looking for a healthy country lifestyle away from the madding crowd of the city. These huge homes were made more attractive by nearby rail access provided by the Putnam Railroad. (COY Planning.)

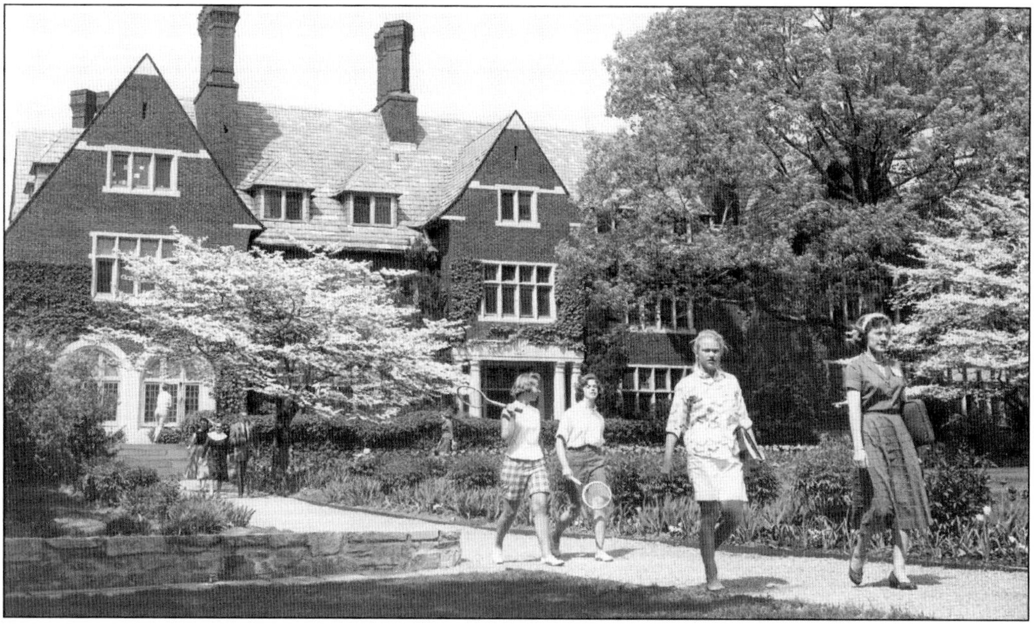

Westlands. Lest wealthy Yonkers east-siders who claim a Bronxville mailing address be neglected, Westlands was home to the philanthropic Lawrence clan, responsible for the founding of Lawrence Hospital and Lawrence Park. Westlands sits in Lawrence Park West in Yonkers and is the main administration building of Sarah Lawrence College. Founded in 1928 by William Van Duzer Lawrence, the college was named for his wife, Sarah "Sadie Lou." (Sarah Lawrence College.)

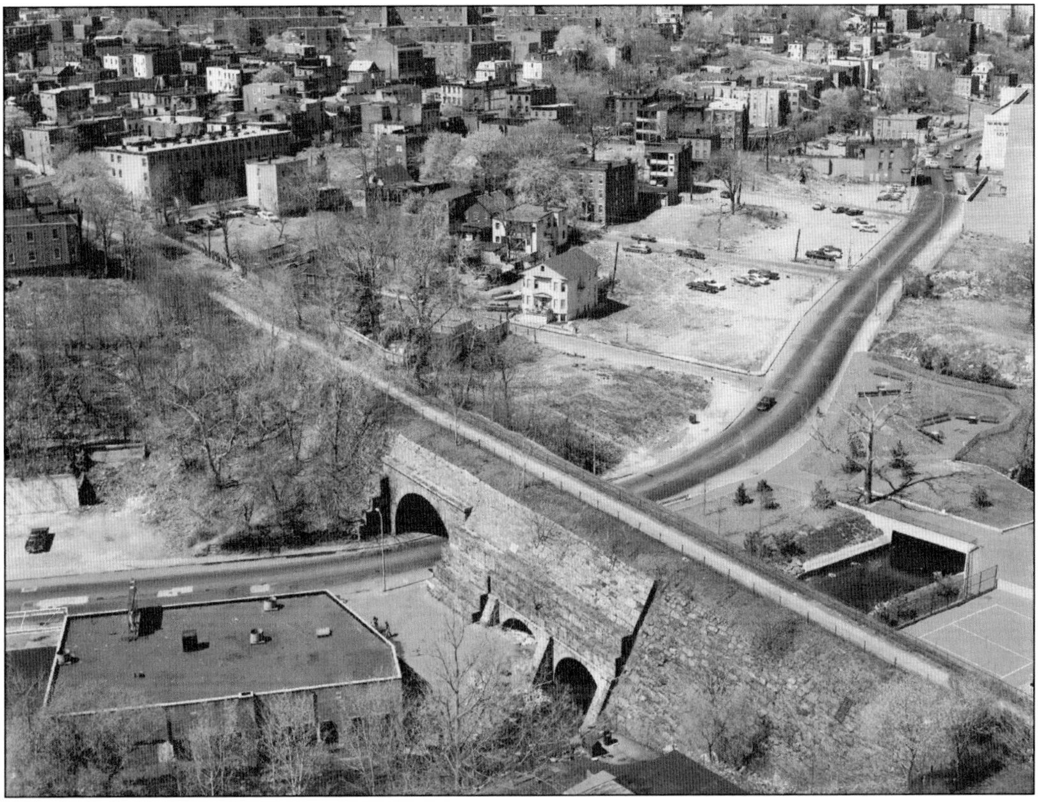

CROTON AQUEDUCT. The Croton Aqueduct, built between 1837 and 1842, brought water from the Croton River south to Manhattan. While initially successful, the gravity-fed system could not keep up with the growth, and it was partially decommissioned in 1940. People can now hike the length of the Old Croton Trail, part of which goes through Yonkers, shown here crossing Nepperhan Avenue. (Westchester County Planning Department.)

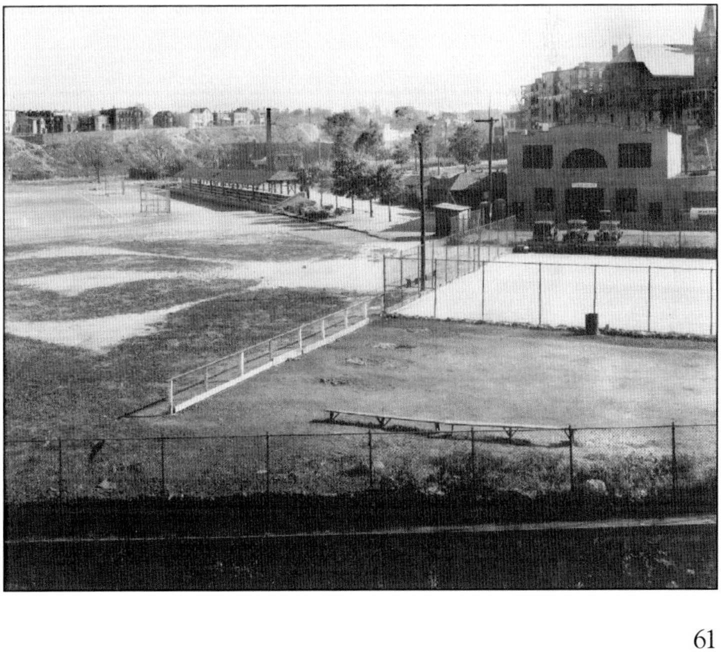

THE GLEN. Yonkers is a hilly city, and the valley formed along the Saw Mill River and the bluffs along Nepperhan Avenue was a popular playground for youth who lived in the densely populated areas around it. It was known as the Glen. (COY Planning.)

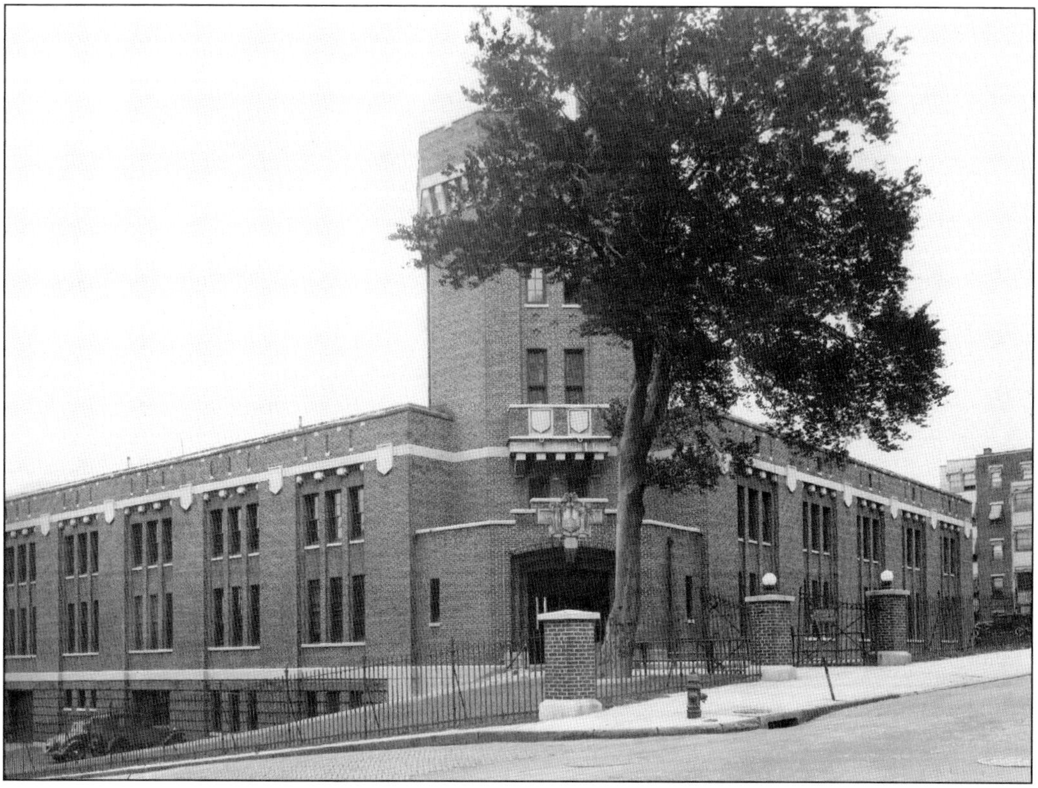

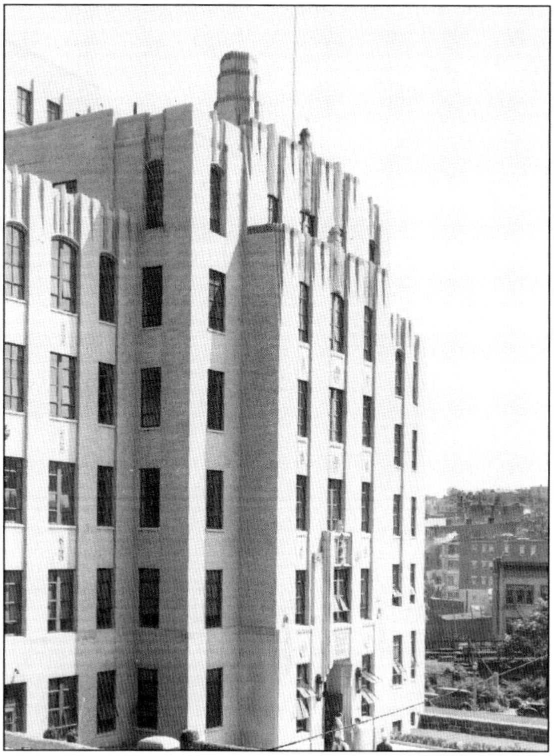

Armory on North Broadway. Yonkers was home to two large armory buildings. This armory on North Broadway still functions as a repository for Army Reserve vehicles and equipment. It also houses the Police Athletic League (PAL), and sporting competitions between groups, such as the Yonkers Police and Fire Departments, are staged here as popular charitable fundraisers. (COY Planning.)

Health Center, 87 Nepperhan Avenue. Built adjacent to city hall, this Art Deco building was originally the health center and also stored records like birth and vaccination records. As city government grew, municipal offices for the Parking Violations Bureau, Department of Housing and Buildings, and other departments were moved into 87 Nepperhan Avenue. (COY Planning.)

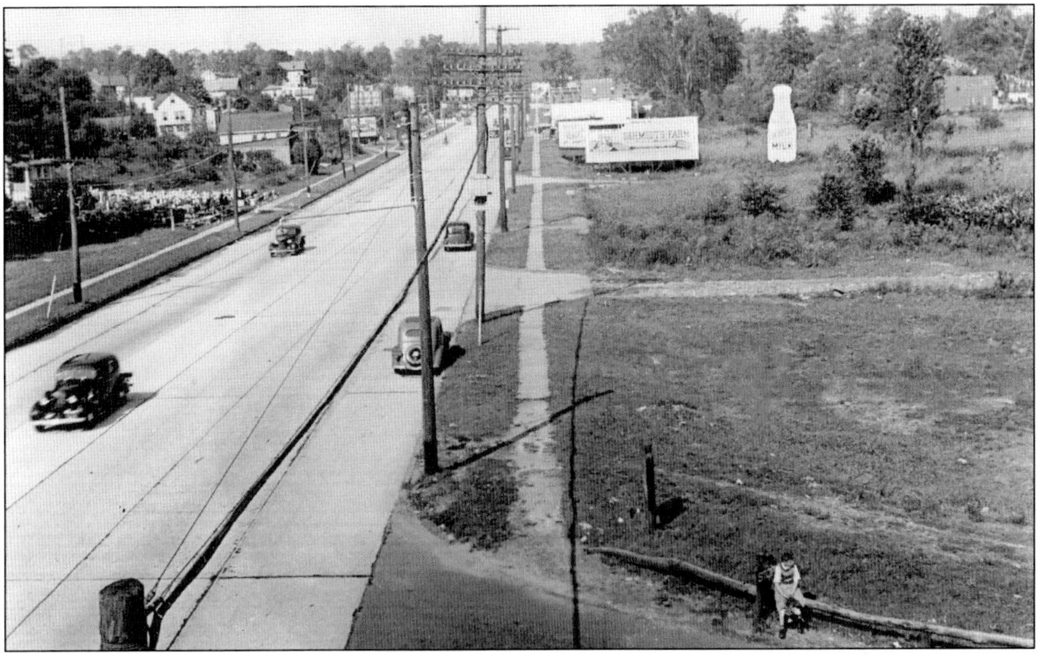

Central Avenue. Shown here in the 1930s, Central Avenue went north—bisecting Yonkers. Spurred by the construction of Cross County Shopping Center in the 1950s and the New York State Thruway (Interstate 95), Central Avenue was expanded to two to three lanes in each direction with jug-handle U-turns, copious traffic signals, and red-light cameras. (BD.)

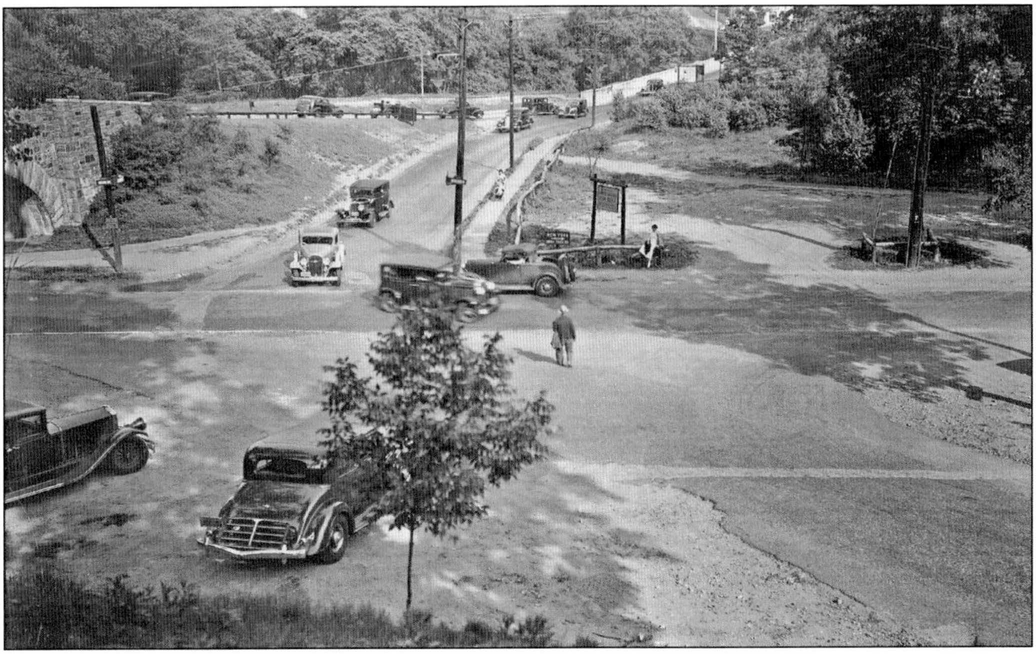

Bronx River Parkway. Built in the 1920s for the Sunday drive, the Bronx River Parkway was just that—a way through a park. Winding narrow roads through woods along streams characterize this roadway notorious for flooding during heavy rains. (Westchester County Planning Department.)

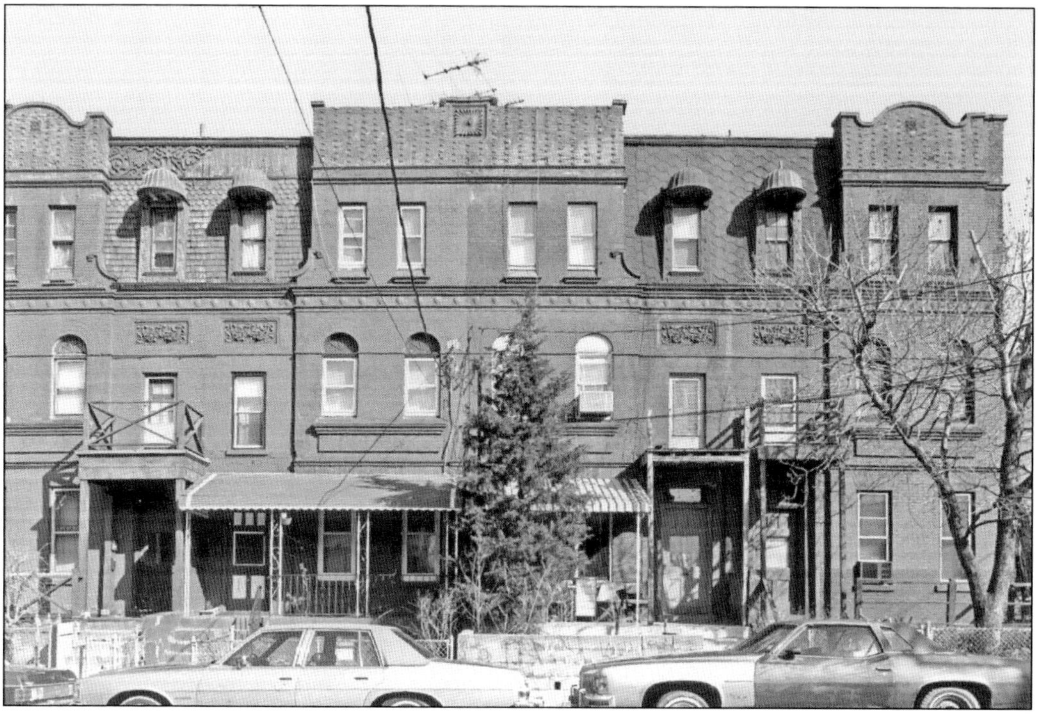

Buena Vista Avenue. These three-story homes on Buena Vista Avenue on the Yonkers waterfront were built to house management-level workers at the Otis Elevator Company and the sugar refineries. Note the unusual canopies and the Dutch influence in the architectural details. (COY Planning.)

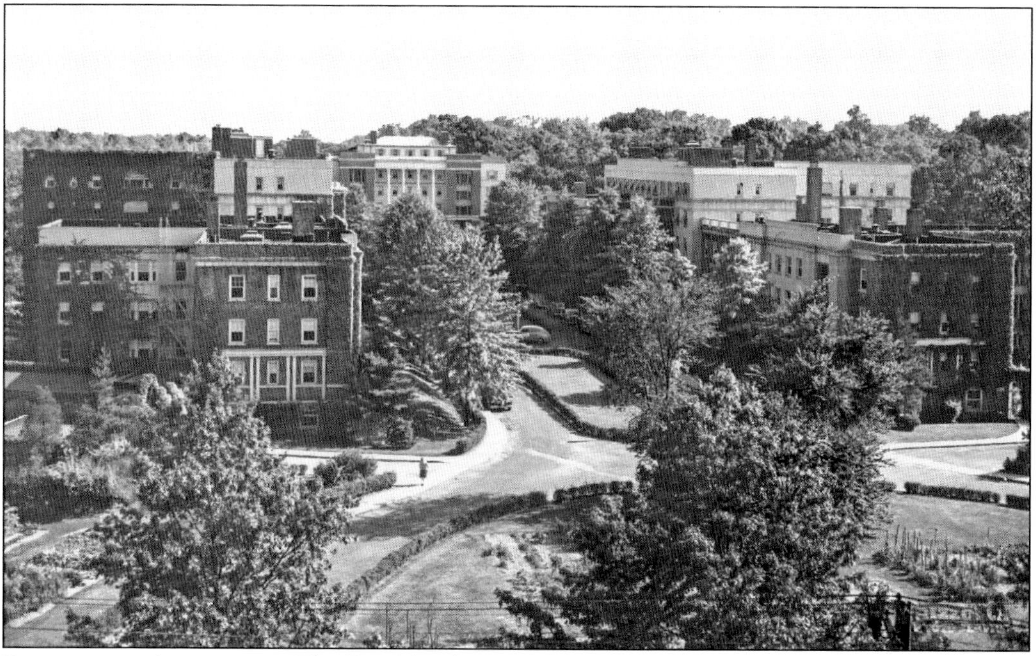

Brooklands Apartments. The Brooklands in eastern Yonkers represent an upscale demographic in cooperative apartments, with spacious grounds and manicured lawns. (COY Planning.)

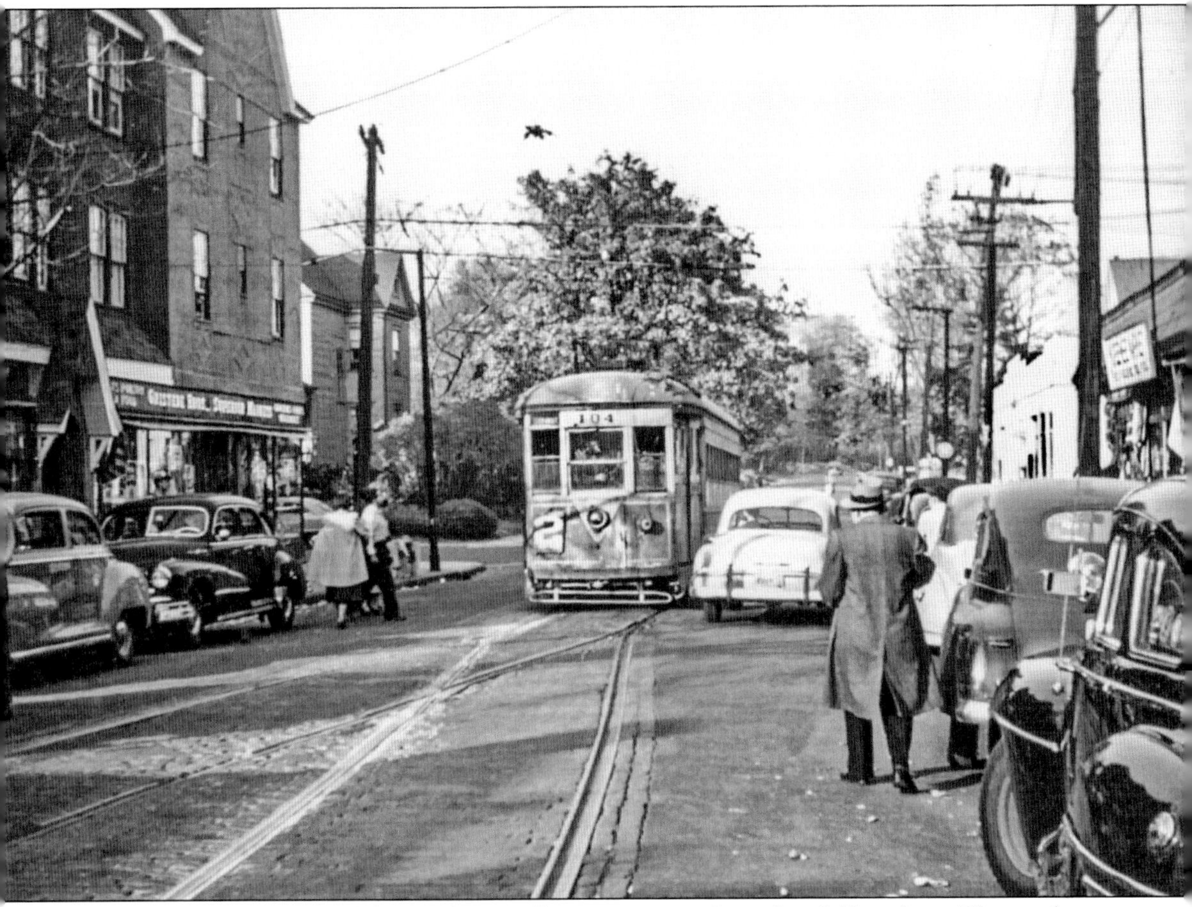

TROLLEY. Another branch of the Yonkers trolley system ran along South Broadway. The tracks were usually considered a nuisance for both drivers and passengers who had to cross traffic to board. The Yonkers trolleys were phased out in 1952, but interest in them has been recently renewed. (YHS.)

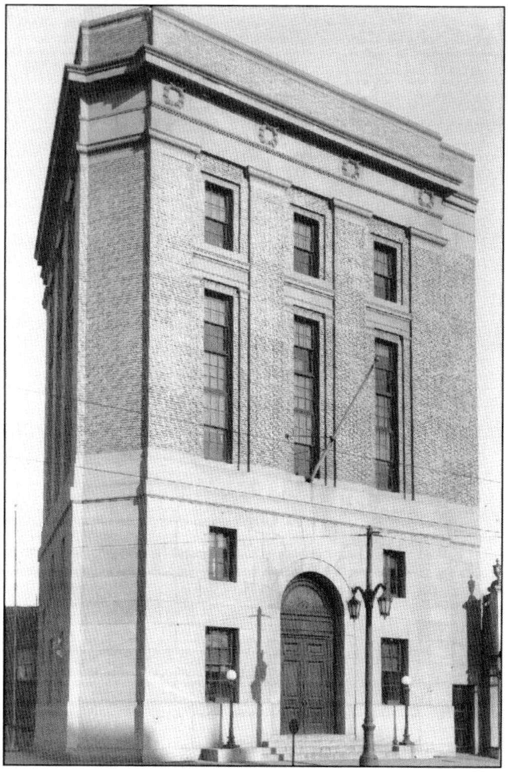

Masonic Temple. Yonkers was home to many fraternal organizations, such as the Masons. The building still stands on the corner of South Broadway and Vark Street, but development around St. Joseph's hospital has threatened it with demolition. (COY Planning.)

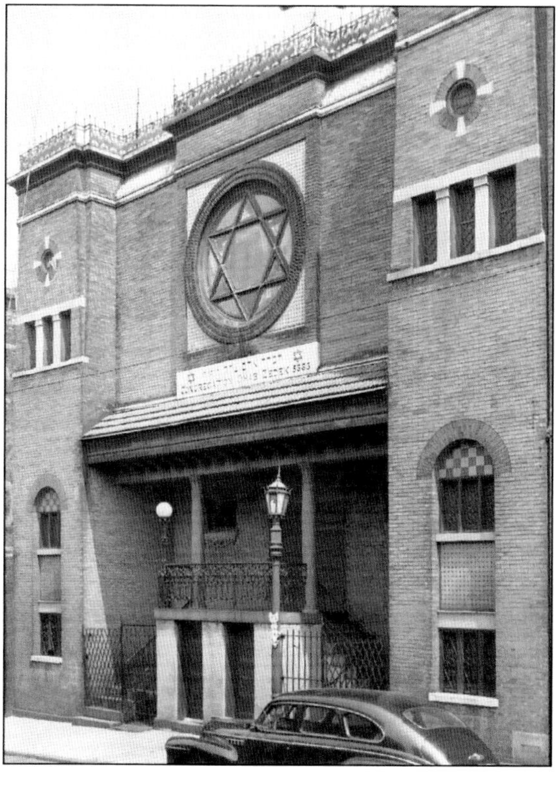

Congregation Ohab Zedek Synagogue. One of the older houses of worship in Yonkers, this synagogue still stands on Hudson Street between Buena Vista and Riverdale Avenues. It is now a Protestant church, the Yonkers Church of God, which has weekly Sunday services. (YHS.)

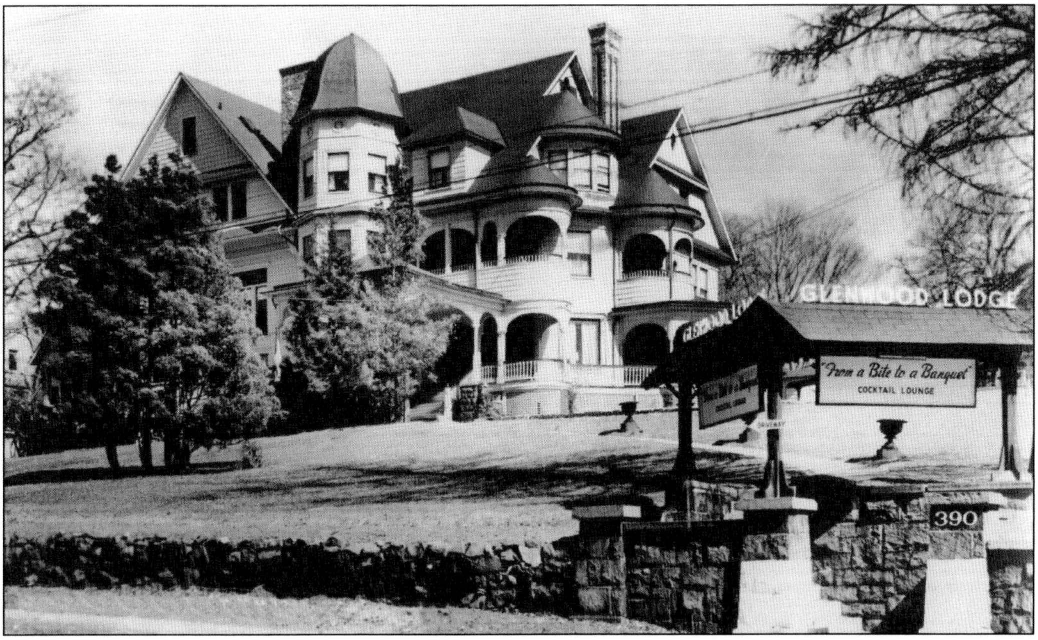

GLENWOOD LODGE. Another magnificent Yonkers home, Glenwood Lodge was located at 300 North Broadway. Like many of its contemporaries, its size, age, and cost of upkeep made affording to own it an expensive proposition and the house was demolished and the property split into building lots for apartments or smaller private homes. (BD.)

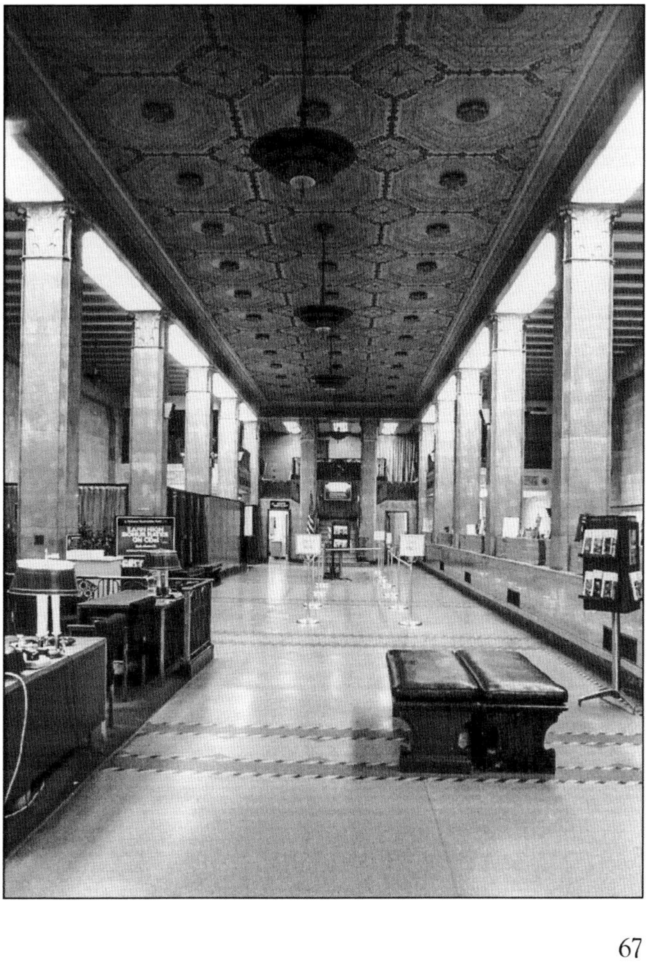

BANK AT 20 SOUTH BROADWAY. The People's Savings Bank was known for its spacious interior decoration, including intaglio lozenges representing various symbols of Yonkers industry, such as locomotives. Its location on the ground floor of a 12-story office building and city hall makes it a convenient place to bank. (COY Planning.)

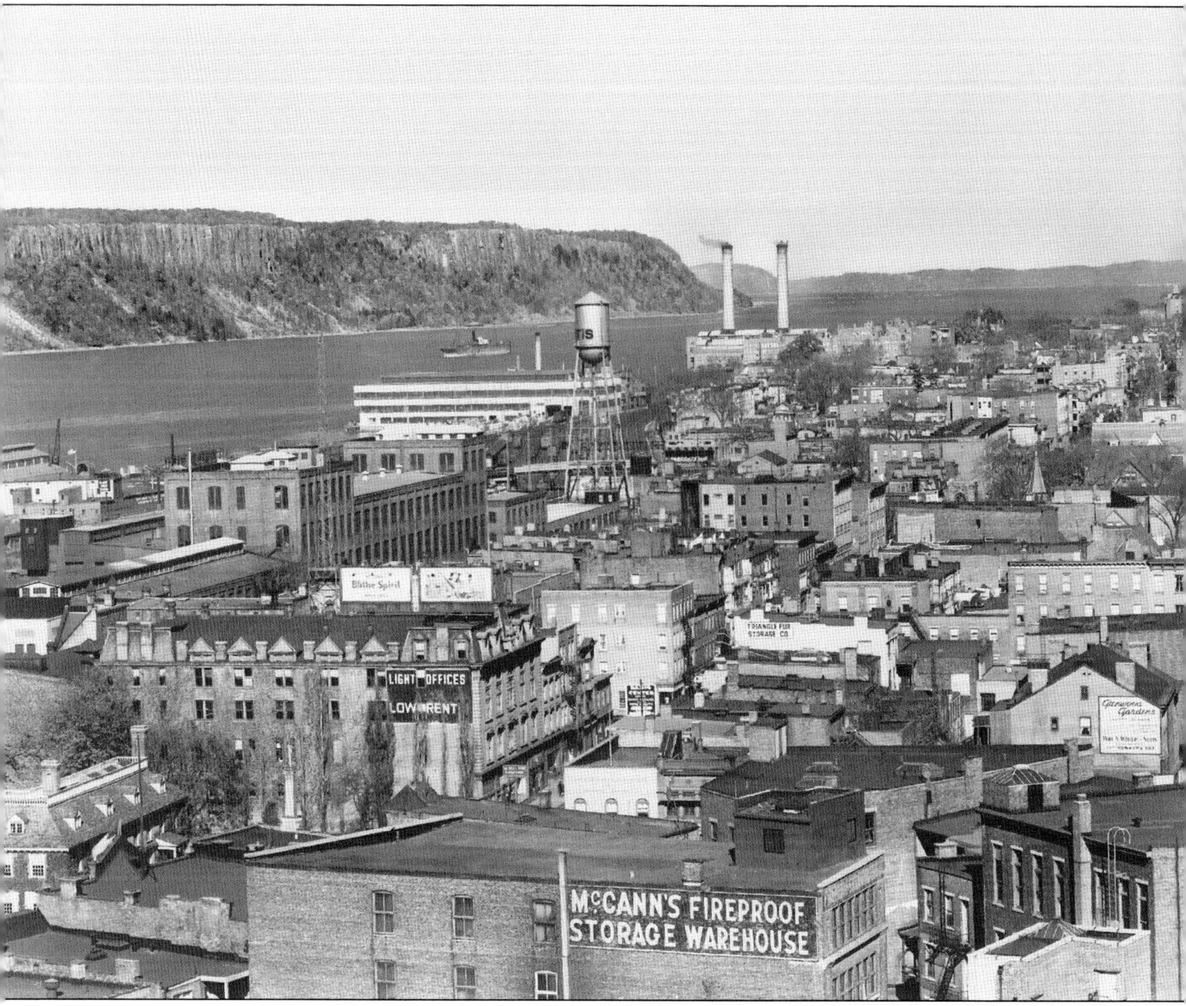

DOWNTOWN PANORAMA. This almost aerial view of downtown Yonkers looks north toward the Hudson River and the Palisades. The iconic twin smokestacks of the Glenwood Power Plant have been a Yonkers riverfront landmark for generations. (YHS.)

Canoe Club, 1892. One of the oldest boating clubs on the Hudson River, the Yonkers Canoe Club is now known as the Yonkers Paddling and Rowing Club (YPRC). These stalwart fellows were competitors for the club in 1892. (Stephen Macknowski.)

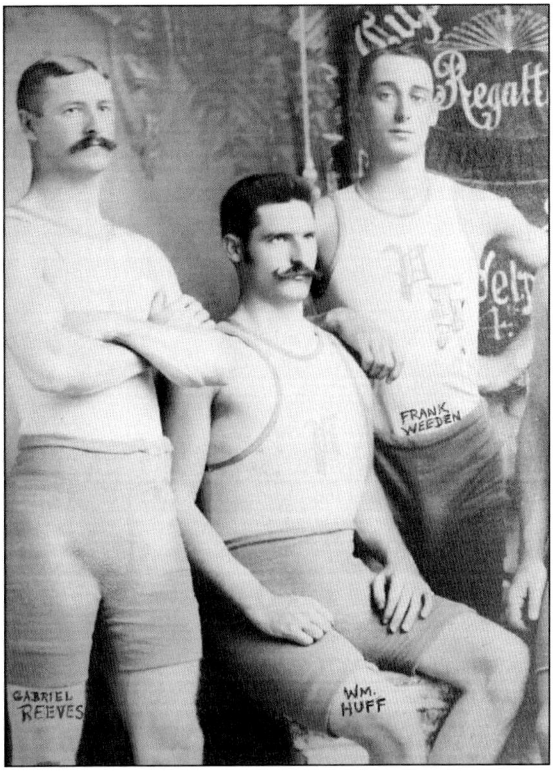

Excursion Boat at Yonkers Pier. Boating on the Hudson has been around since Henry Hudson documented his exploration of the river that bears his name. Robert Fulton's *Clermont* plied the lower Hudson River, and the tragedy of the fire that claimed the *Henry Clay* was succeeded by the ferries and dayliners that took Yonkersites to picnic in Alpine, Bear Mountain, or Coney Island. (YHS.)

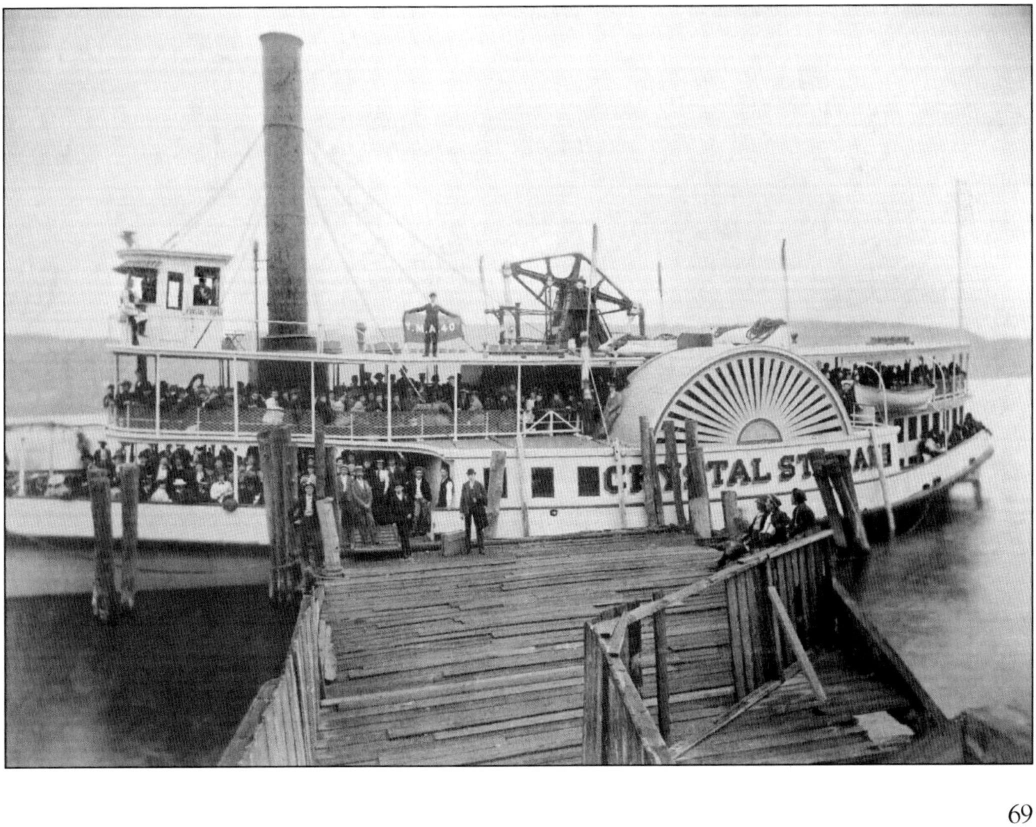

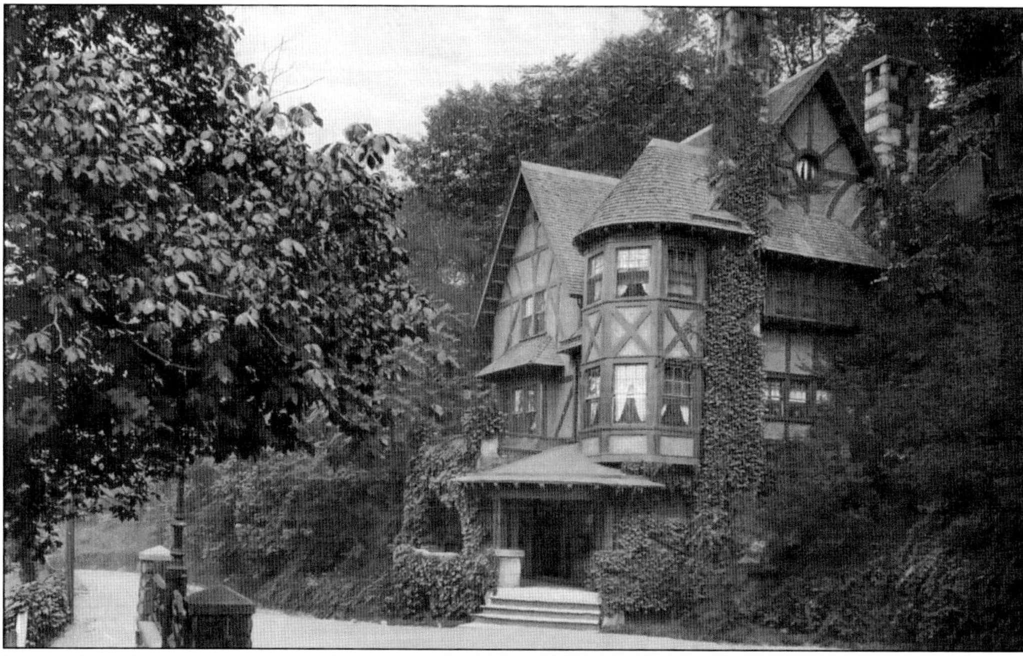

Park Hill Elevator House. To make home ownership in the Park Hill section of Yonkers even more attractive, a railroad to New York City was built. To make it easy for these upscale commuters to get from home to coach, this elevator house was built. (YHS.)

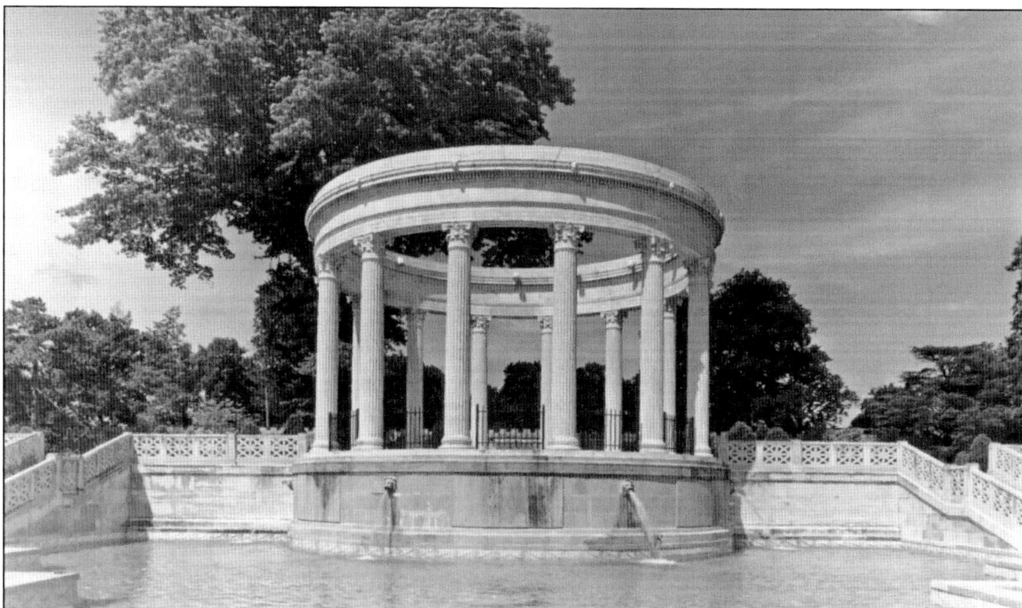

Grecian Temple, Untermyer Park. The gardens belonging to Samuel Untermyer were designed by Welles Bosworth in 1912, in the style of a Persian garden with walls and a large impressive gateway. The garden contains a circular temple with a magnificent mosaic in the center with a head of Medusa, symbolizing two water elements—most likely the fountains in the garden and the Hudson River, which it overlooks. The gardens and temple are a popular place for photographs. (COY Planning.)

Five

Blue Collars to Blue Bloods

Yonkers is truly a melting pot, both ethnically and economically. The New York Central Railroad (now Metro-North's Hudson Line) train made Yonkers easily accessible and the location for the country manses of the very wealthy. Industrialists like Samuel Untermyer, Samuel Tilden, Robert Parkhill Getty, Ethan Flagg, Rudolph Eickemeyer, Leo Baekeland, William Boyce Thompson, the Cochran and Andrus families, and many others built enormous castle-like homes along Warburton Avenue and North Broadway, staggered so as to maximize the view sheds west toward the Hudson River and Palisades. Tilden, who ran for president in 1876, shares the distinction of winning the popular vote but losing the election in a disputed count in the electoral college. Leaving one of the largest estates of the time, he died a bachelor in 1886 at his palatial home, Greystone. The Untermyer Park Conservancy has taken on the task of restoring the gardens and grounds, now called Untermyer Park in honor of subsequent owners, to their former splendor.

A similar phenomenon occurred along the east side of Yonkers where the Harlem Division brought the wealthy to Bronxville and Scarsdale. Once the superrich built mansions here, American Realty, a turn-of-the-century real estate development company, built high-end tract housing in places like Park Hill, which was serviced by its own train spur accessed from the elevator house. Armour Villa and Cedar Knolls communities were built on the east side in the mid-1890s.

A need for people to maintain these properties and work for their owners attracted immigrants coming from Europe. True to human nature, the turn-of-the-century wave of European immigrants settled together, founded churches and schools, and established food stores and bakeries. The Nodine Hill section of Yonkers became home to Polish, Ukrainian, and Italian populations. Pasta and pierogi existed side by side. Irish immigrants tended to settle in Woodlawn along the Bronx border to the south and in Woodstock Park in the northwest corner of the city. A large Portuguese population settled in central Yonkers. In the late 1950s, many Hispanics and African Americans came to Yonkers and the diversity expanded. An influx of Arabic people settled in the southwest portion of Yonkers in the 1980s. Yonkers is said to have 38 distinct neighborhoods, and it would be safe to say that each neighborhood contains about five different ethnicities.

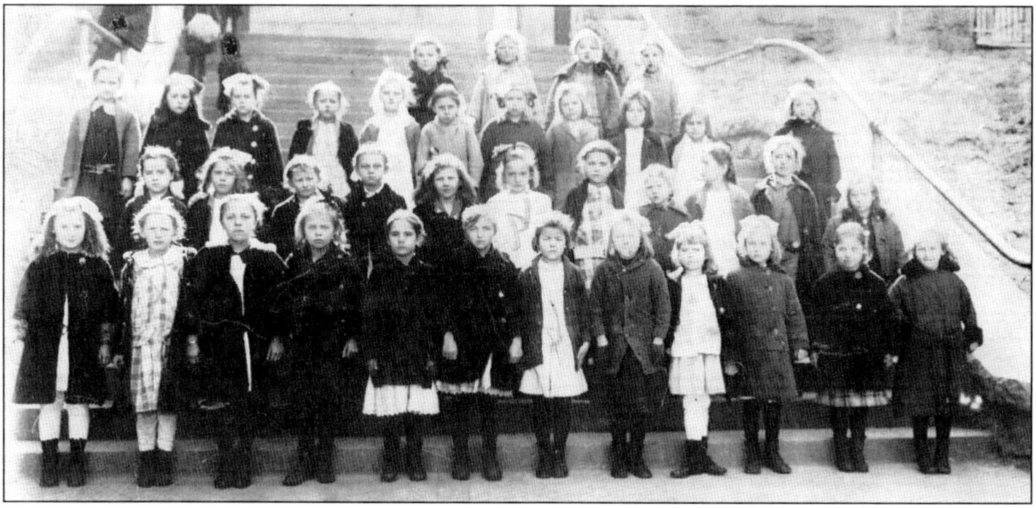

St. Casimir's Kindergarten Graduation, 1910. Yonkers had a large immigrant population at the turn of the 20th century, primarily from Eastern European countries. There was a large, devoutly Roman Catholic Polish population on Nodine Hill that built St. Casimir's Church and Grammar School. This is the kindergarten graduation class of girls in 1910. (Joan Jennings.)

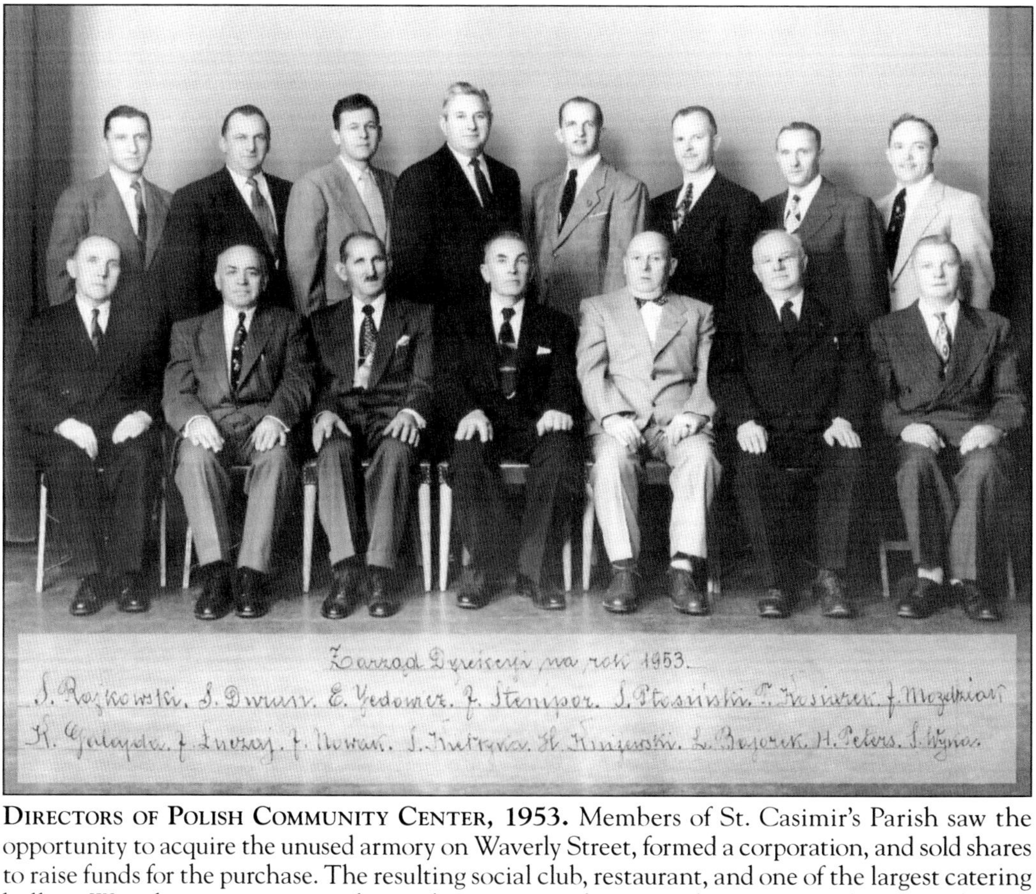

Directors of Polish Community Center, 1953. Members of St. Casimir's Parish saw the opportunity to acquire the unused armory on Waverly Street, formed a corporation, and sold shares to raise funds for the purchase. The resulting social club, restaurant, and one of the largest catering halls in Westchester was put on the market in 2012, after more than 65 years. (Toni Gugliotti.)

St. Mary's Roman Catholic Church, 1908. Irish immigrants, another devout Roman Catholic population, raised funds to build the Immaculate Conception (St. Mary's) Church. Many of the Irish were quarrymen and masons and did the work on this magnificent church themselves. Its spires, like those of St. Casimir's, are Yonkers landmarks. (Bill Tarmaz.)

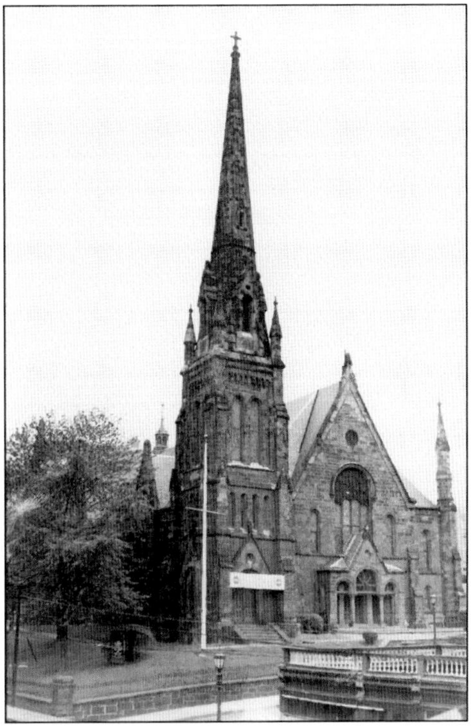

St. Mary's Graduating Class. Typical of parochial grammar school students, these boys wear uniforms. This is the eighth-grade graduating class of St. Mary's in 1946. (South Yonkers Photos.)

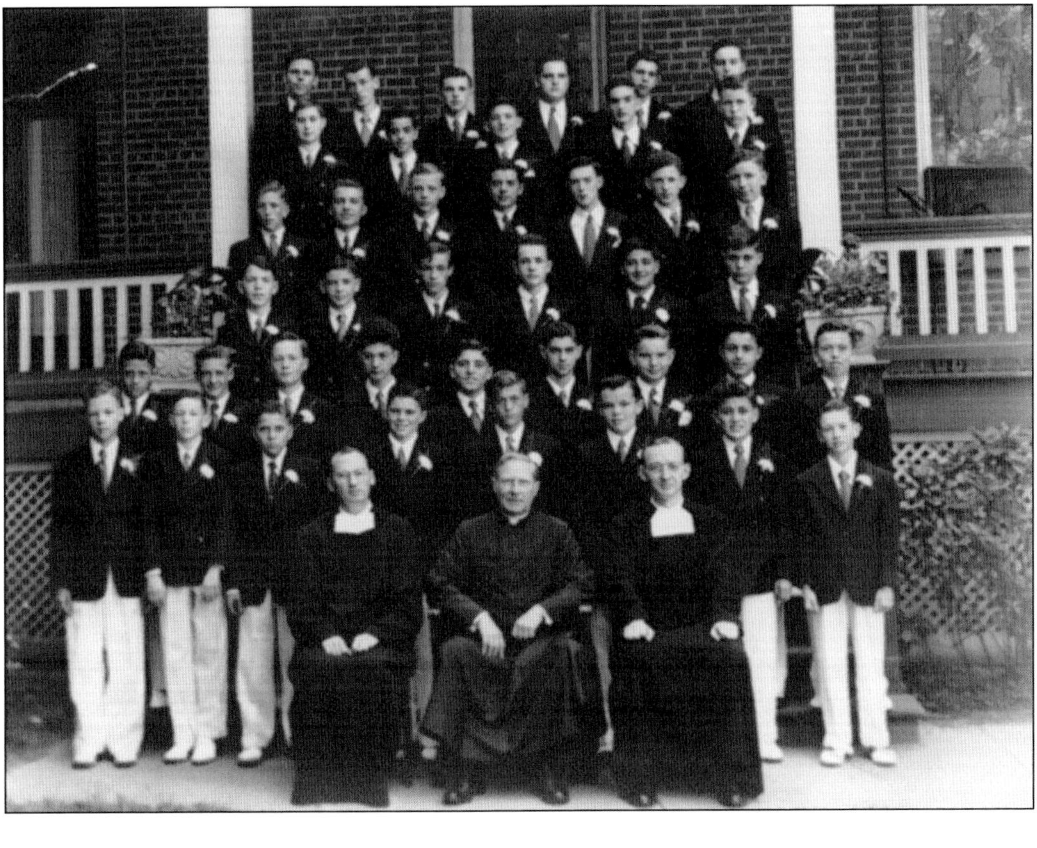

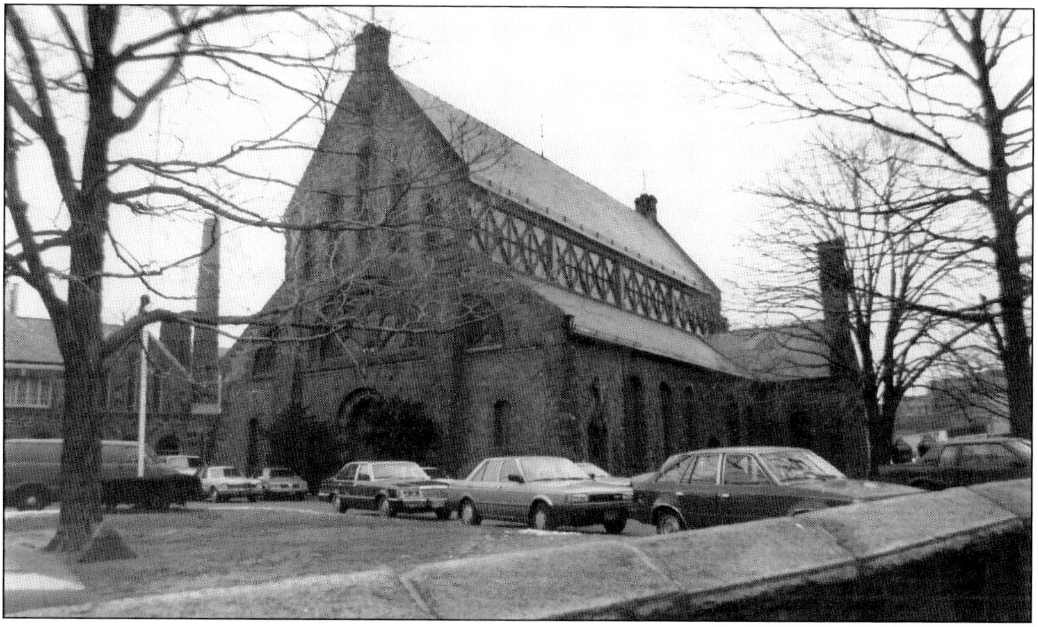

St. John's Church. The oldest Episcopal parish in Westchester (1693), St. John's Church, as it stands today, has a chapel originally financed by Frederick Philipse III in 1753. The large edifice designed by Edward Tuckerman Potter was built in 1858. A historic building listed in the National Register of Historic Places, St. John's remains an active parish. (Steve Asaro, architect.)

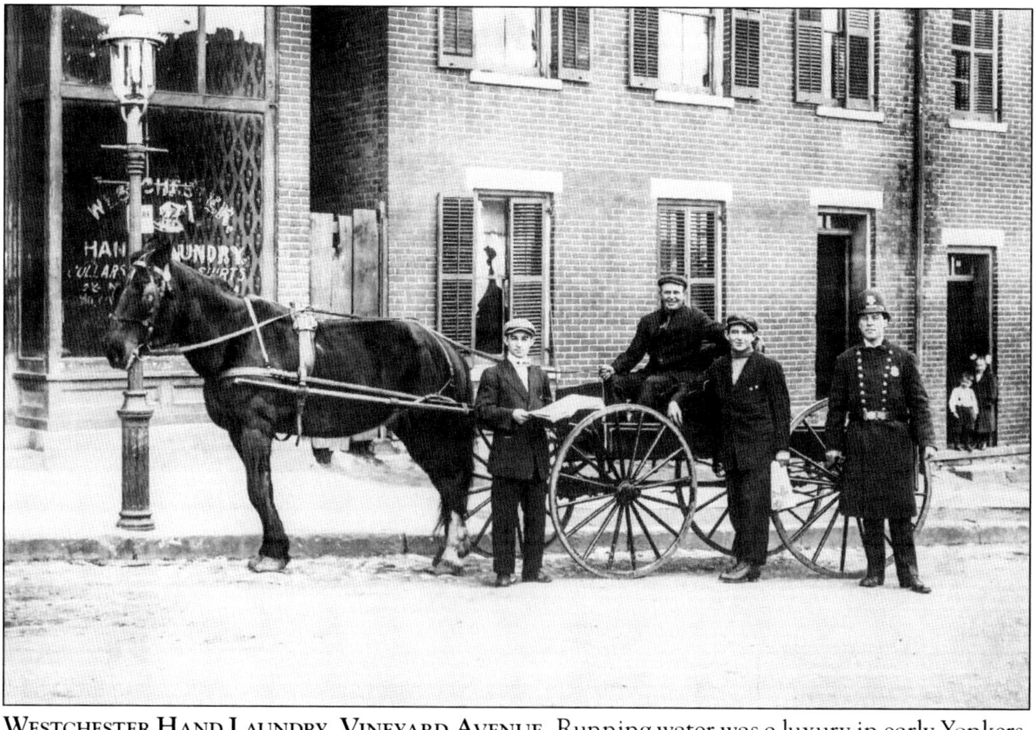

Westchester Hand Laundry, Vineyard Avenue. Running water was a luxury in early Yonkers. These employees of the Westchester Hand Laundry on Vineyard Avenue picked up and dropped off in the laundry's horse-drawn buggy. (Hanrahan family.)

OPPENHEIMER MEATS, 1918. Supermarkets did not exist in the early 20th century. Housewives shopped almost daily at butcher shops, bakeries, and green grocers. (YHS.)

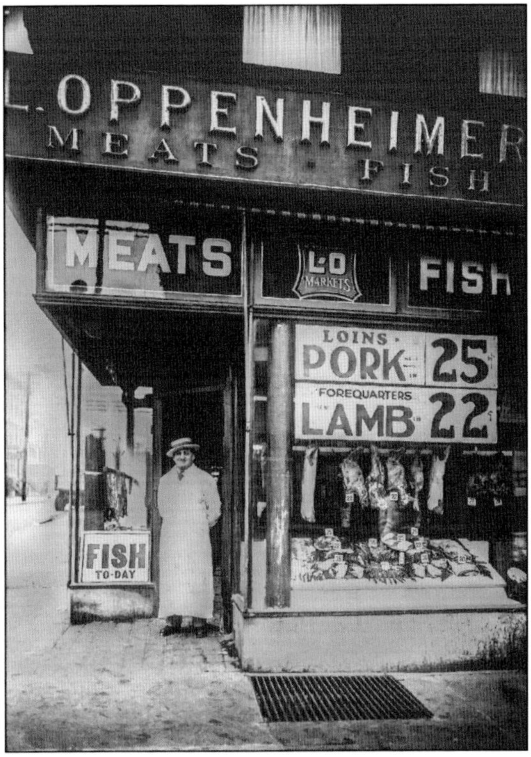

MIKE'S MEAT MARKET, 1922. Mike's Meat Market, located on New Main Street just east of Getty Square, had a large complement of butchers. They also had a patriotic streak and a sense of humor—note the American flag made from sausage and chop meat in honor of Washington's Birthday in 1922. (Joan Jennings.)

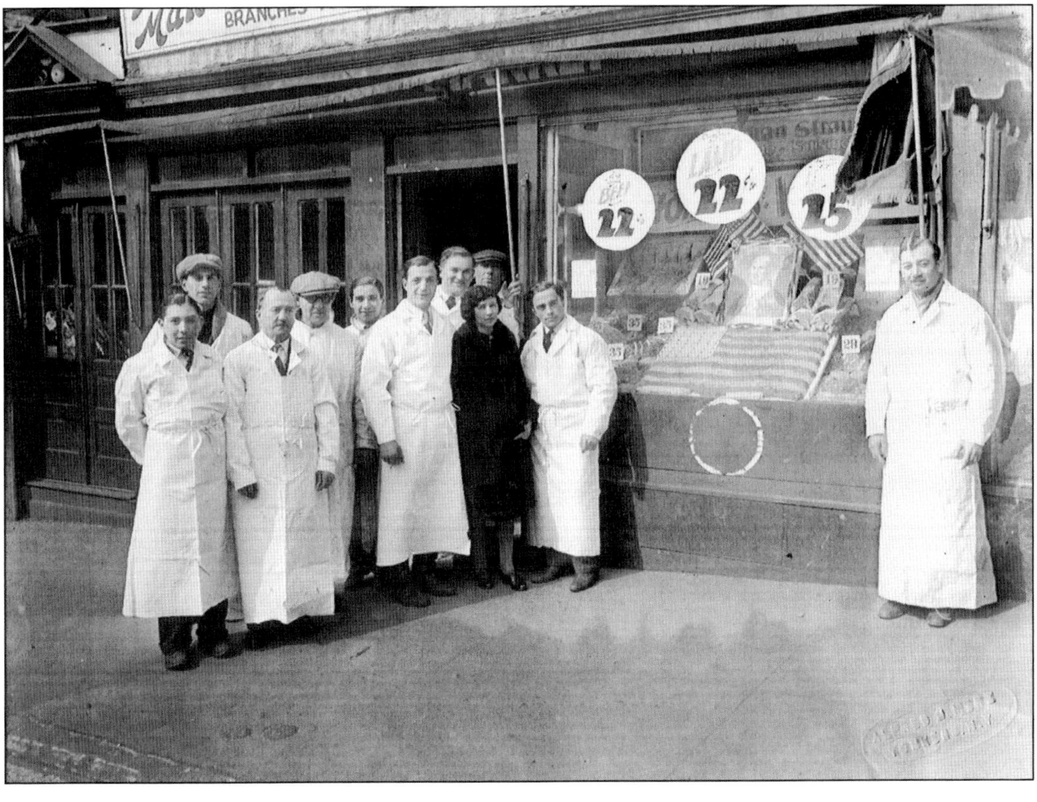

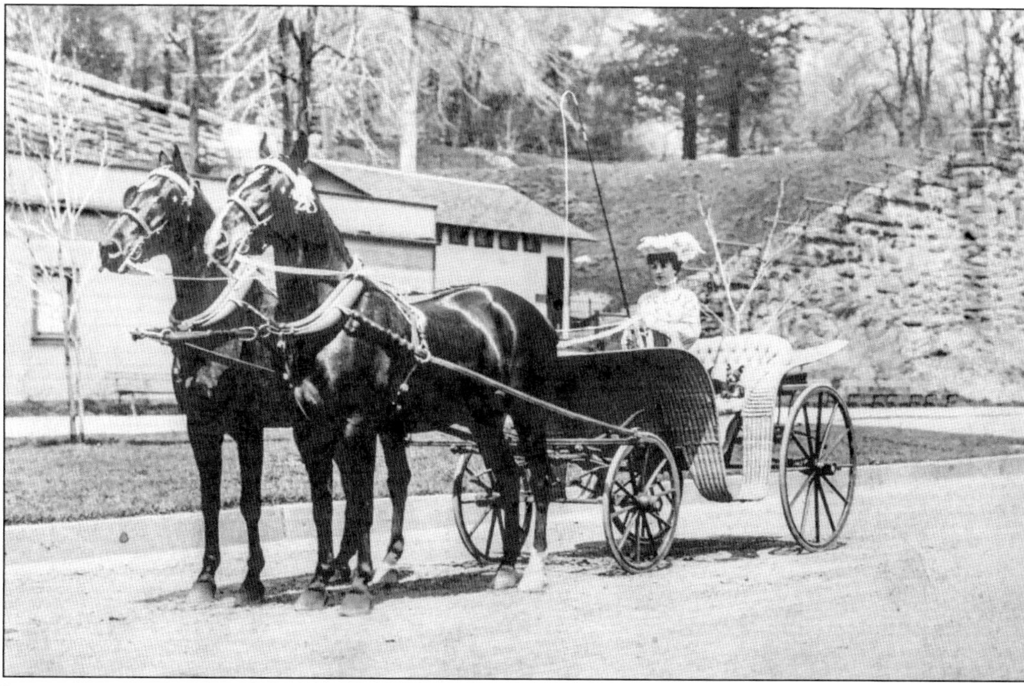

Mrs. Morrissey, North Broadway. When Mrs. Morrissey wanted to shop or go calling on her friends, she just hitched up her horses and jumped into her carriage. One can trust she kept up a modest pace so her hat did not blow off. (Terry Sanchez.)

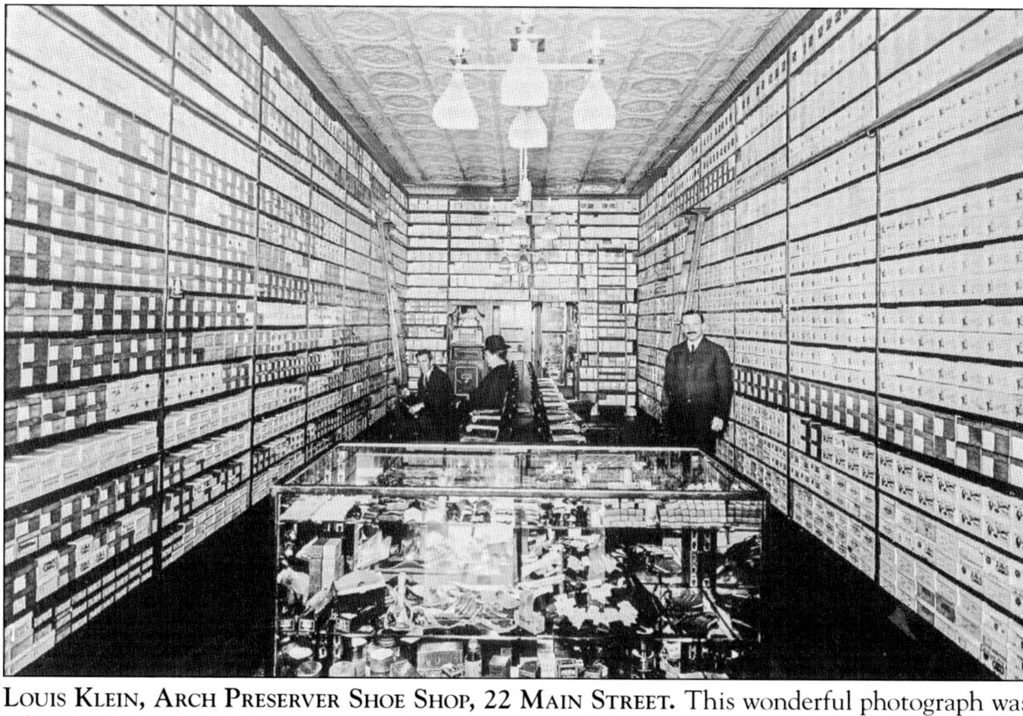

Louis Klein, Arch Preserver Shoe Shop, 22 Main Street. This wonderful photograph was taken in the early 1920s as part of a business survey of downtown businesses. The precision of the shoeboxes is a work of art. (Mina Klein Crasson.)

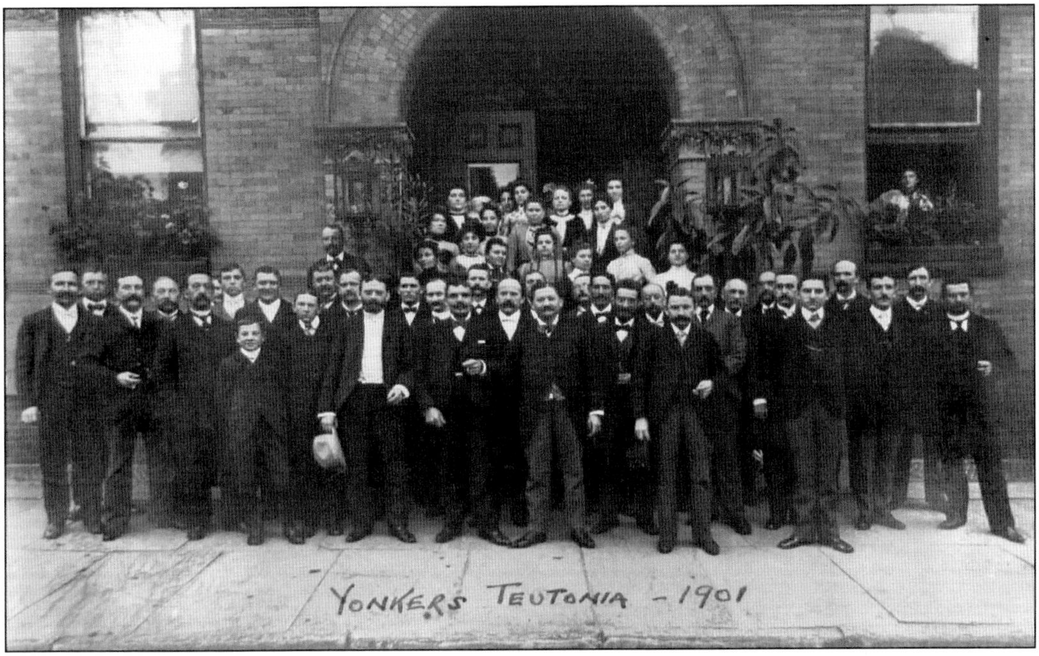

TEUTONIA HALL. This German group was considered a turnverein, or social club. This enormous building on Buena Vista Avenue contained offices and a large hardwood-floored dance hall, where the group held dances and other civic and fellowship activities for the Germans of Yonkers to participate in. (YHS.)

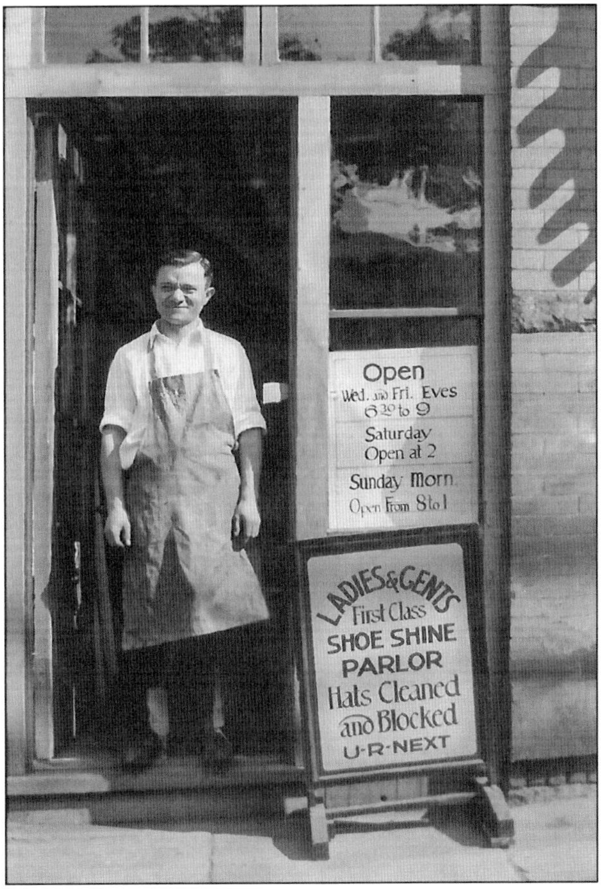

JOSEPH GIANNOTTO, LAWRENCE STREET. Although there is still a shoemaker in Getty Square (Harry's Shoes on North Broadway), shoemakers were once much more plentiful as people tended to repair their shoes rather than replace them. (Giannotto Morris families.)

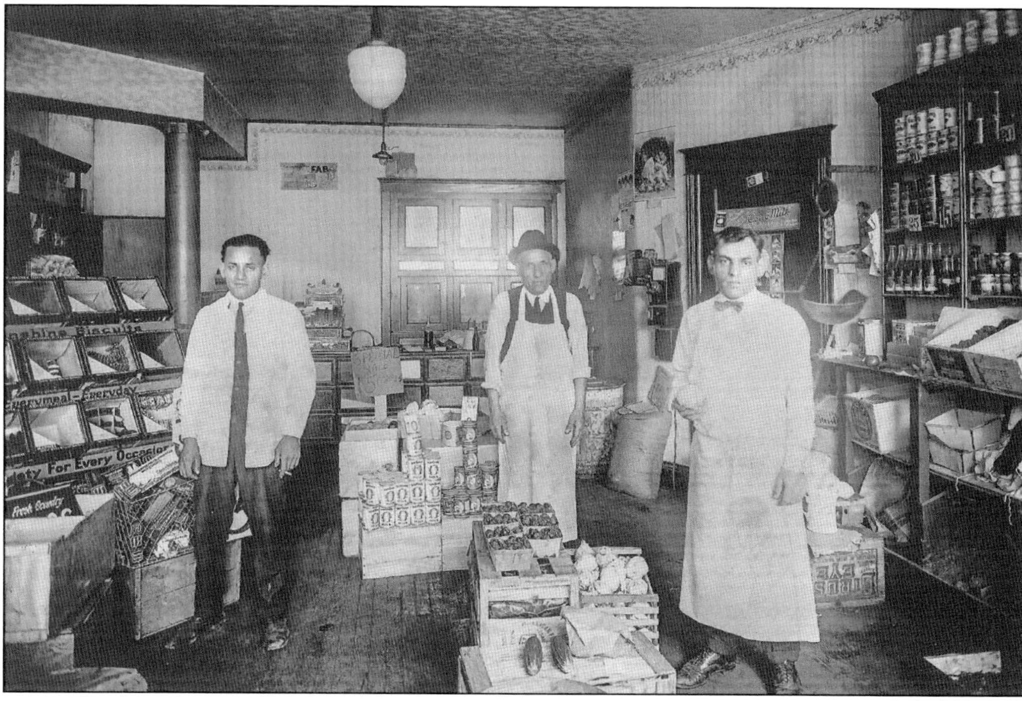

George Schliman Grocery at 202 Riverdale. George Schliman's grocery store was on 202 Riverdale Avenue, an area with commercial establishments bordering on a residential district. (Schliman family.)

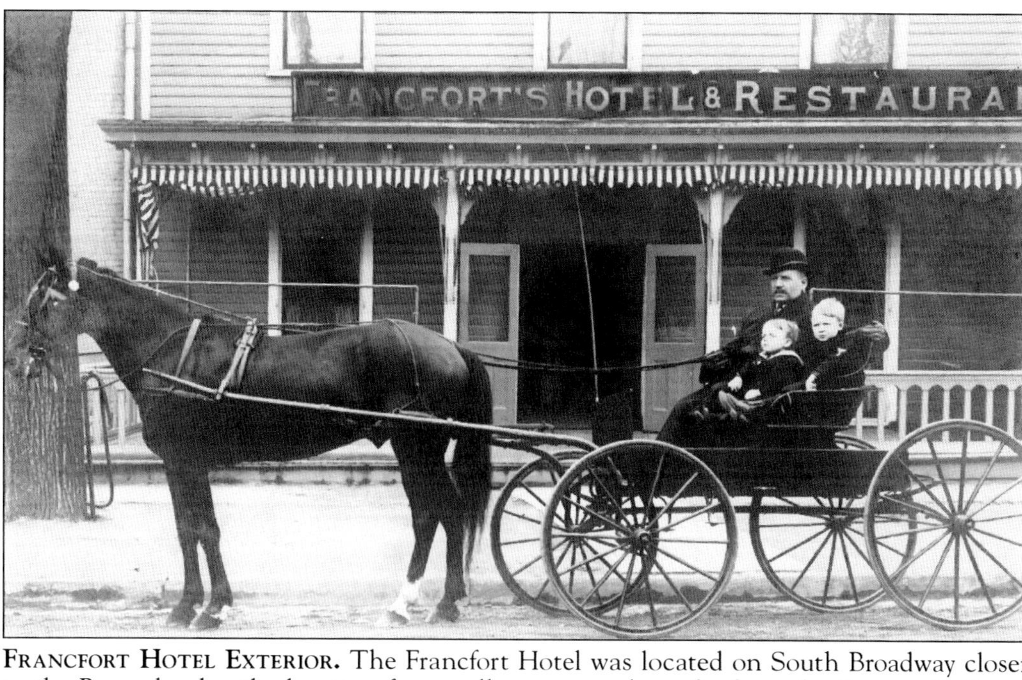

Francfort Hotel Exterior. The Francfort Hotel was located on South Broadway closer to the Bronx border, the location for a trolley route and not far from the Putnam Railroad line. (YHS.)

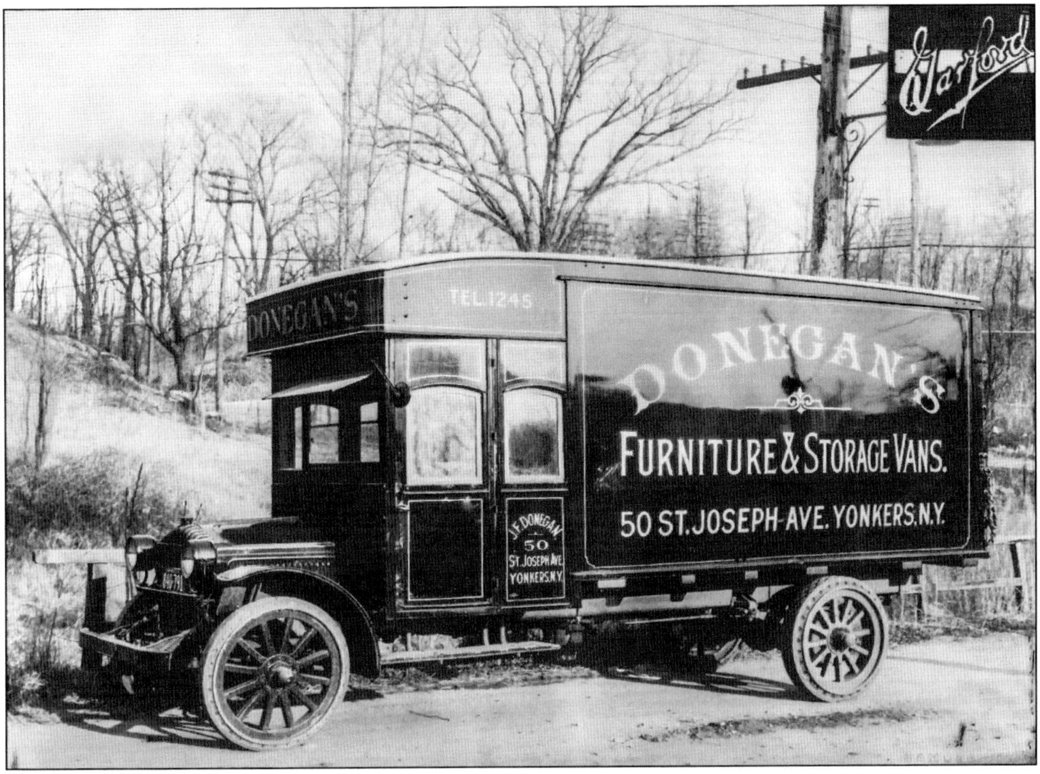

DONEGAN'S MOVING CAMDEN STUDIOS. Donegan's Moving Company had quite the ornately decorated moving truck, especially for that era. (Hanrahan family.)

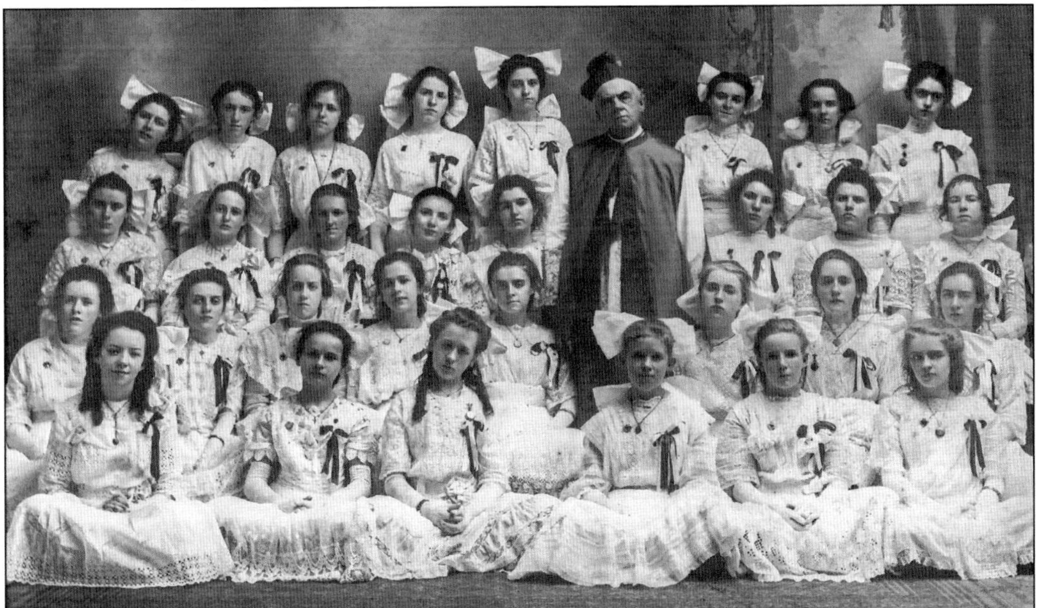

ST. JOSEPH'S GRAMMAR SCHOOL, 1920s. St. Joseph's Roman Catholic Church and School was located on Ashburton Avenue. This grammar school graduation photograph was taken in the 1920s. (Joyce Pidel.)

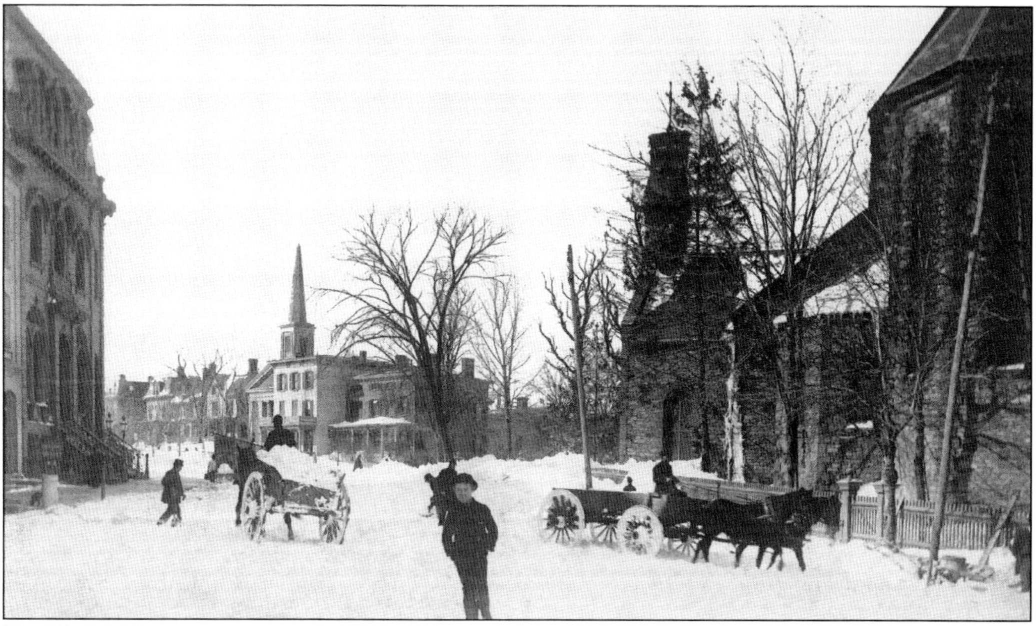

THE GREAT BLIZZARD OF 1888. One of the signature weather events of the 19th century was the Great Blizzard of 1888 that dumped up to 50 inches of snow in the New York metropolitan area in March of that year. It remains one of the worst blizzards in United States history. This view is looking south on South Broadway at Hudson Street. (YHS.)

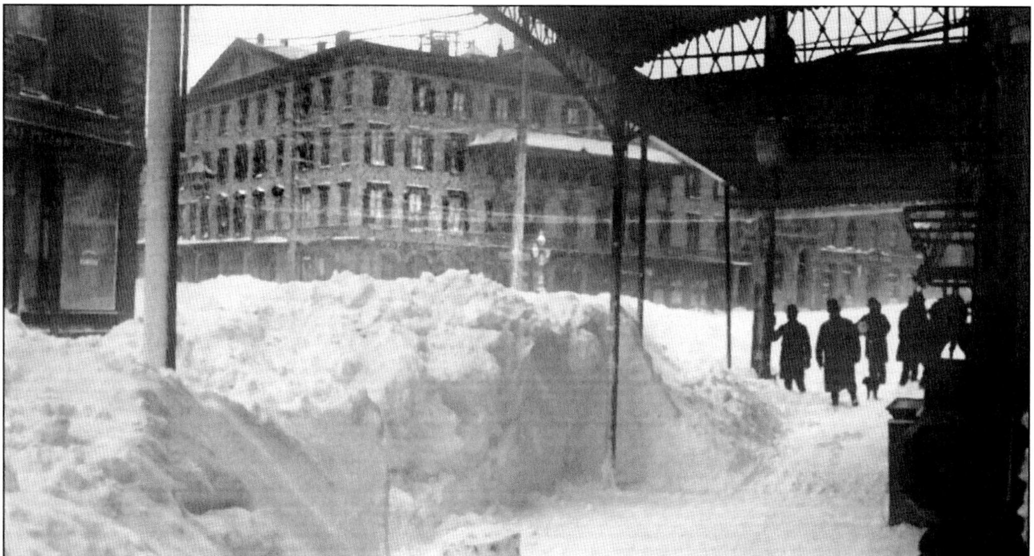

GREAT BLIZZARD OF 1888 AT GETTY SQUARE. Seen here is a view of Getty Square looking toward the Getty House in the background. Note policemen under the awnings of a local business. (YHS.)

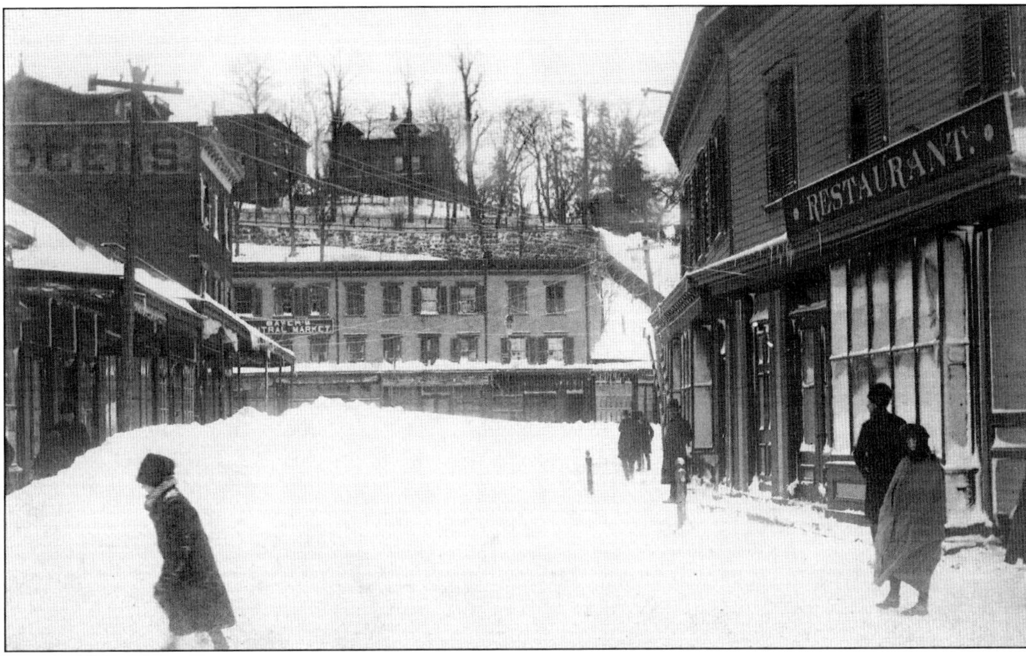

GREAT BLIZZARD OF 1888, MANOR HOUSE SQUARE. The view in this photograph is looking east toward Manor House Square from Warburton Avenue. (YHS.)

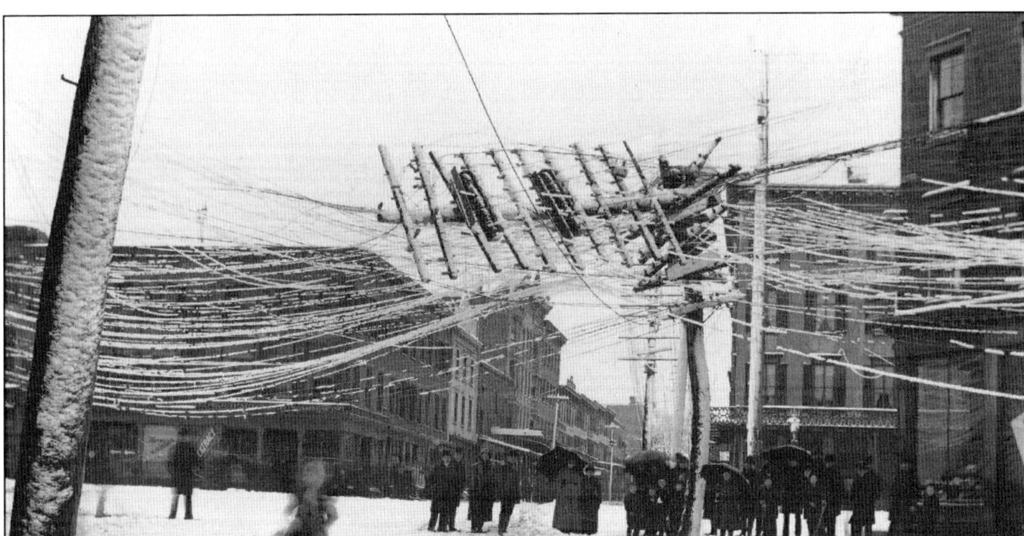

GREAT BLIZZARD OF 1888, MAIN STREET, LOOKING EAST. Ice-encrusted telephone and electrical lines have collapsed under the weight as onlookers try to navigate through Getty Square. (YHS.)

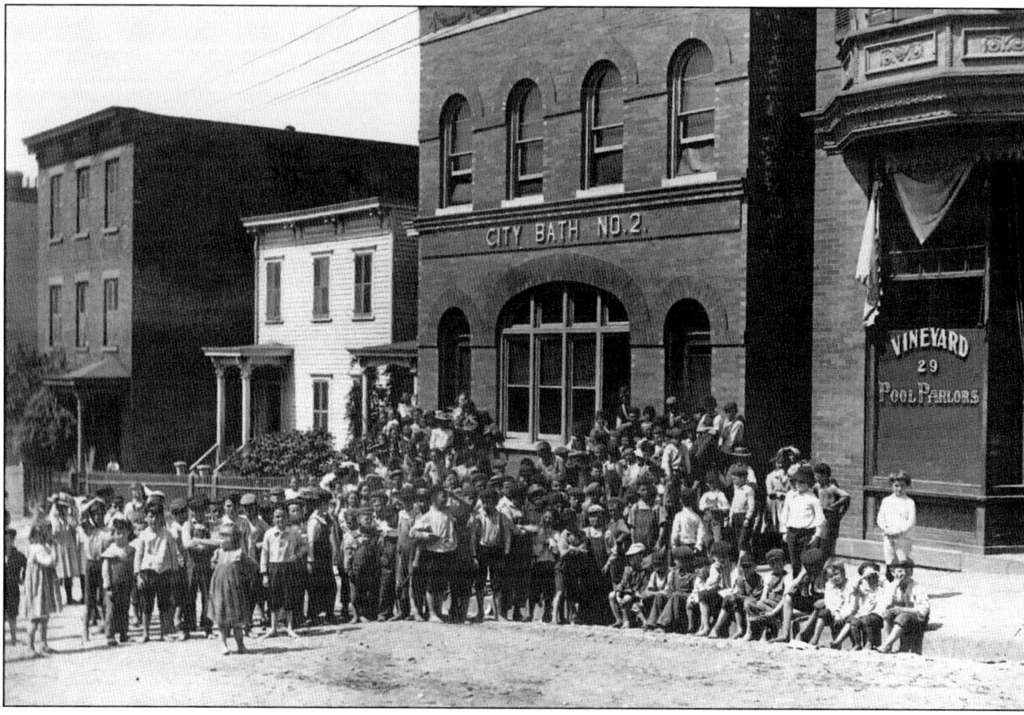

City Bath No. 2. Yonkersites had to keep clean at the public baths. Housing that had indoor plumbing only had cold water (cold-water flats), so the tradition of the Saturday-night bath was born. Yonkers had four public baths; only one remains and is designated as a landmark. The buildings had incredibly ornate tile work in the pools and on the walls. (COY Planning.)

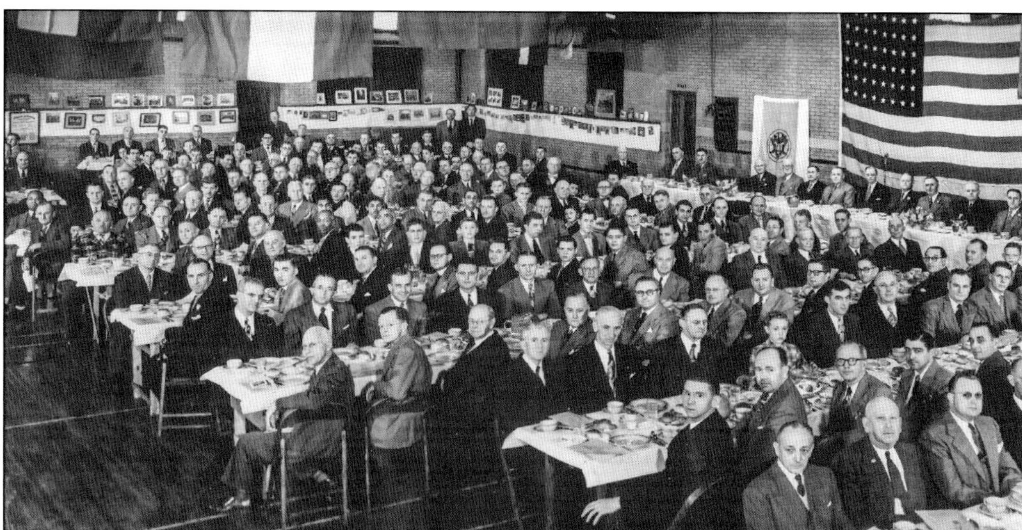

YMCA Centennial. The downtown boasted two large Ys—the YMCA (Young Men's Christian Association) on Riverdale Avenue and the YWCA (Young Women's Christian Association) for women on South Broadway. This wonderful example of crowd photography was taken on the occasion of the 100th anniversary of the YMCA in its gym. (YMCA.)

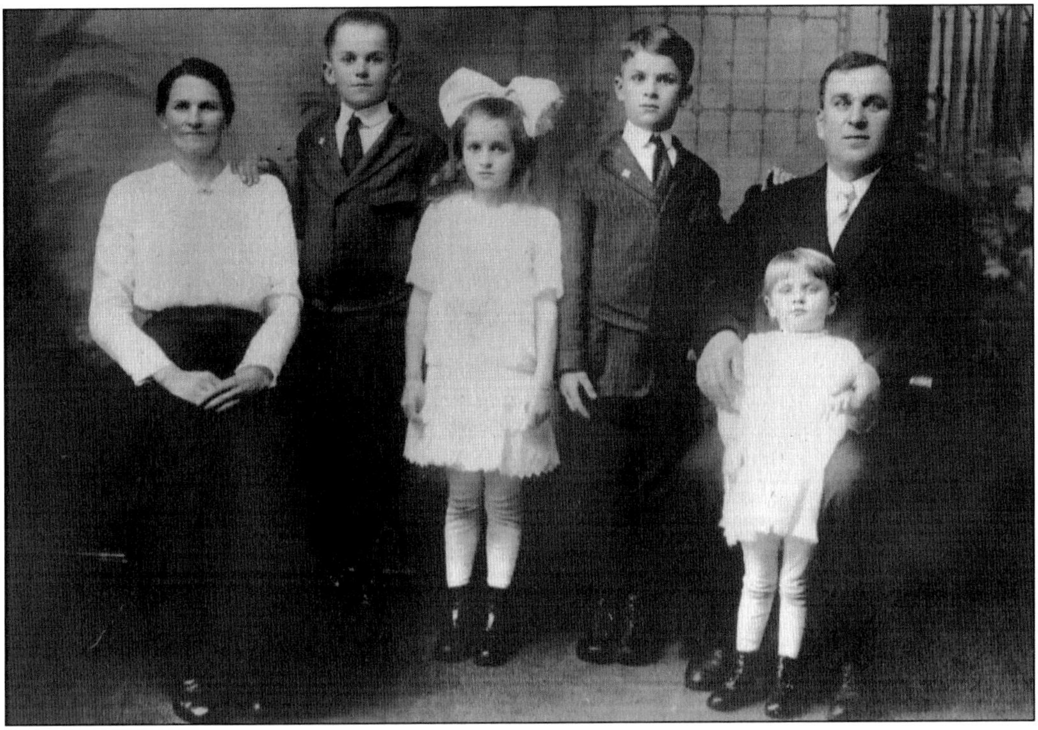

Poroski Family, c. 1920. The Poroskis were typical of families of that era. Unlike with 21st-century families who photograph everything every minute, the tradition was to dress up, go to a photographer's studio, and have a portrait taken. This image was made around 1925. (Joan Jennings.)

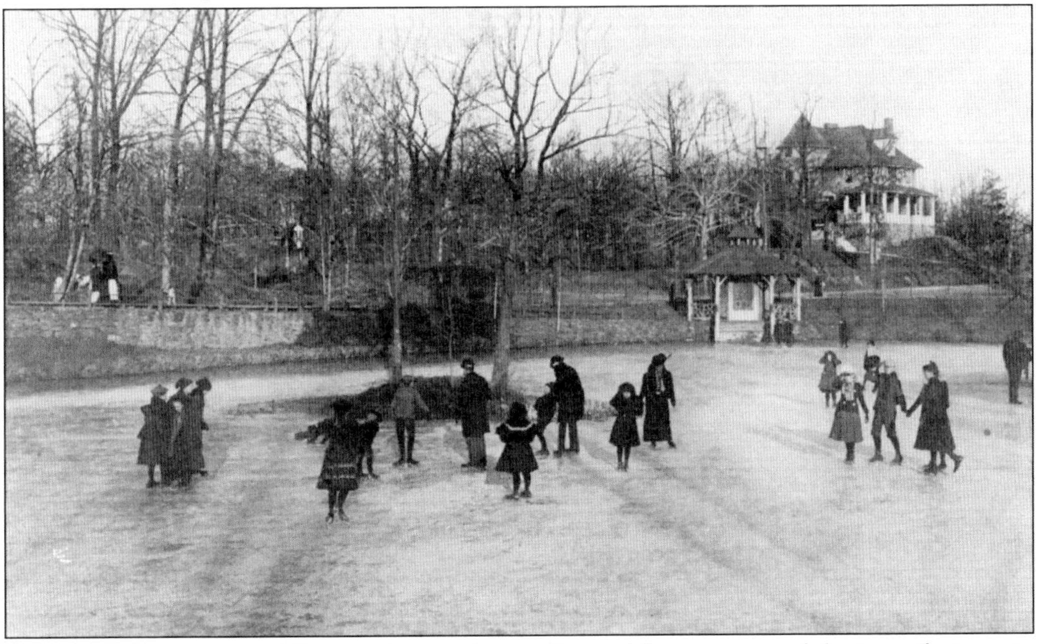

Park Hill Lake in the Winter. Ice-skating on frozen lakes was one of the joys of winter in the early part of the 20th century. This shallow lake was in front of the Park Hill Racquet Club, which is still an active tennis and swim club, and this location is now tennis courts. (YHS.)

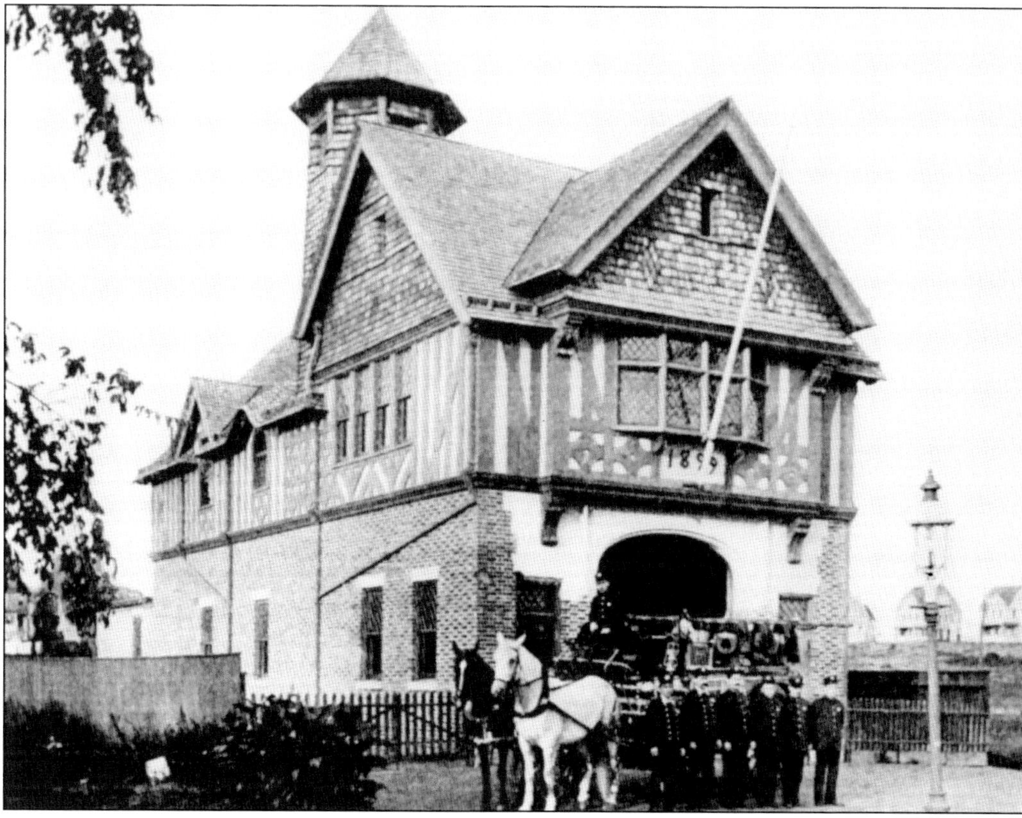

SHONNARD PLACE FIREHOUSE. This ornate Tudor-style firehouse is still in use and houses the Fourth Precinct Police Headquarters and adjacent firehouse. The horse-drawn pumpers are things of the past and come out for parades and celebrations, usually drawn by human volunteers. (YFD.)

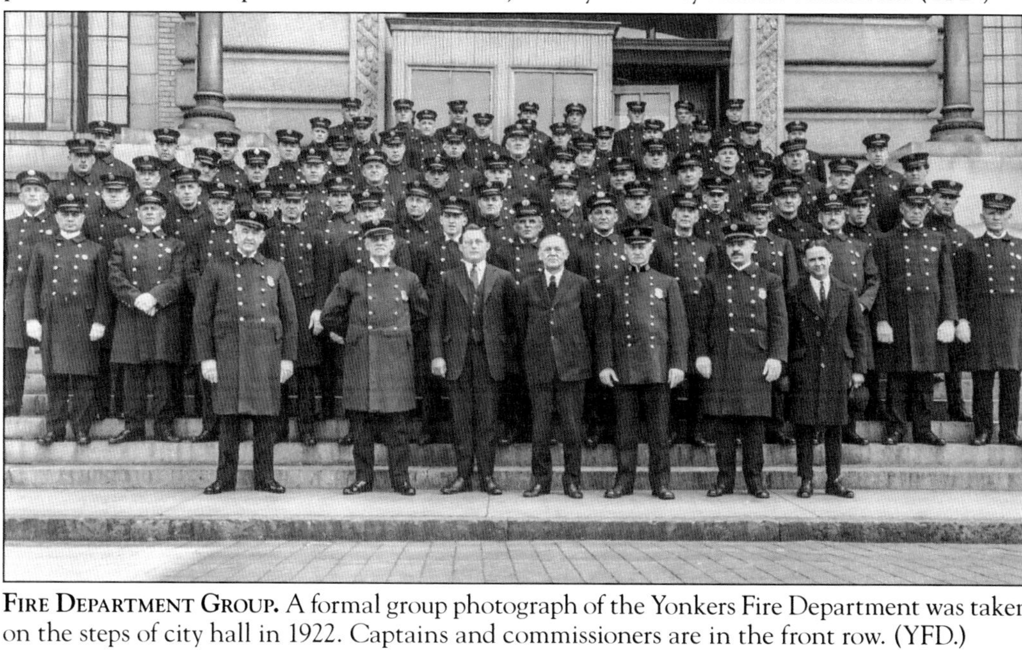

FIRE DEPARTMENT GROUP. A formal group photograph of the Yonkers Fire Department was taken on the steps of city hall in 1922. Captains and commissioners are in the front row. (YFD.)

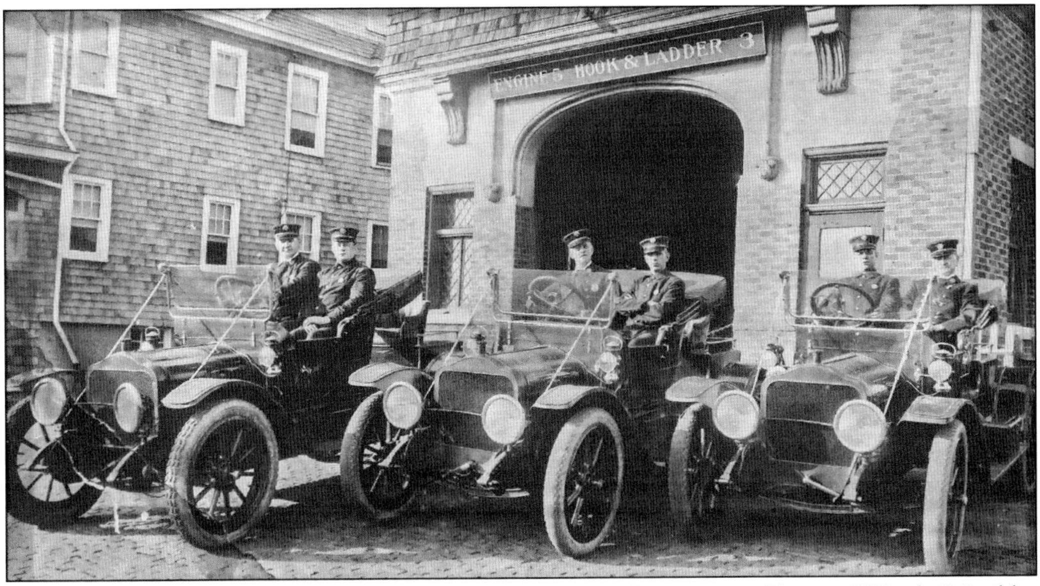

ENGINE NO. 5, 1920s. This great old shot of Yonkers Fire Department Engine 5 Hook & Ladder 3 almost reminds one of a fire-department version of the Keystone Kops. (YFD.)

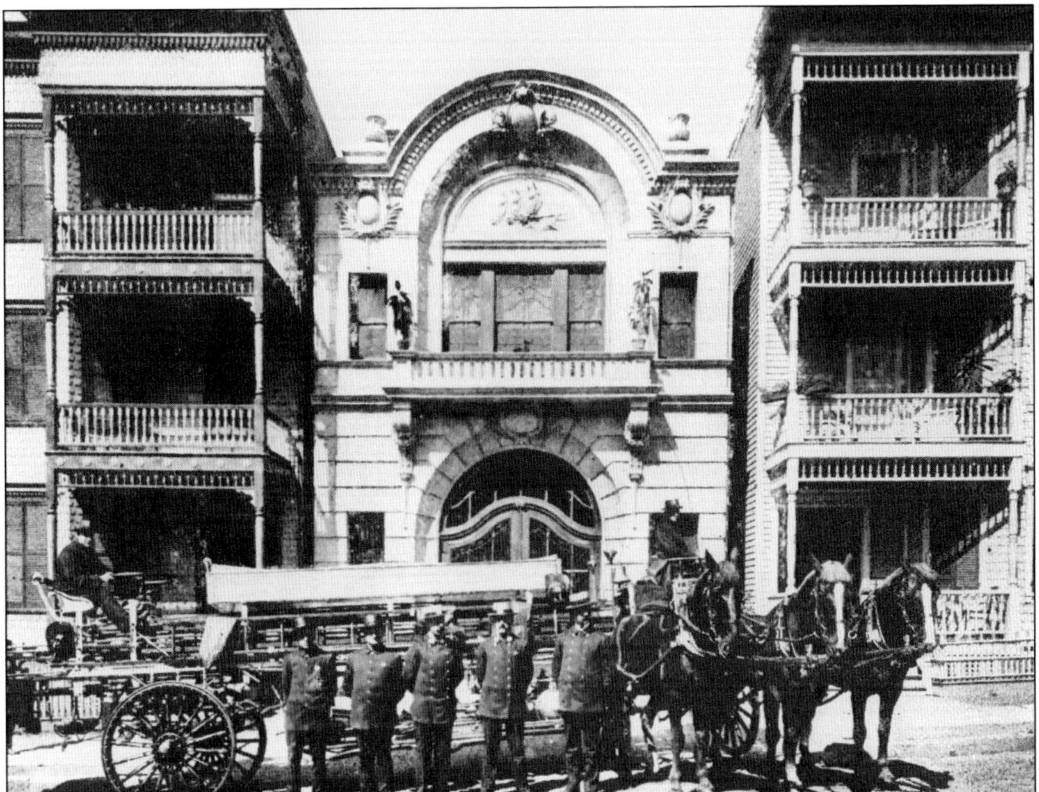

OAK STREET FIREHOUSE. Oak Street is located in the densely populated, wood-frame house area Nodine Hill, and this firehouse is still an active one. The wonderful intaglio of four straining horses in an ornate, almost Palladian arch gives this firehouse incredible character. (YFD.)

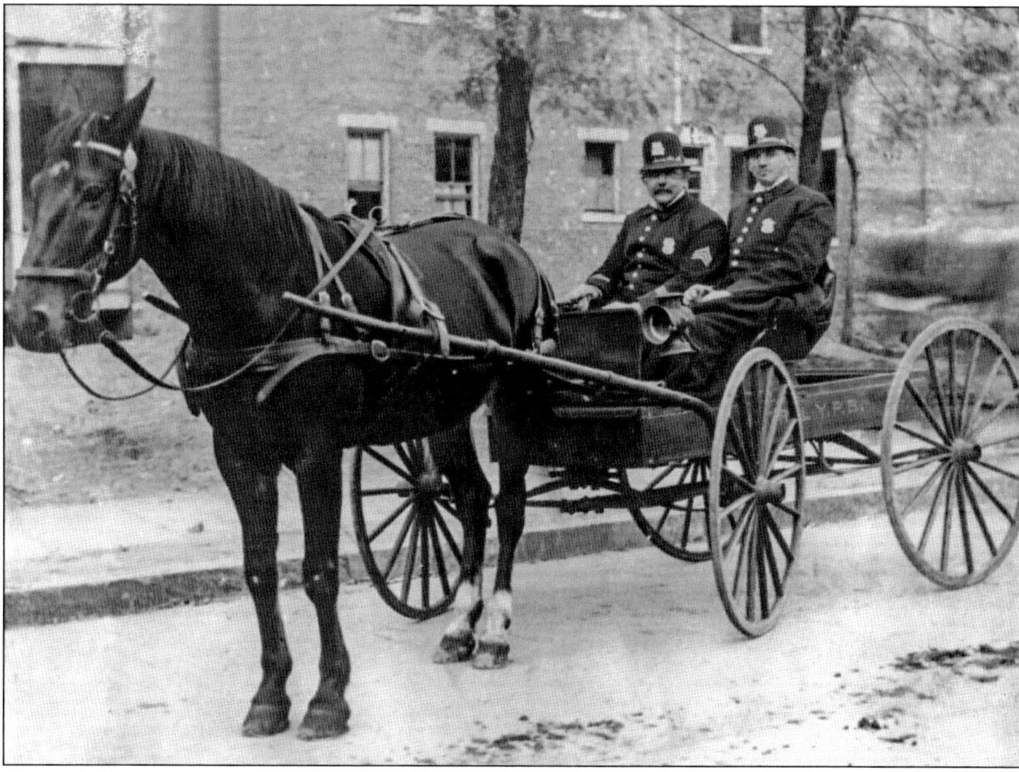

POLICE WAGON, C. 1913. Yonkers's finest chased criminals from horse-drawn carriages in the 1900s. The horses were stabled in the rear of the then police headquarters on Dock Street on the waterfront. (YPD.)

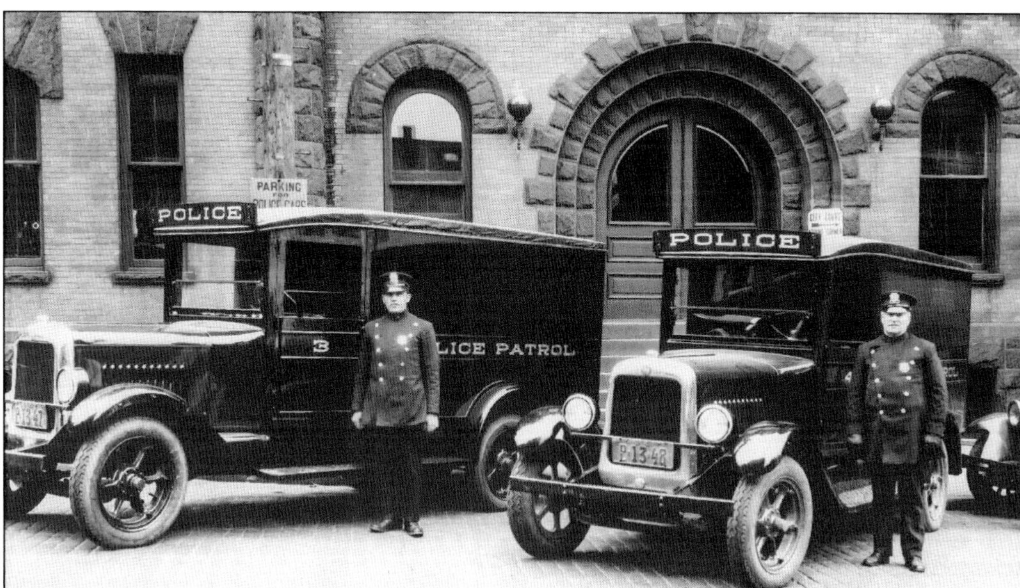

PADDY WAGONS, 1927. These paddy wagons, so called because of the predominance of Irish in the police department, were used to haul criminals off to jail. (YPD.)

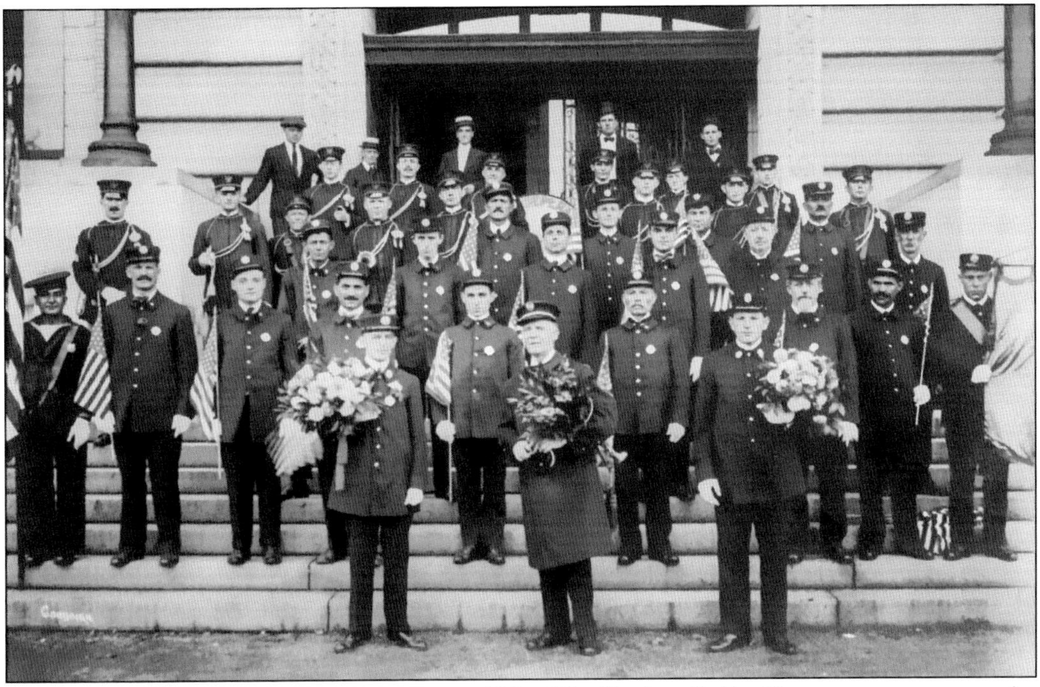

First Department Group Photograph, 1920s. The Yonkers Police Department poses on the steps of Yonkers City Hall for a formal group photograph of the first department. (YPD.)

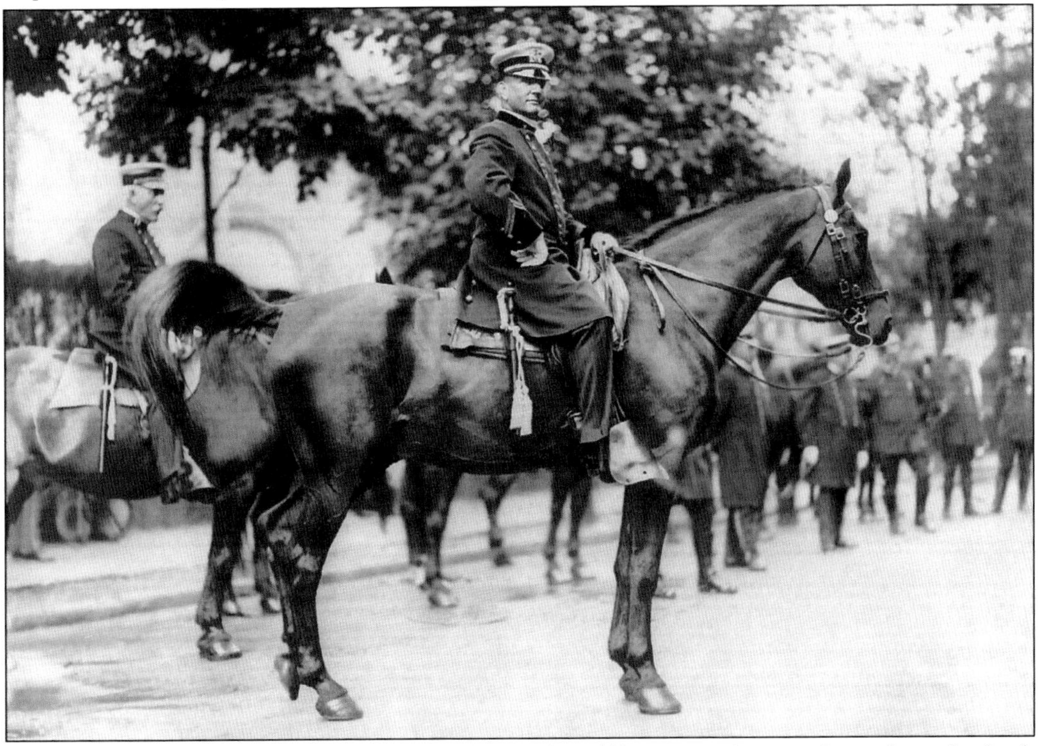

Chief Daniel Wolff. Yonkers police chief Daniel Wolff inspects the patrolmen from the back of his fine steed. (YPD.)

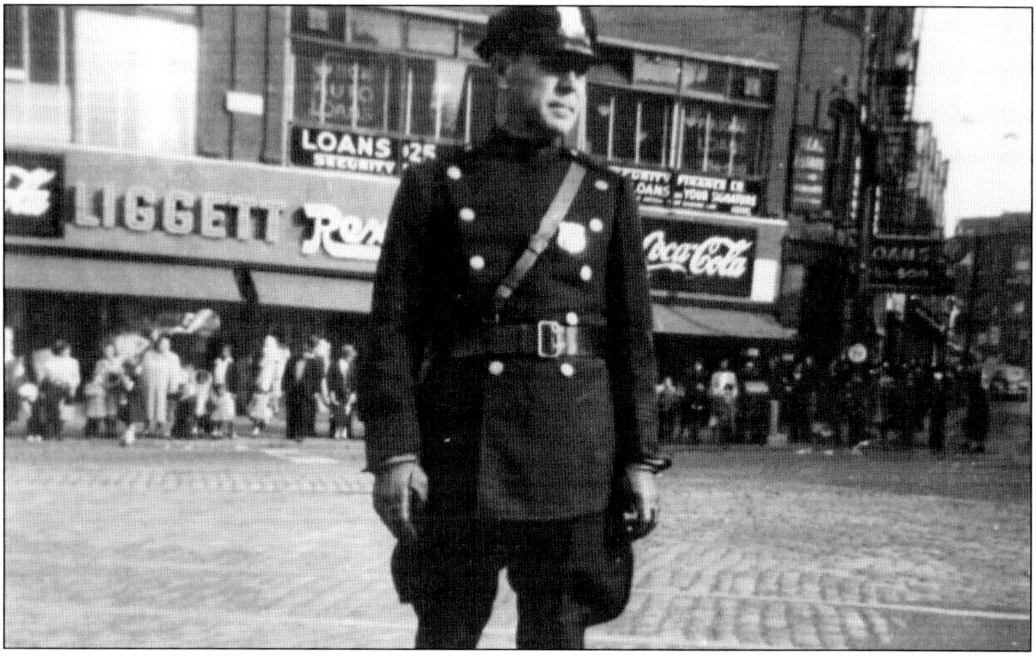

Police in Getty Square. The backbone of the police department was the foot patrolman who also directed traffic. Given the octopus-like configuration of the square, with two-way traffic coming and going from all streets, this cop had his work cut out for him. Note the trolley tracks in the pavement. (YHS.)

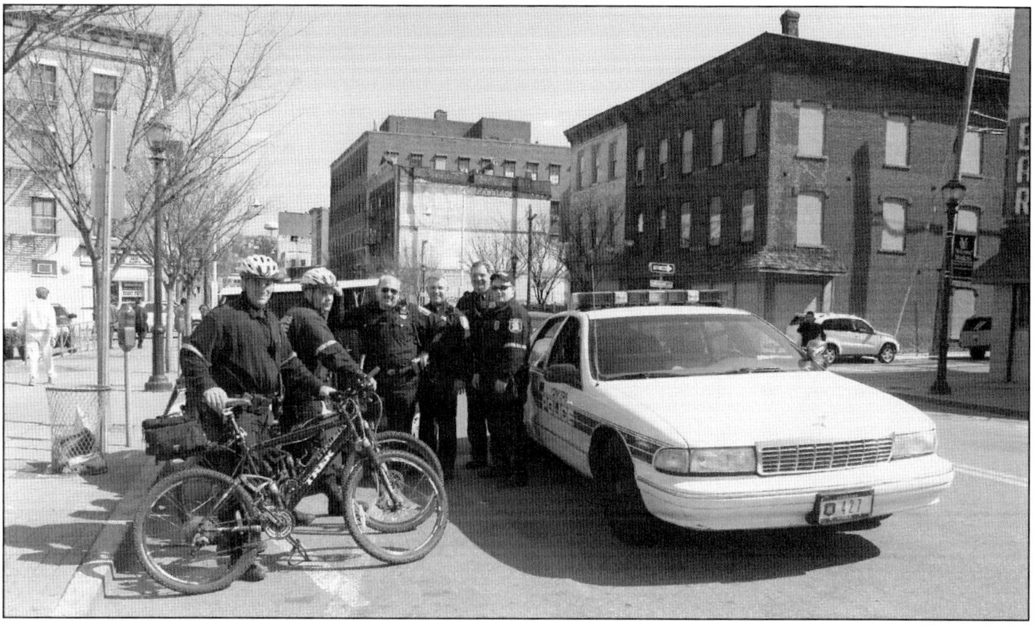

Police Bike Patrol on Main Street. Research showed that the short narrow streets, alleyways, and now one-way traffic made criminal pursuits on bicycle to be the most effective way to make a collar. These downtown bicycle cops pose with a traffic control officer in a golf cart and a patrolman in a sector car. The buildings in the background were demolished and replaced with a six-story apartment building. (Joan Jennings.)

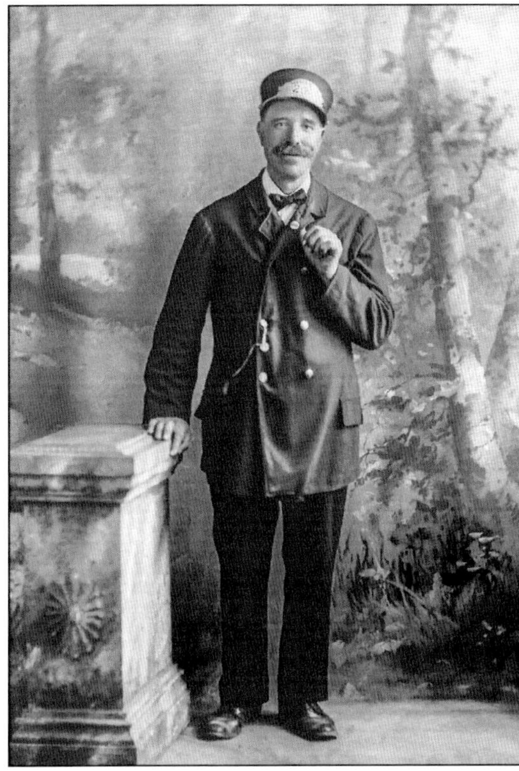

Michael Grad, Trolley Driver. Michael Grady could have been a lord of the realm. He is so proud of his trolley driver's uniform in this studio portrait. (Kay Amicone.)

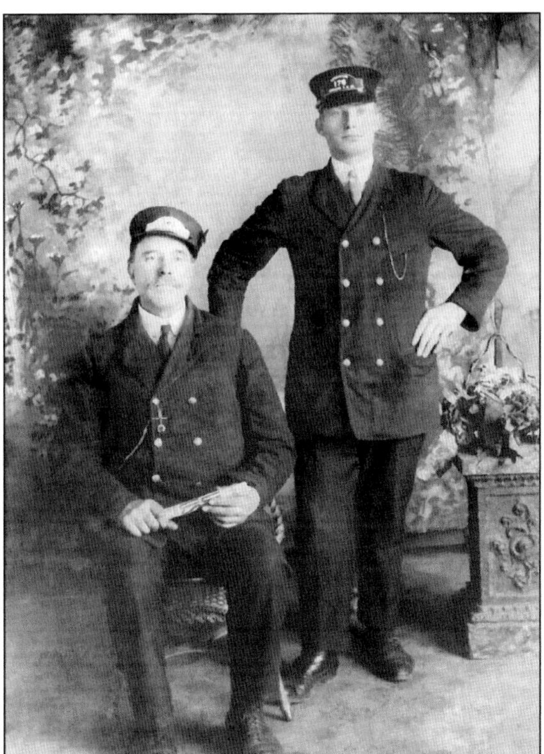

Two Trolley Drivers. Michael Grady and his unidentified partner strike a pose in their trolley driver finery. (Kay Amicone.)

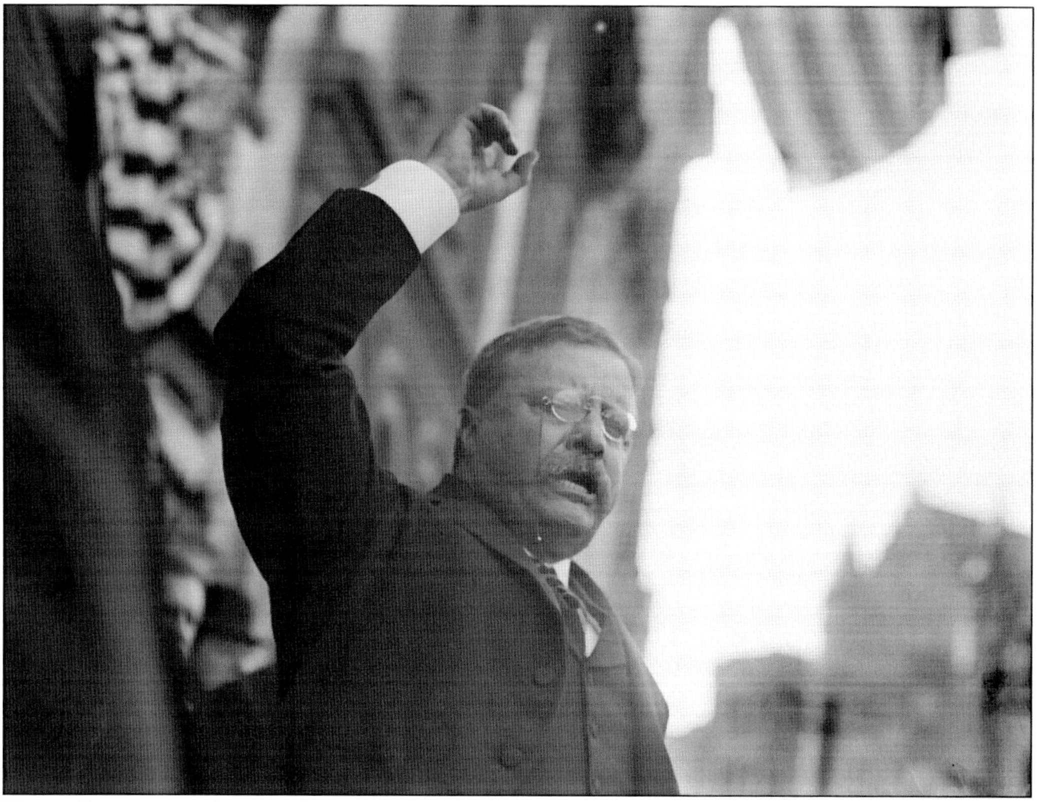

TEDDY ROOSEVELT GIVING SPEECH IN YONKERS. Yonkers has been a destination for presidential speeches since Teddy Roosevelt stopped by Getty Square in 1912. Notice the Hollywood Inn in the background. (Library of Congress.)

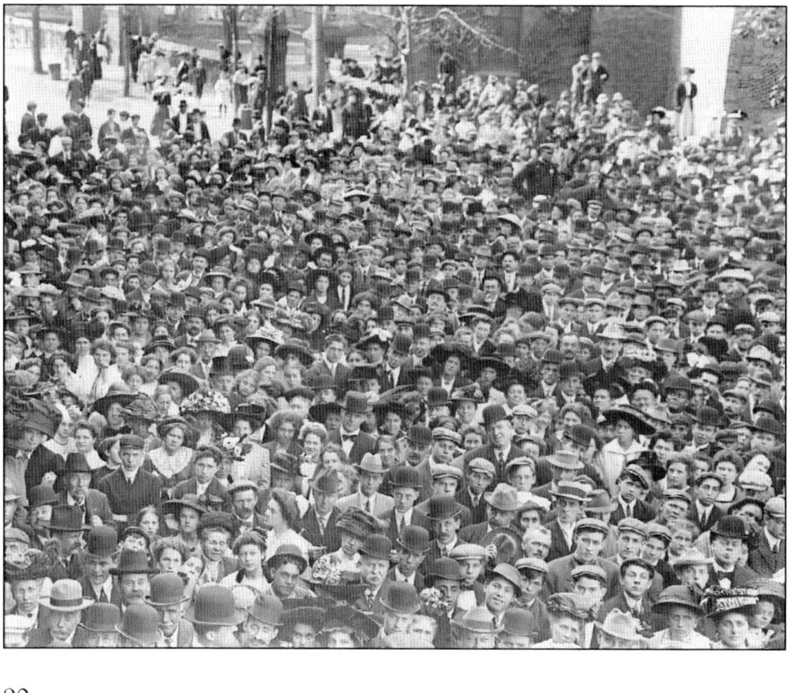

CROWD AT ROOSEVELT SPEECH IN YONKERS, 1912. Yonkersites turned out in vast numbers to hear the hero of San Juan Hill speak from his bully pulpit. Note the predominance of hats—one of the primary products of Yonkers hatmakers. (Library of Congress.)

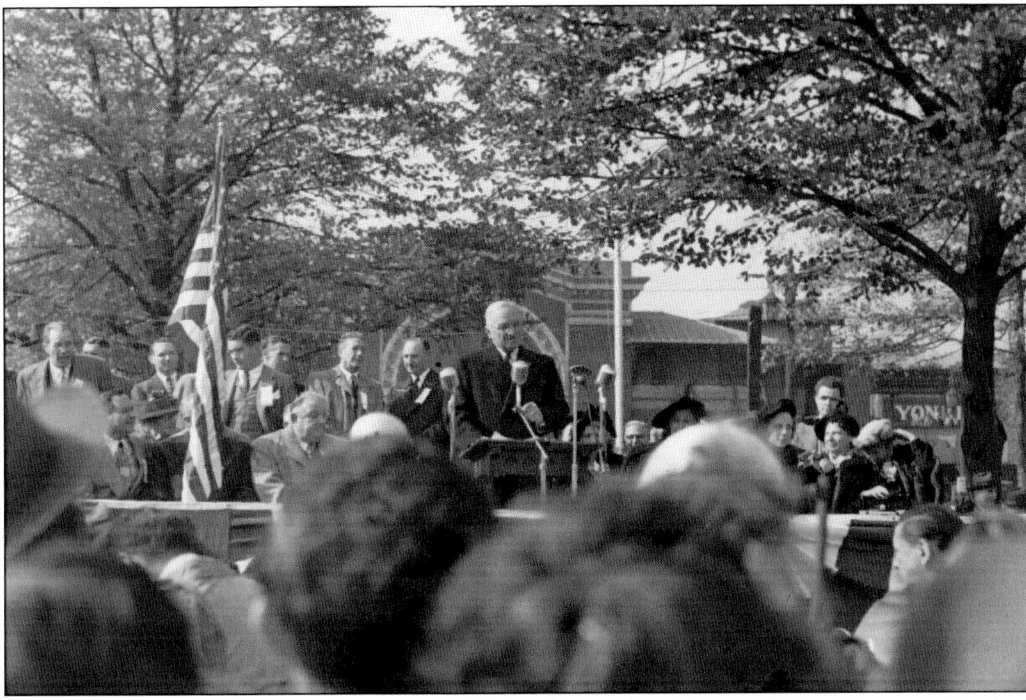

TRUMAN IN LARKIN PLAZA. Harry Truman stopped by Larkin Plaza in front of the main Yonkers Train Station in 1946. (Richard Moore.)

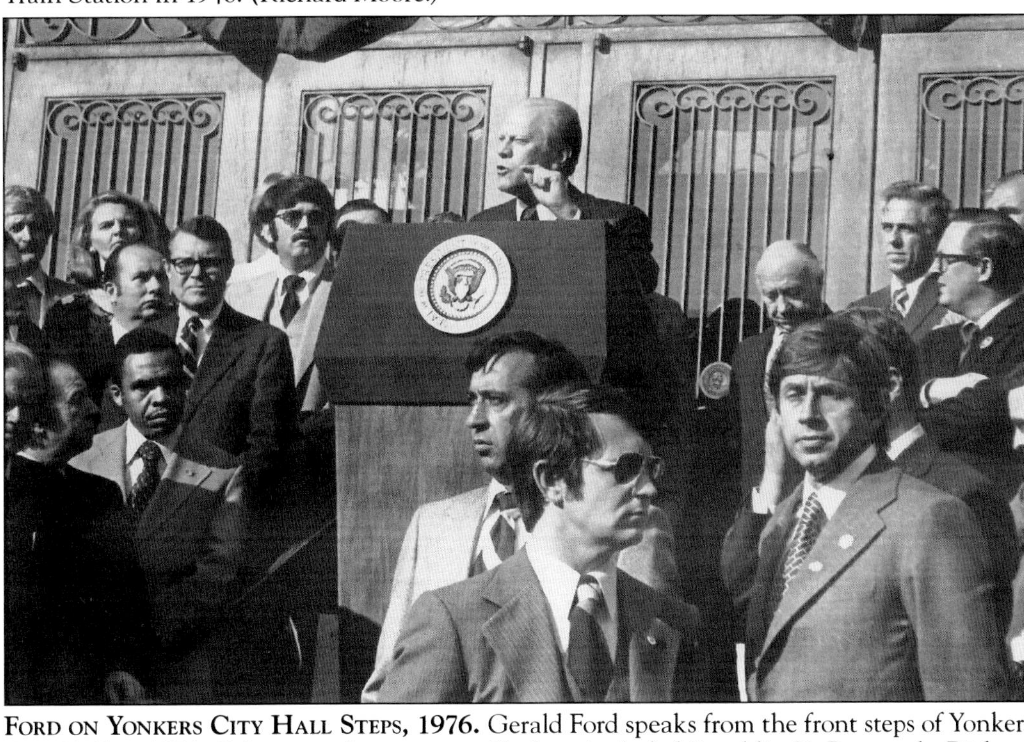

FORD ON YONKERS CITY HALL STEPS, 1976. Gerald Ford speaks from the front steps of Yonkers City Hall in 1976. Other presidents to visit Yonkers included Franklin D. Roosevelt, Richard Nixon, and John F. Kennedy. (Richard Moore.)

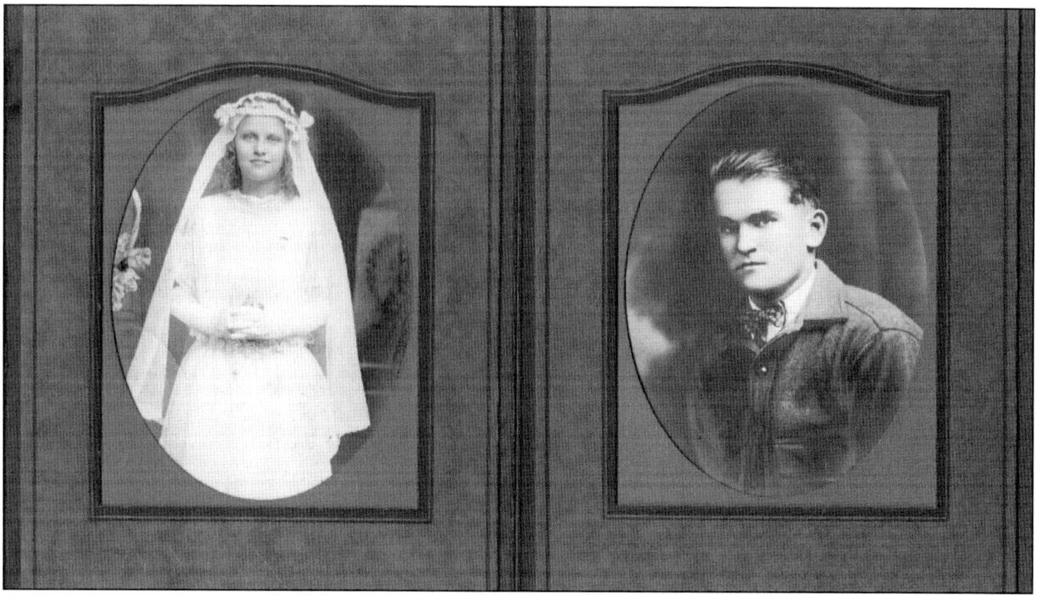

Communion and Portrait Studio Portraits. Life moments were commemorated in studio portraits mounted in custom folders. This young lady had just made her First Holy Communion, and this young man may have just graduated from school or begun a trade. (Joan Jennings.)

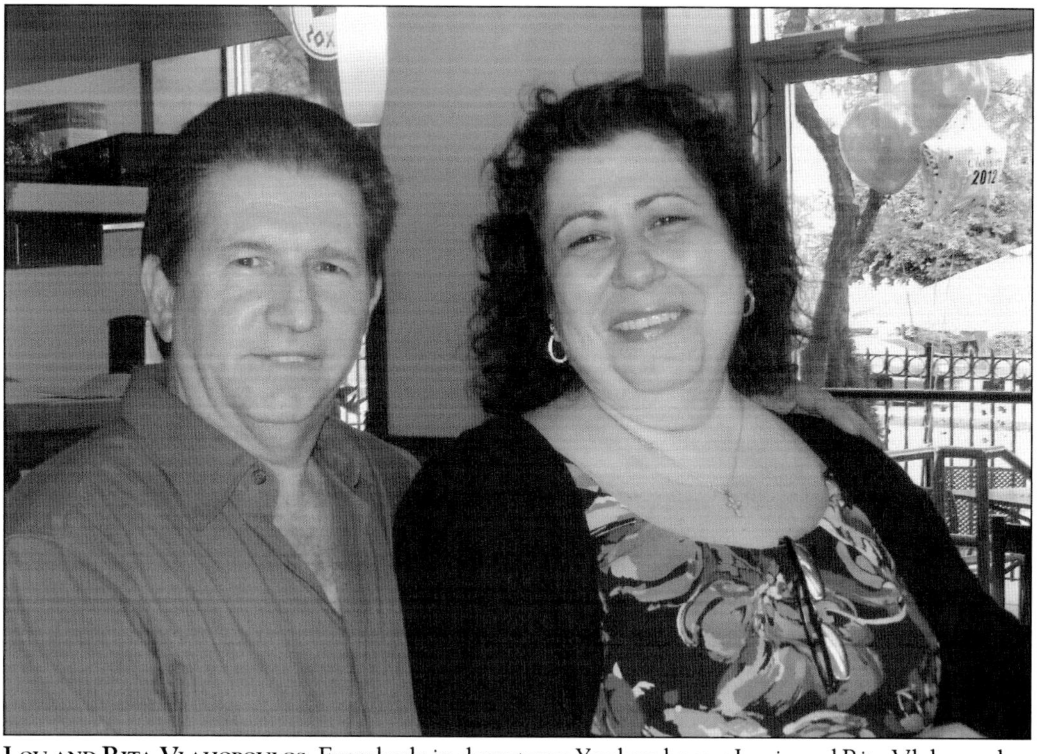

Lou and Rita Vlahopoulos. Everybody in downtown Yonkers knows Louie and Rita Vlahopoulos, working seven days a week as owners of prosperous luncheonette Galaxy, now Paxos. Their patrons watched the Vlahopouloses' three daughters—Barbara, Joanna, and Maria—grow up. (Joan Jennings.)

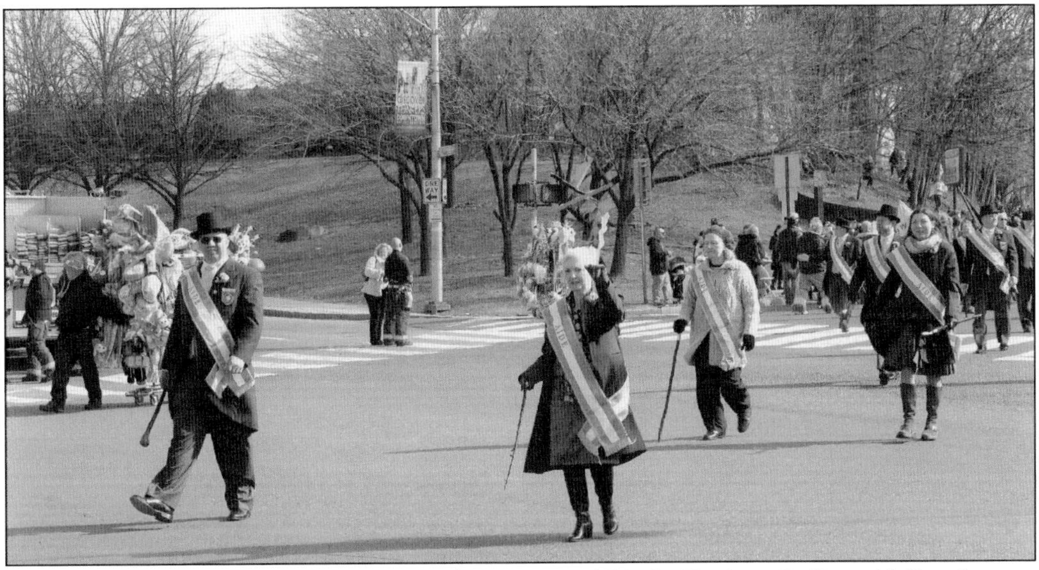

YONKERS SAINT PATRICK'S PARADE. A tradition since 1956, the Yonkers St. Patrick's Parade steps off on the first Sunday in March. Several events such as the "Changing of the Sash," a Sunday-morning mass at St. Mary's Roman Catholic Church (Immaculate Conception, built by Irish immigrants), the parade, and a dinner dance complete the celebrations. Pictured, from left to right, are parade aides Kenny O'Brien, Kathleen Ennis, Mary Teague (owner of the Tyrone House, one of the oldest businesses in Yonkers), and Eileen Collum. (Donna Davis.)

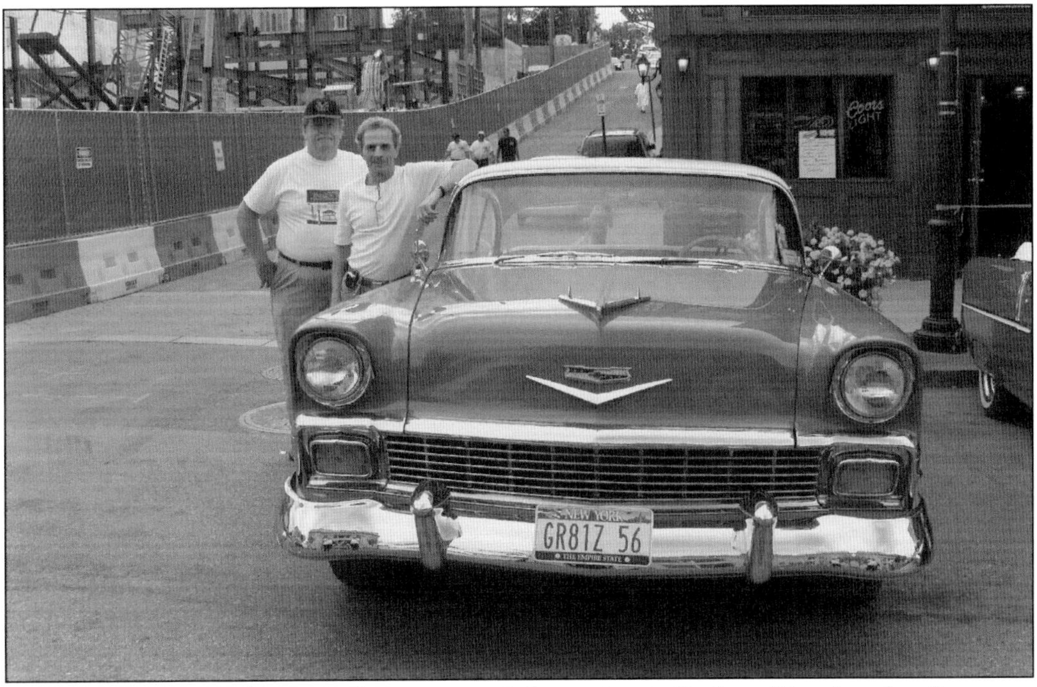

1956 CHEVY. A popular annual event in mid-September is Yonkers Riverfest that features a display of "Rockin' Rods," vintage cars from the 1950s and 1960s. Here, Andrew C. "Andy" Betts (left) visits with 1956 Chevy owner Phil Pepe, while the car is on display in front of the Tyrone House. (Joan Jennings.)

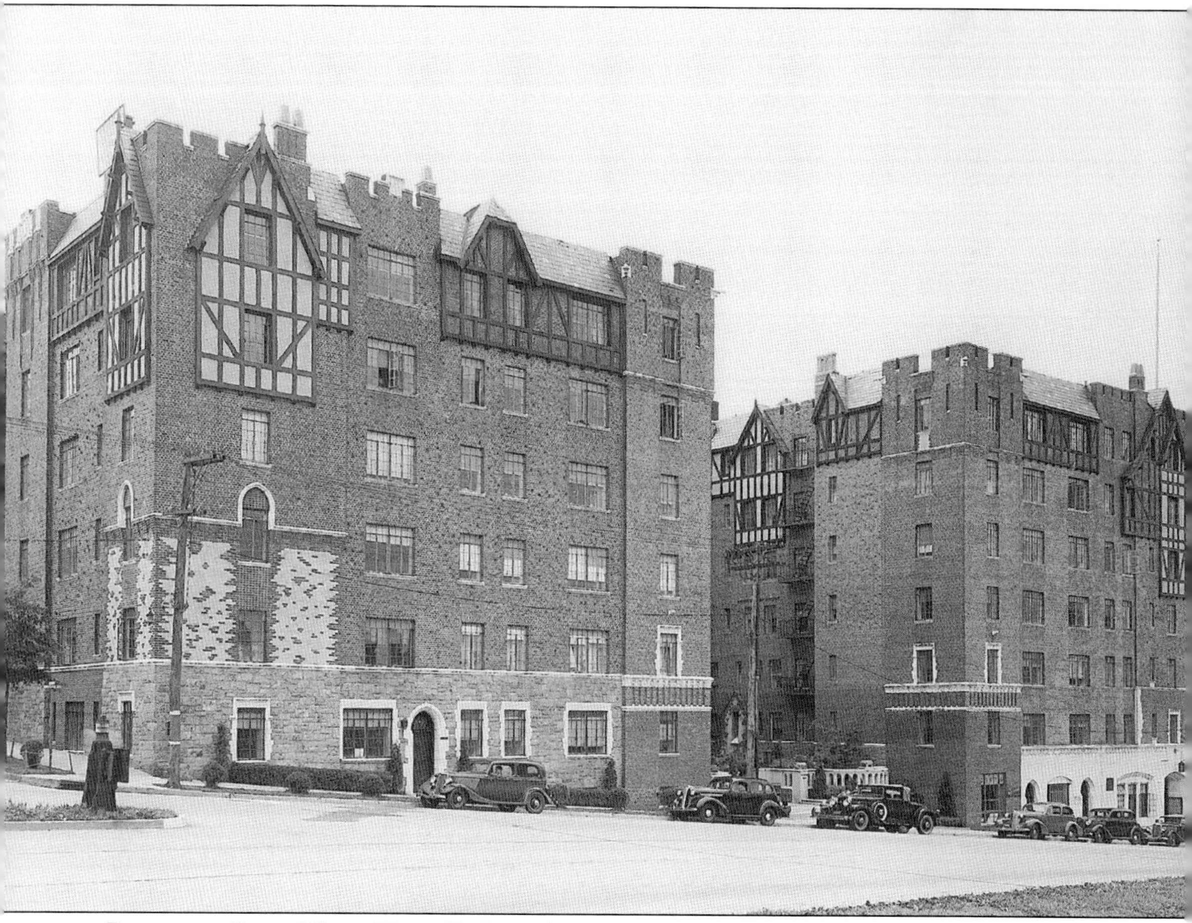

Pondfield Road West. These Tudor-style apartments on Pondfield Road West in east Yonkers had an architectural style and features seen around the city. (COY Planning.)

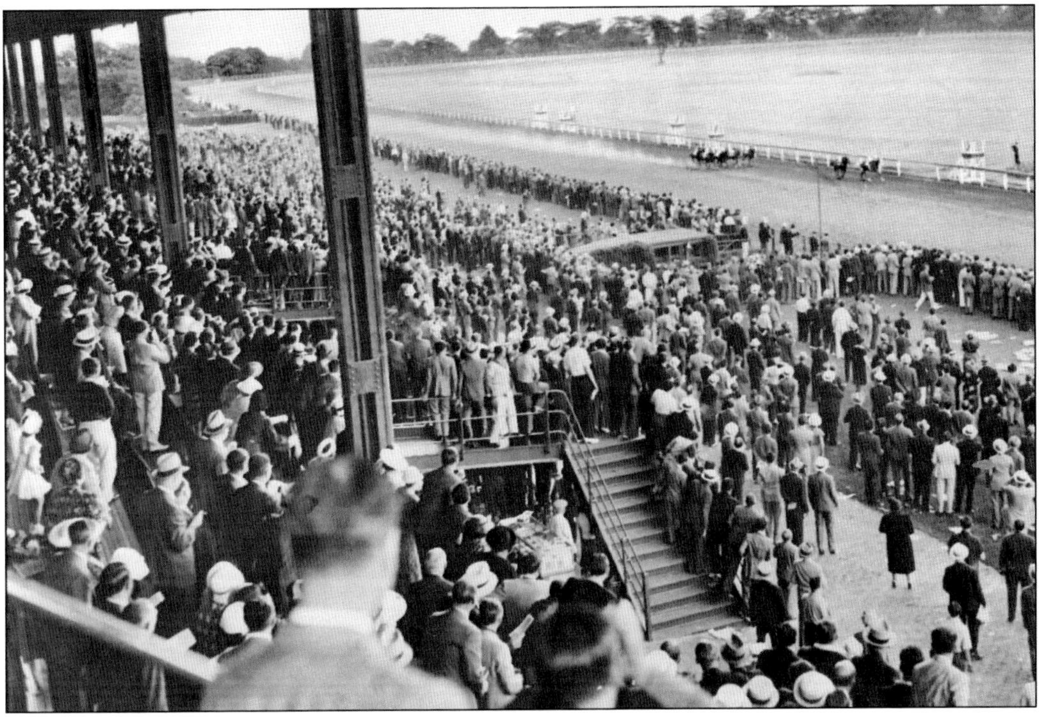

Yonkers Racetrack, 1950s. Starting its life as the Empire Raceway, where legendary car racer Barney Oldfield once roared around the track, Yonkers Race Track (shown here in the 1950s) has once again become Empire, now with video slot machines and gaming tables. (COY Planning.)

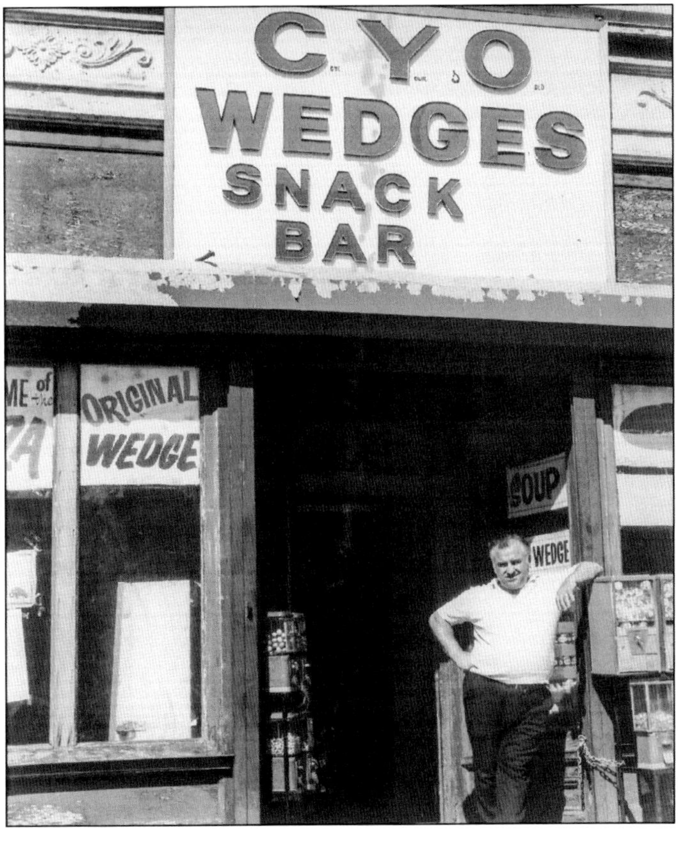

CYO Wedges at 205 Nepperhan Avenue. The proprietor of CYO Wedges takes a break in the front of his store at 205 Nepperhan Avenue. Along with rubber-soled athletic shoes, a sandwich made from cold sliced meat and cheese is called by a multitude of names. In Yonkers, yo, it's a wedge! (Joe Forlivio.)

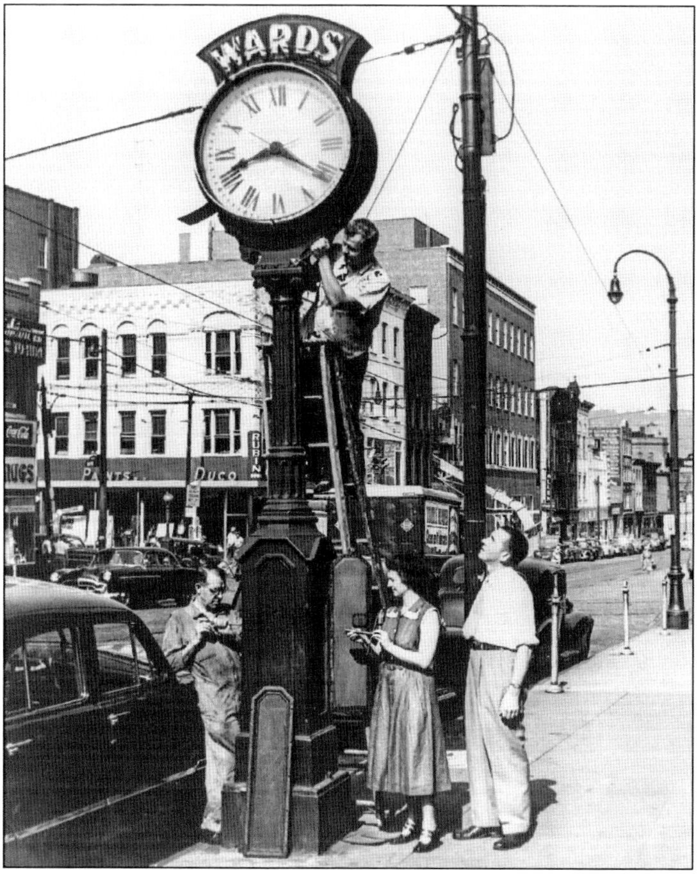

CLOCK REPAIR. Ward's Jewelers on Main Street wanted to make sure its shoppers knew what time it was, a habit owners hoped would lead to the purchase of an expensive wristwatch. The building behind the clock, Rubin's Paint, was torn down and is now the site of Richard Haas's trompe l'oeil mural *Gateway to the Hudson*. (COY Planning.)

FIRST DAY OF SCHOOL. The children in this photograph are dressed up for the first day of school. The housing at Riverview Place on Nodine Hill was three-story buildings with basement storage bins, small backyards, and white picket fences around microscopic front rose gardens with hopscotch numbers scrawled on the slate sidewalks with chalk. (Joan Jennings.)

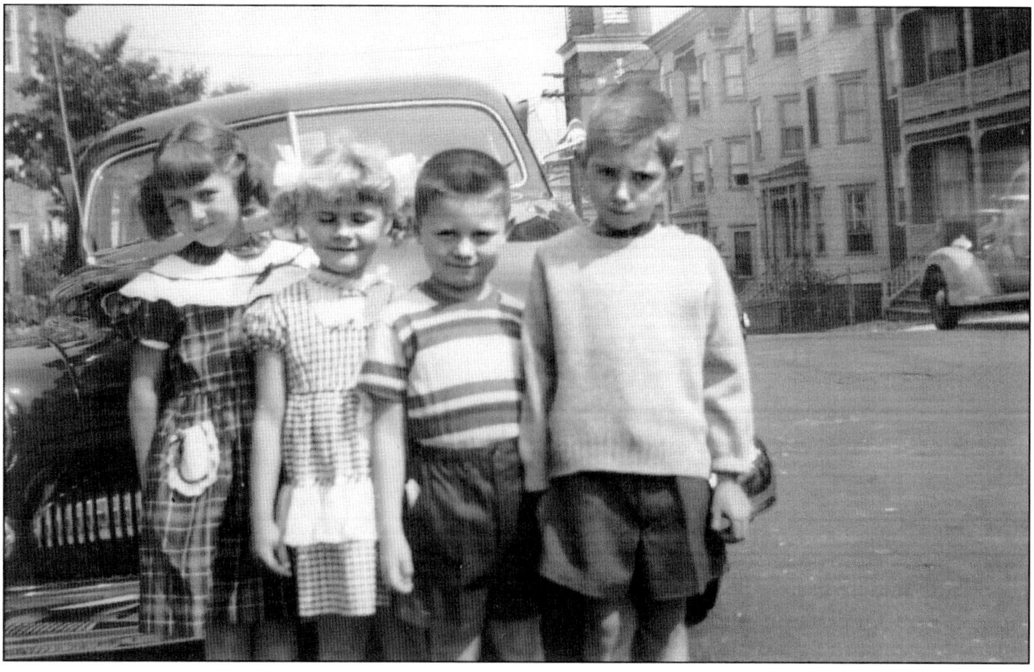

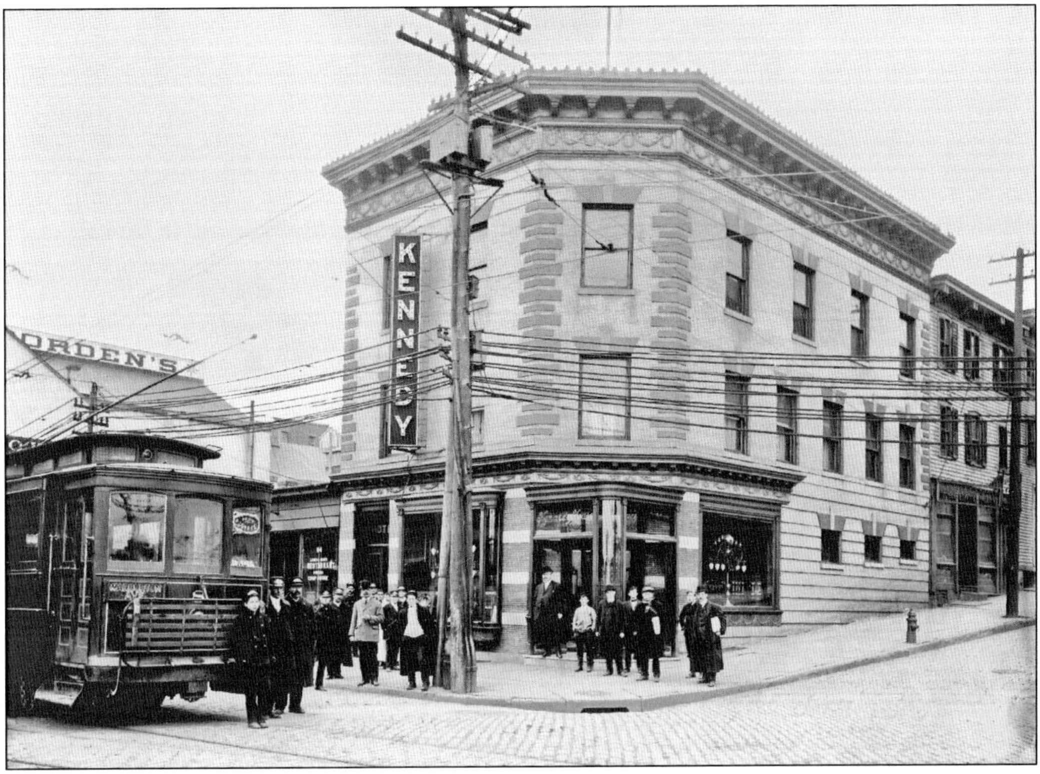

Kennedy Saloon, Main Street and Buena Vista Avenue. The Kennedy Hotel was built to accommodate the new train travelers on the New York Central Railroad. The ground floor became the Kennedy Saloon, which in turn became the Tyrone House in the 1950s. When the hotel was scheduled for demolition, the T-House, as the locals called it, moved three stores east on Main Street, where it remains today. (YHS.)

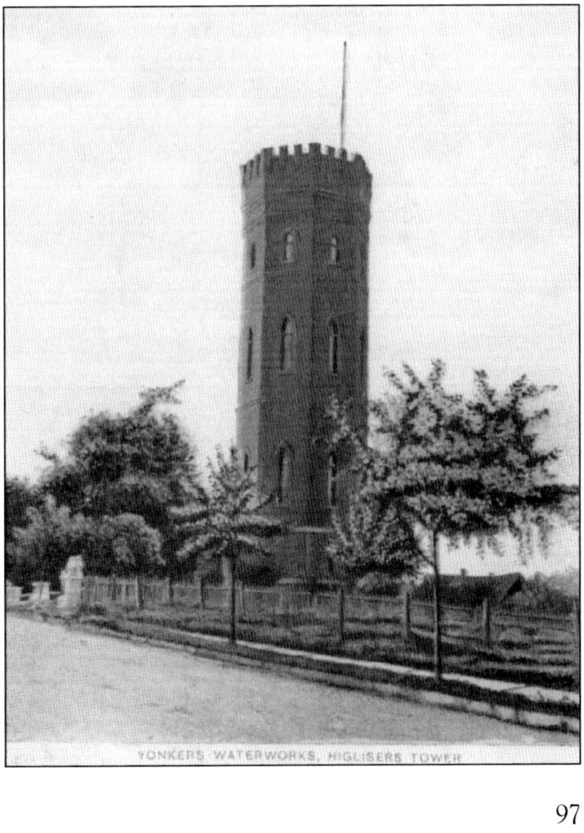

Water Tower at Reservoir. As part of the Croton Aqueduct water supply, Yonkers had a large reservoir in an area now bounded by Palmer and Tuckahoe Roads. This tower was used as a vantage point to survey water levels in the reservoir. The land on which it stood was filled in and, today, most residents are not aware it ever existed. (YHS.)

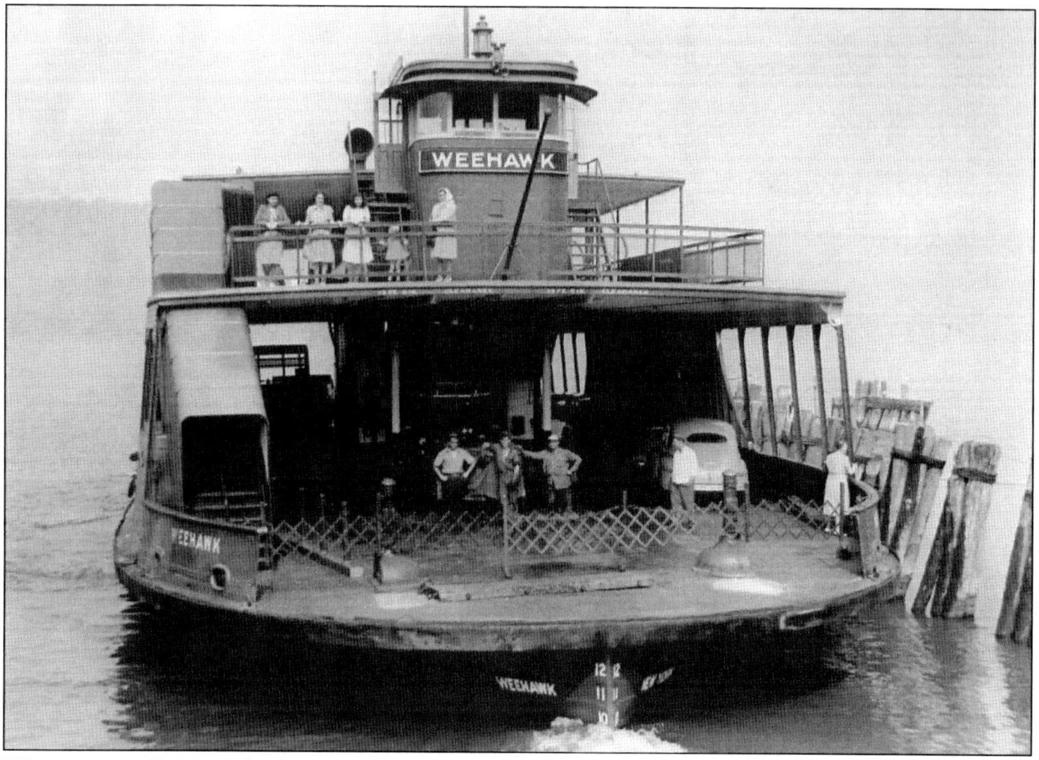

WEEHAWKEN FERRY. The big treat in the 1950s was to take the brand-new cars that Yonkersites only drove on Sundays down to the Weehawken Ferry, where they drove them up the ramp onto the boat to be ferried across the Hudson River to picnic at Alpine. (BD.)

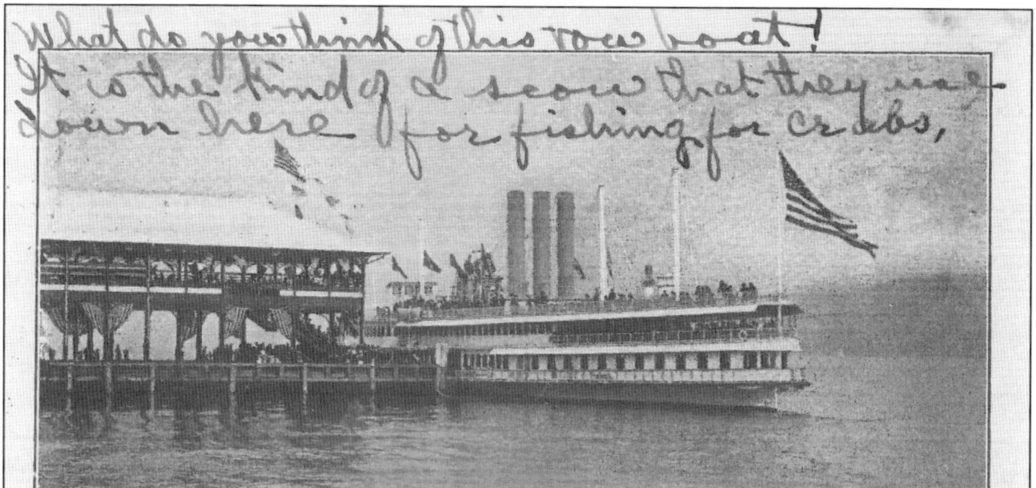

DAYLINER AT PIER. If one just wanted a boat ride, the dayliner could take passengers all the way to Albany or for a family picnic on Coney Island. These huge ships pulled up to the Yonkers Pier, and passengers embarked from both the upper and lower levels. (YHS.)

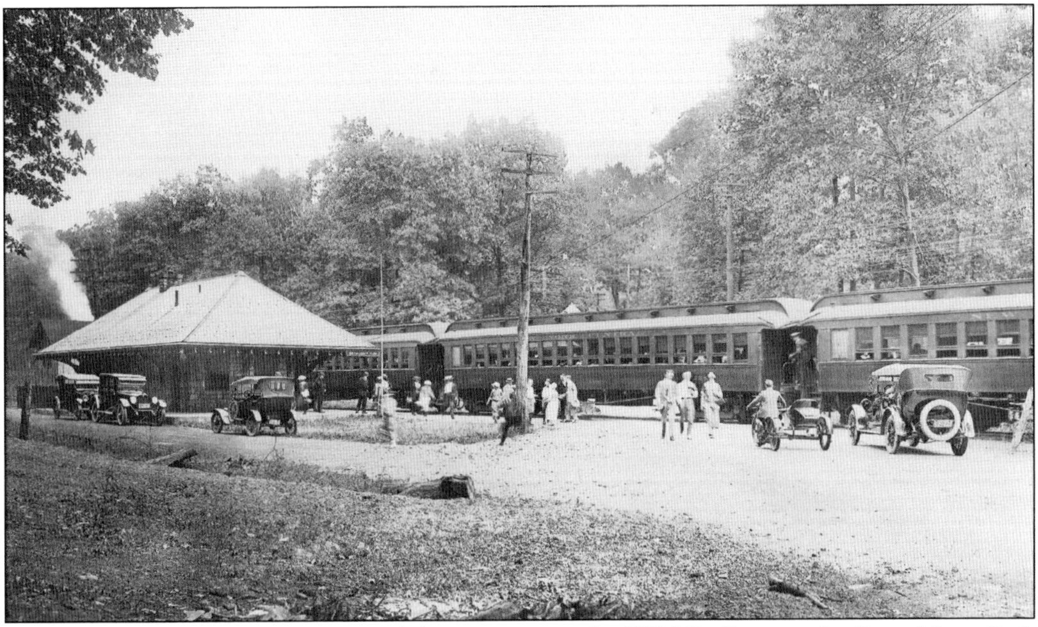

Bryn Mawr Park Station. One of the stations on the "Old Put" route, the Bryn Mawr Park Station was adaptively reused as a local produce market that featured model trains running around the store on tracks installed just below ceiling level. (COY Planning.)

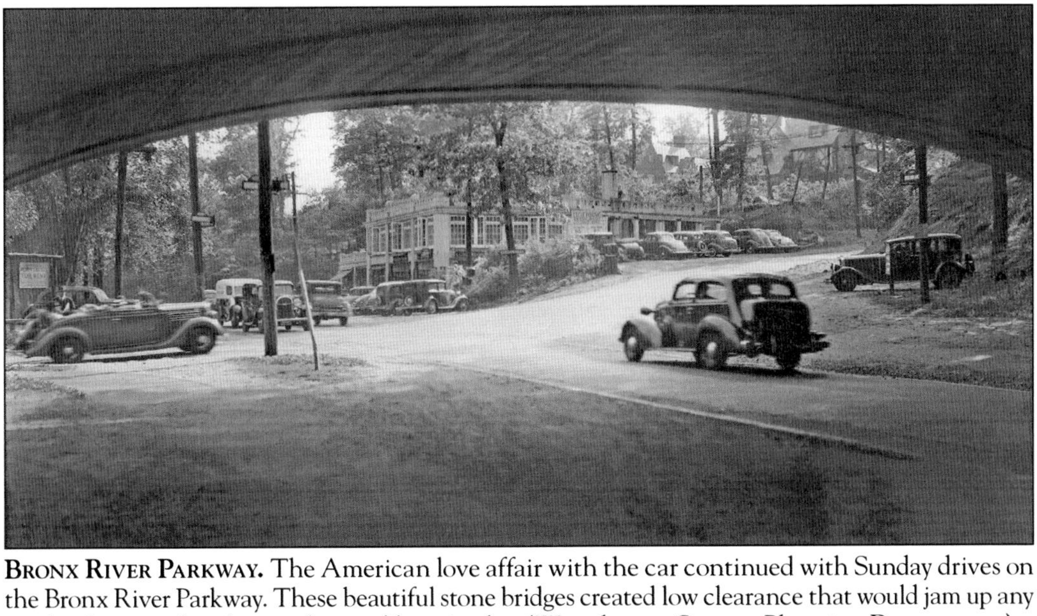

Bronx River Parkway. The American love affair with the car continued with Sunday drives on the Bronx River Parkway. These beautiful stone bridges created low clearance that would jam up any trucks that wandered onto the road by mistake. (Westchester County Planning Department.)

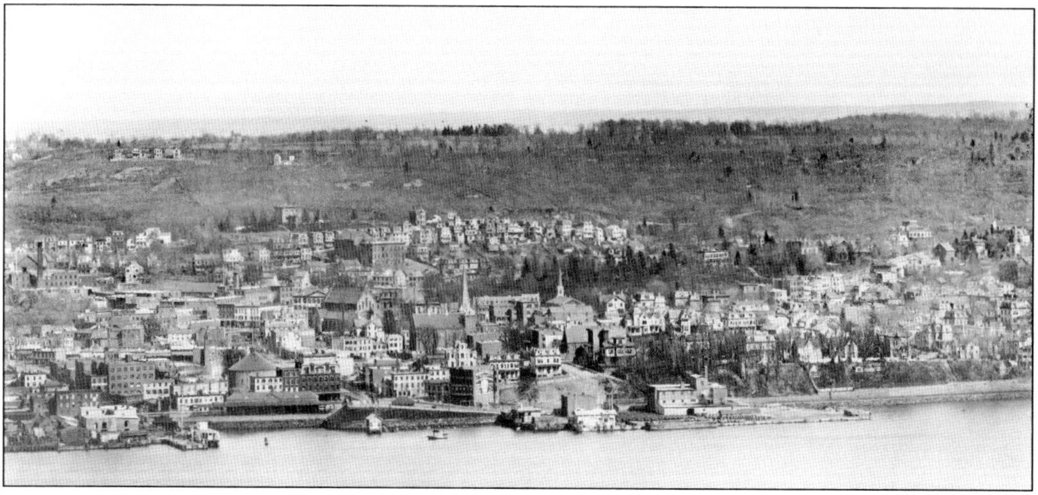

PANORAMA. This very early 1868 photograph of the Yonkers waterfront was taken from the Palisades. The photographer walked along, taking photographs as he went, stitching them together. This image is one of six that compromise a complete photograph of the shoreline from Riverdale to Hastings. (Yonkers Public Library)

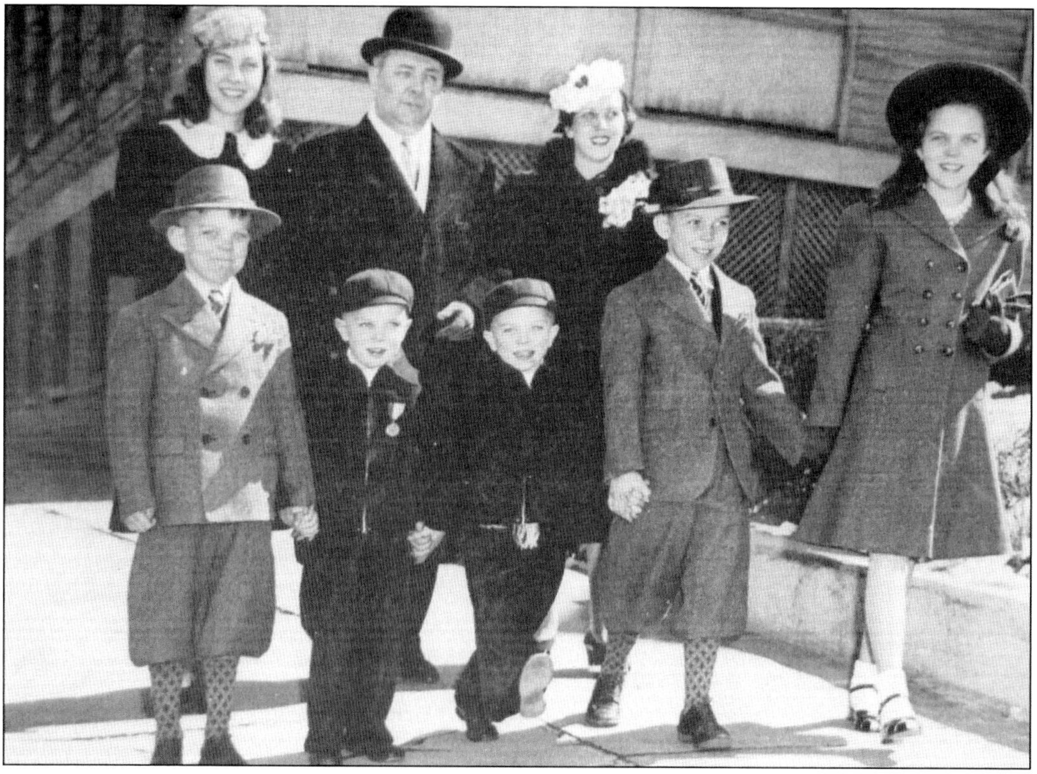

JOHN FLYNN AND FAMILY, 1939. The Flynn family has lived in Yonkers for at least three generations. This photograph of the Flynns on their way to church in 1939 is representative of the Yonkers upper middle class of the day. The family's funeral home is one of the oldest businesses in Yonkers. (Flynn.)

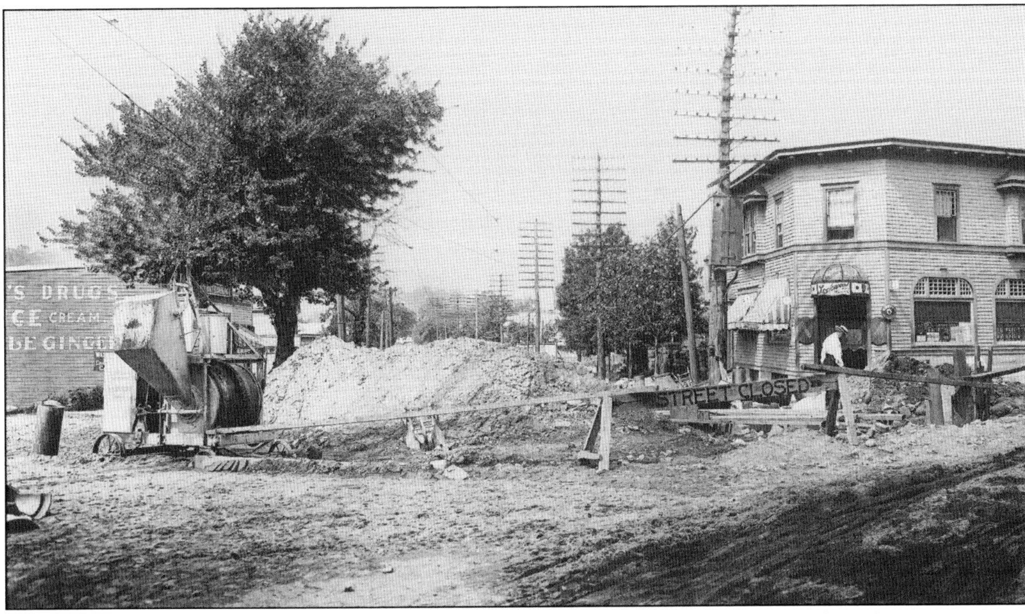

Saw Mill River Road, Looking North at Lockwood Avenue. New modes of transportation mandated new roads. These trenches were dug in preparation for paving at the intersection of Saw Mill River Road and Lockwood Avenue. (COY Planning.)

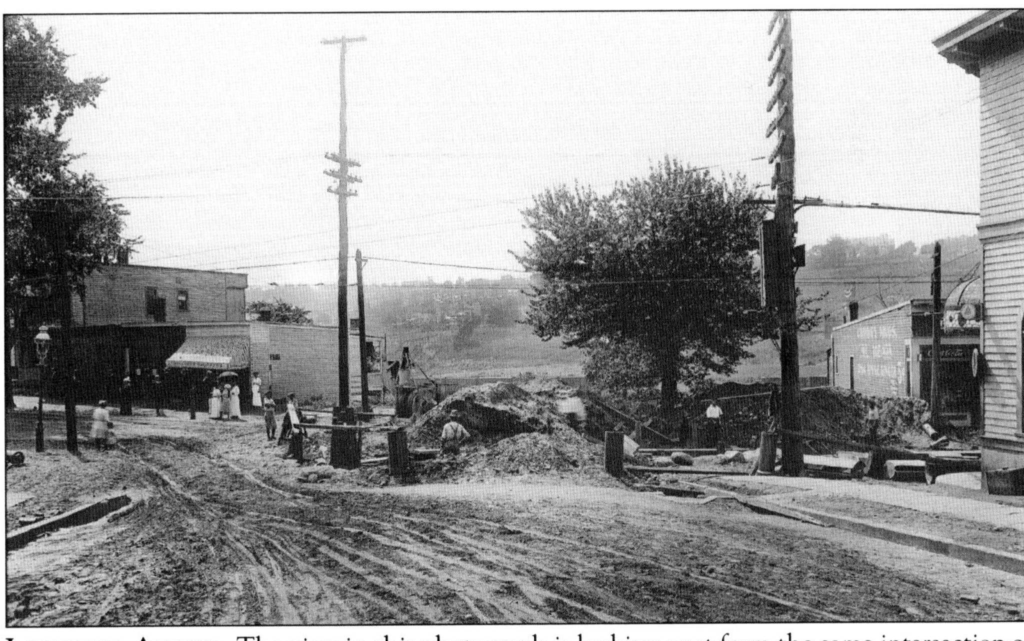

Lockwood Avenue. The view in this photograph is looking west from the same intersection as road-building progresses. (COY Planning.)

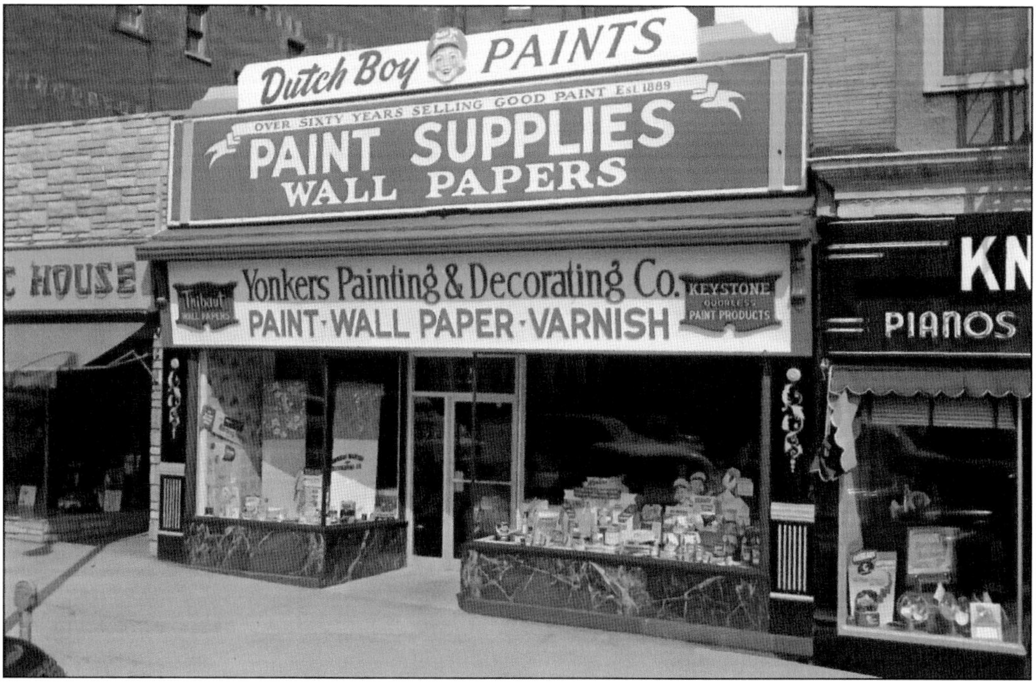

Yonkers Paint, 22 Warburton Avenue. Only recently closed, Yonkers Paint and Glass had the distinction of being one of the oldest businesses in town along with the also shuttered McVicar Roofing. Rubin Hardware and the Tyrone House have operated for seven and five decades respectively and continue to thrive. (BD.)

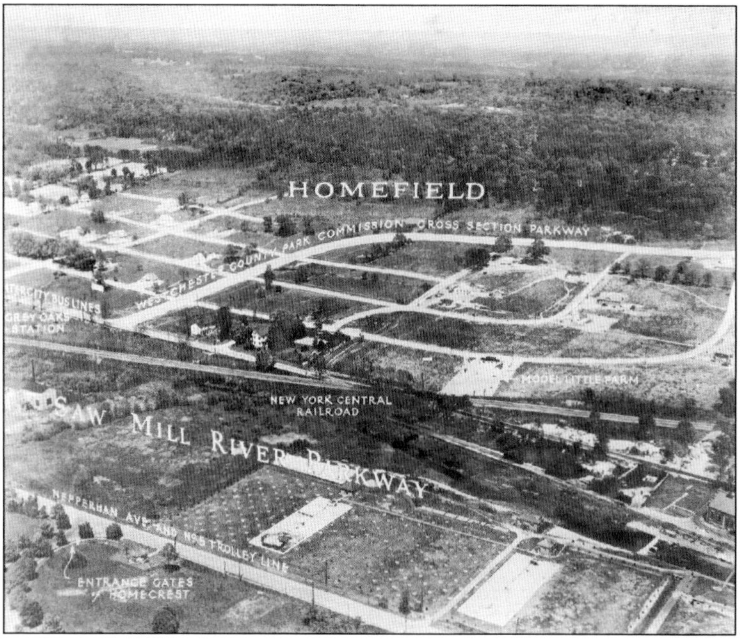

Homefield, Cross Hill at Nepperhan Avenue. This aerial shot shows the middle-class housing development called Homefield. There are many distinct residential neighborhoods in Yonkers characterized by certain types of structures and architectural styles. (Marianne Winstanley.)

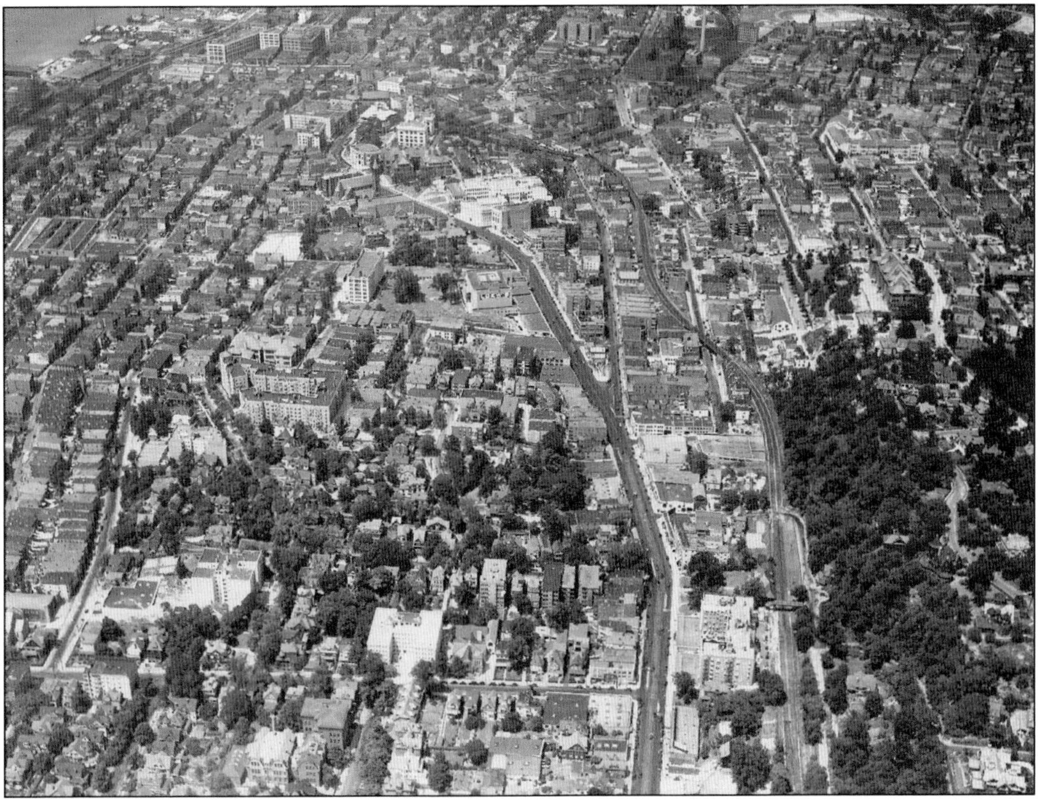

AERIAL. This aerial shot shows the varied and congested nature of building in downtown Yonkers. The road in the lower center is South Broadway, which splits, becoming New Main Street to the right. The other dark path is the "Old Put" rail line, which heads to its terminal station at 30 South Broadway. Note the Carnegie library adjacent to city hall. (COY Planning.)

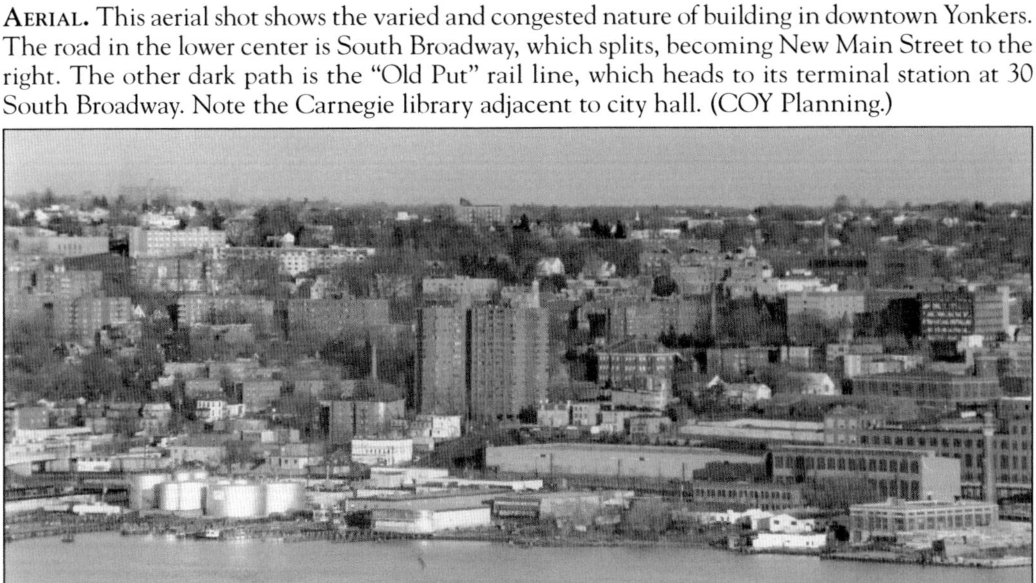

WATERFRONT AT ALEXANDER STREET, TANK FARM. Taken from the Palisades across the river from Yonkers, this photograph shows the industrial nature of the Yonkers waterfront. The large silver circular structures were the Tarricone "tank farm," removed using brownfield remediation funds in the early 2000s. (COY Planning.)

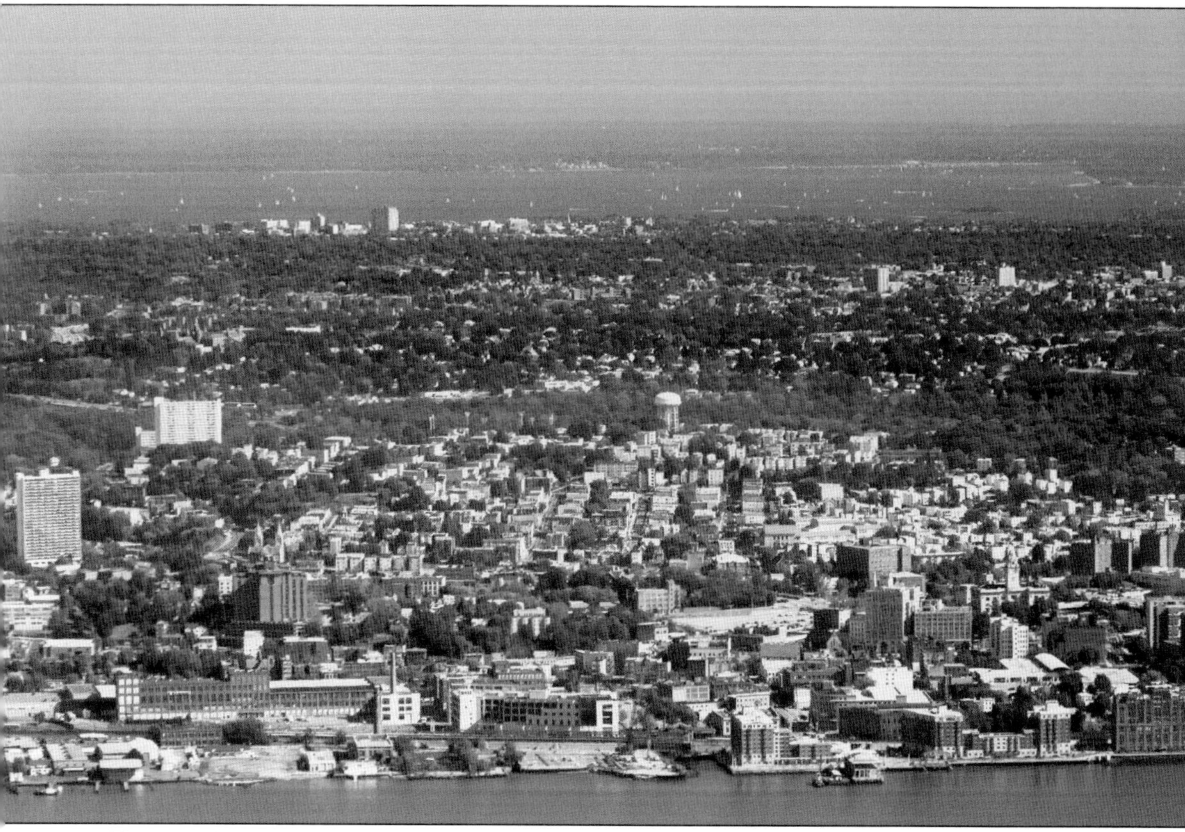

Yonkers Aerial View, 2003. In the space of a few years, industrial uses have given way to new residential buildings on the Yonkers waterfront. In the background of this aerial is the Long Island Sound, giving a good perspective on the extent of Yonkers when looking from the west on the Hudson River to the east. While there are still industrial uses on the Hudson riverbank, note the apartment buildings in proximity to the pier in the front center; the large building in the right foreground was an old power plant adaptively reused for cooperative housing. Note the high density of the population in the foreground, while the midsection has more trees and greenery, denoting the prevalence of single-family residential structures. The white water tower sits atop Nodine Hill and is another Yonkers visual landmark. (Joan Jennings.)

Six

From Van der Donck to Van der Donck Park

What had been Adriaen Van der Donck's extensive patroonship—purchased by the Philipse family, lost as a spoil of war to private owners, becoming Yonkers Village Hall, then abandoned for a new City Hall and slated for demolition—has come full circle. The Manor Hall, built alongside Van der Donck's mills, was saved by a philanthropist and donated to New York State as a museum. The Saw Mill River, once the pristine source of fish and game for the local Lenape tribes, became an open sewer, threatening the populace with the horrors of cholera so that its dams were torn down in 1892 to make the waters flow. With the river still a problem 30 years later, the Army Corps of Engineers funneled its waters into a flume and covered it over. A parking lot and small park was built over the flume, and Yonkers continued to grow and build around it. From prosperity to decline, the river ran unnoticed and unremarked under the downtown that it had birthed.

In the latter years of the 20th century, New York governor George Pataki vowed to see the river uncovered so that one day, citizens could see the river that was the source of the city. Surprisingly, his dream was actually realized. The waters of the river were cleaned. Teams of volunteers cut back invasive vines; tires, baby carriages, and even old cars were removed from the riverbed. The waterway that residents had derisively called a creek, a sewer, and other epithets now saw the return of fish and wildfowl. The City of Yonkers, under the aegis of Jim Pinto (director of Downtown and Waterfront Development for the city), the Yonkers Planning Department (Mario Caruso), Groundwork Hudson Valley (Ann-Marie Mitroff, Andrew Boyd, and Bob Walters), and others from the Friends of Philipse Manor Hall, the Yonkers Historical Society, and Riverfront Library (Susan Thaler), created historic and ecologic educational signage about this now delightful river. This engineered park features include riffles that aerate the water, a fish ladder that enables the American eel to return up the river, nets to trap trash, and ecologically accurate plantings that would recreate the riverbank familiar to the Lenape. Local artist Haifa Bint-Kadi, with the assistance of local Yonkers High School volunteers, installed a mosaic showing the life cycle of the American eel from the Saw Mill River to the Sargasso Sea. Historic statues like *The Hiker*, a Spanish-American War memorial, and the Gold Star Mothers monument joined Vinnie Bagwell's "*The First Lady of Jazz*" *Ella Fitzgerald* around the parkland and train station.

Yonkers had come full circle—from Adriaen Van der Donck, the "Jonkheer" who gave the city its name—to Van der Donck Park. Excelsior!

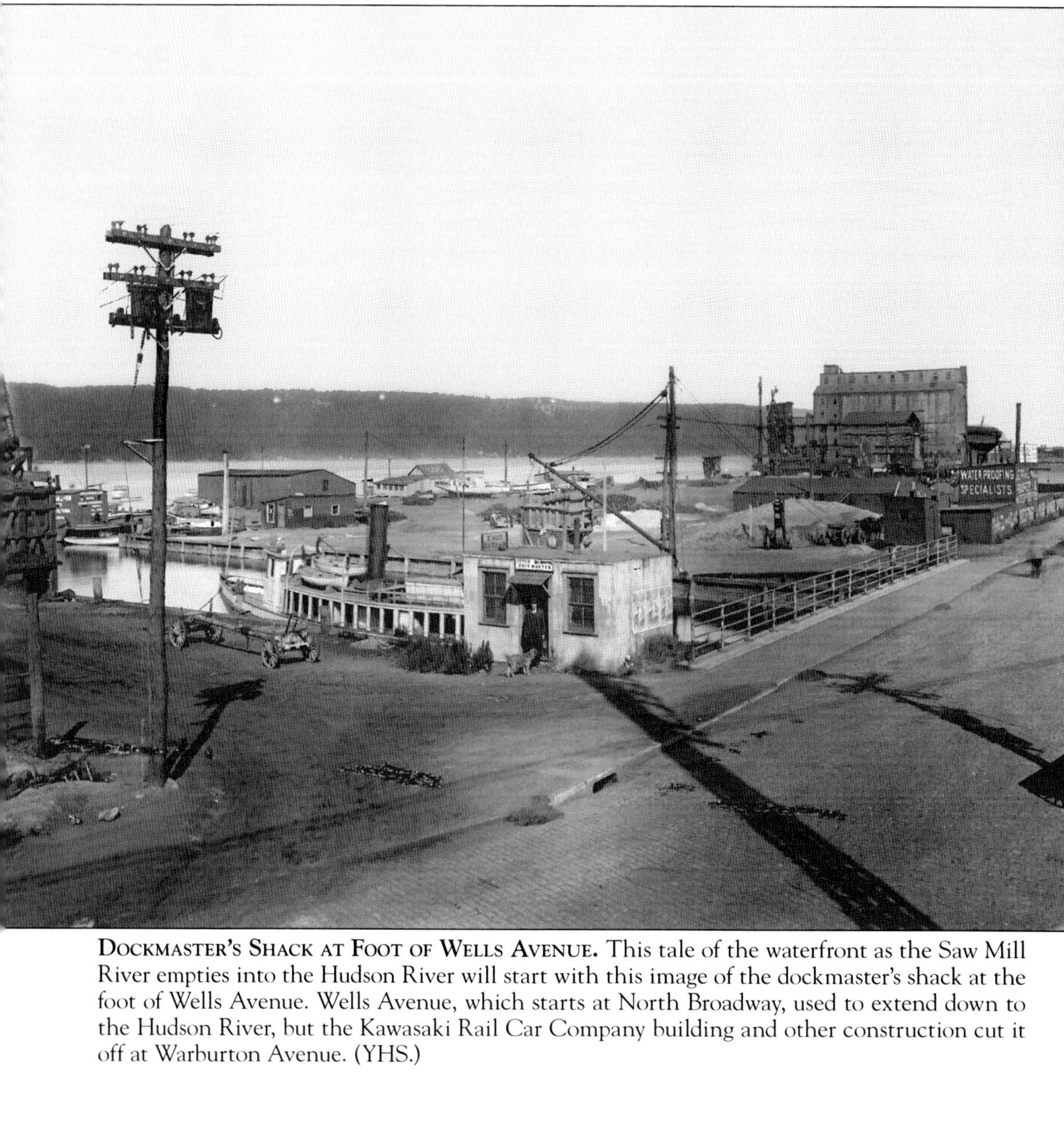

Dockmaster's Shack at Foot of Wells Avenue. This tale of the waterfront as the Saw Mill River empties into the Hudson River will start with this image of the dockmaster's shack at the foot of Wells Avenue. Wells Avenue, which starts at North Broadway, used to extend down to the Hudson River, but the Kawasaki Rail Car Company building and other construction cut it off at Warburton Avenue. (YHS.)

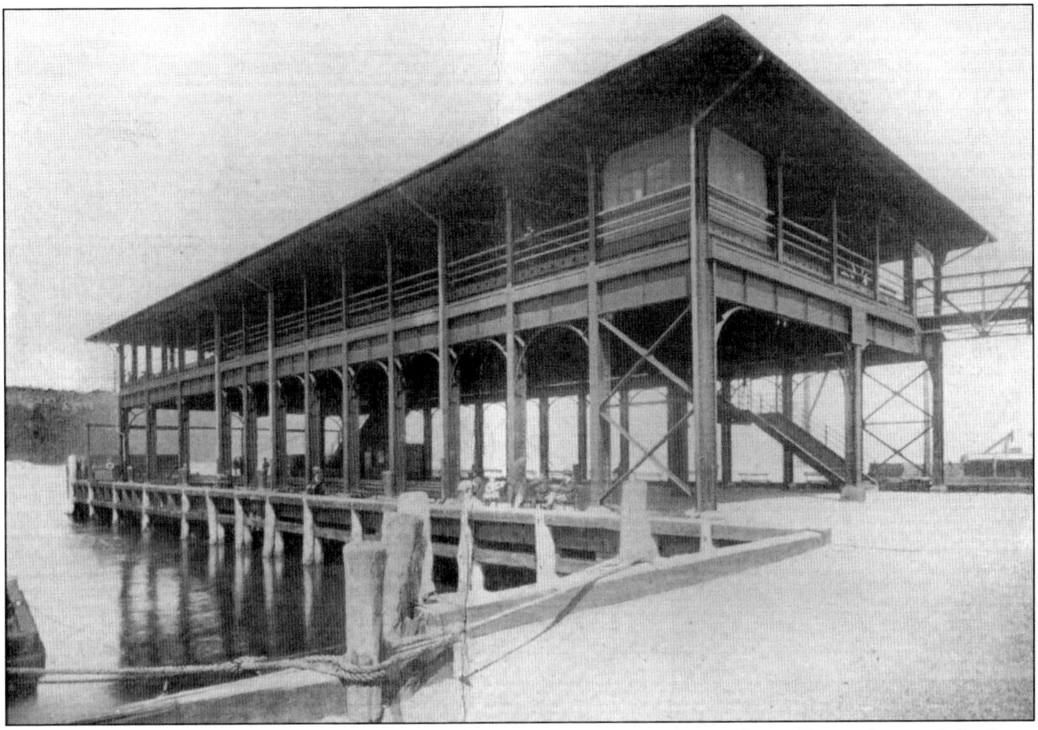

Pier with Walkway. This image of the Yonkers Recreation Pier shows the walkway (top right) where passengers for the ferries or dayliners docked at the pier could walk to or from the main Yonkers Train Station when it was located at a height level even with the walkway. (Mary Hoar.)

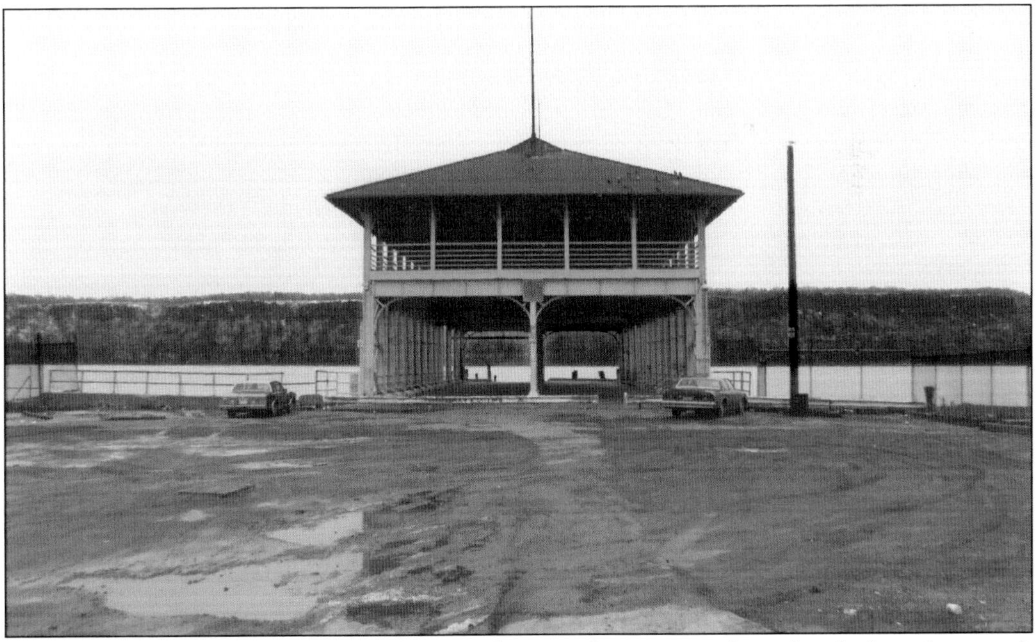

Pier 1977. For many years in the mid-1970s, the waterfront was neglected and relatively unused. This stark photograph of the pier shows a veritable wasteland around this old Victorian steel structure on the Hudson River. (Steve Asaro, architect.)

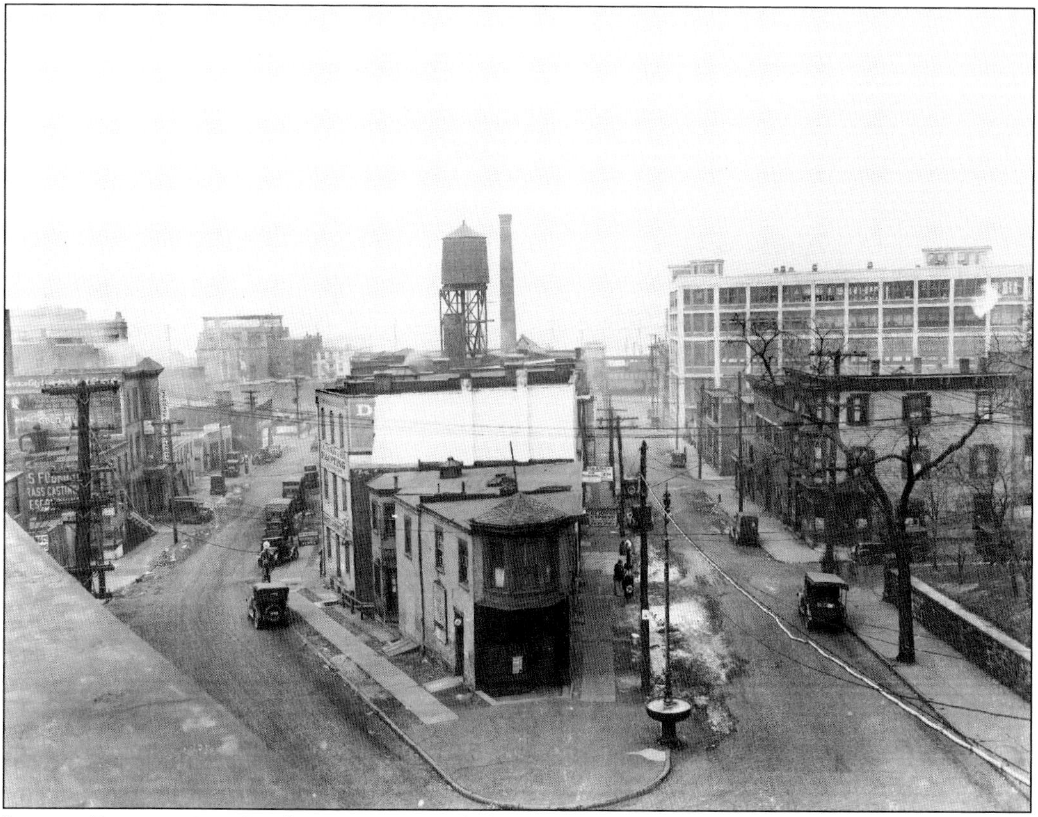

LARKIN PLAZA, 1910. Looking west toward the Hudson River, one can see how congested with buildings the area around the Saw Mill had been. Because of the triangular configuration of the buildings at the east end, it was called "the Wedge." (HRM.)

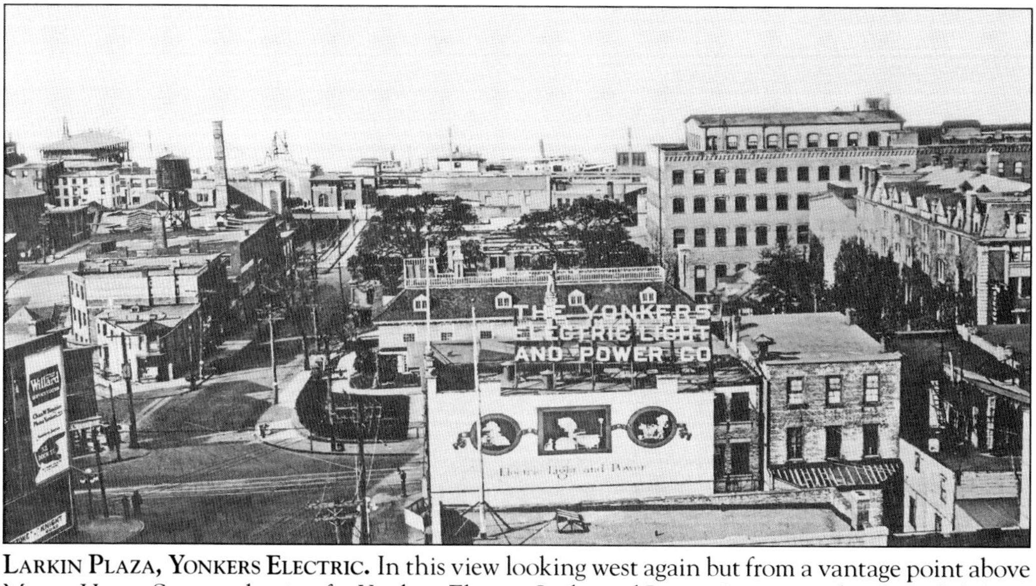

LARKIN PLAZA, YONKERS ELECTRIC. In this view looking west again but from a vantage point above Manor House Square, the sign for Yonkers Electric Light and Power Company, the roof of Philipse Manor, the Warburton Theater, and the Otis Elevator buildings can all be seen. (YHS.)

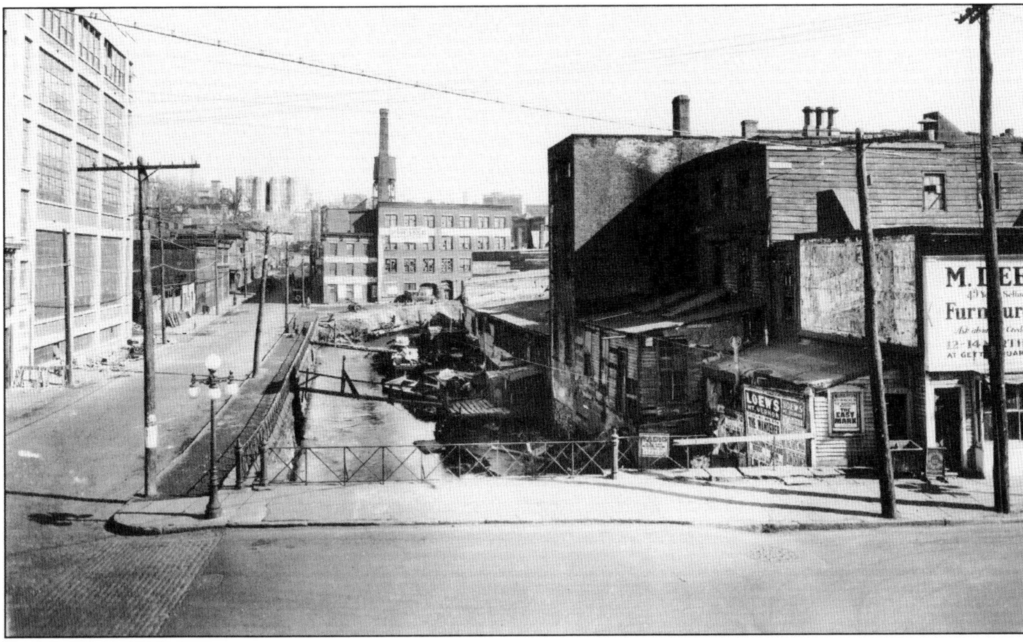

LARKIN PLAZA. Construction over the decades squeezed the Saw Mill River into narrower and narrower channels. The river can be seen on the left, along with Dock Street with one of the Otis Elevator buildings. (YHS.)

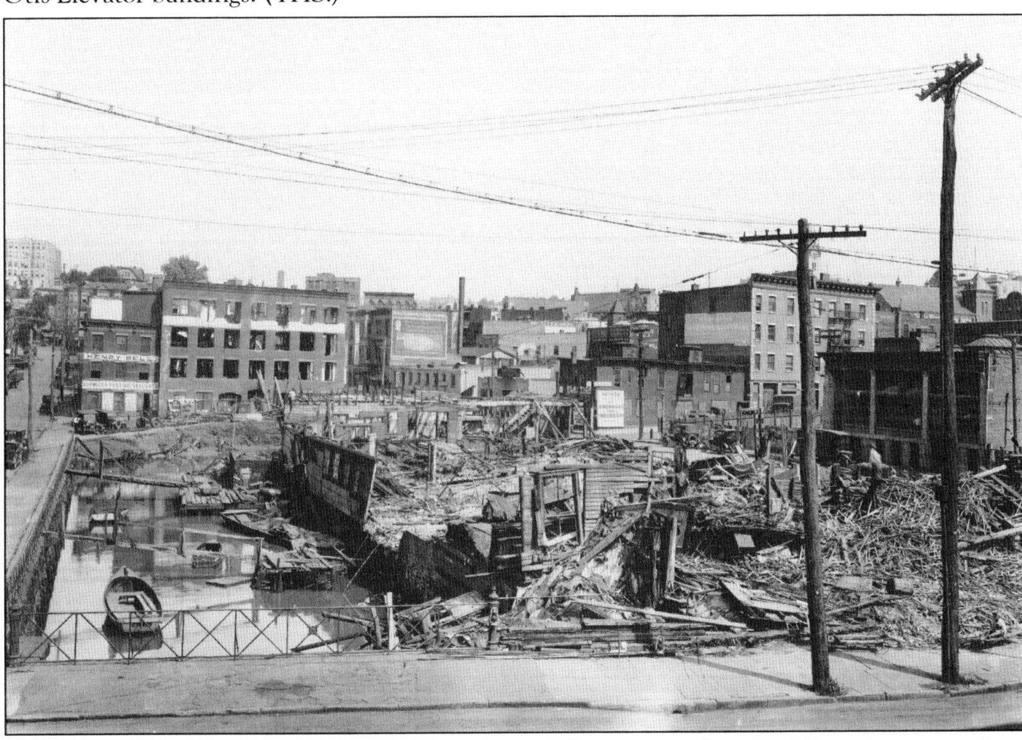

LARKIN PLAZA OPEN, SHOWING RIVER. Many of the surrounding buildings have now been demolished in preparation for installing the flume, covering the river, and paving it over for a park and parking lot. (YHS.)

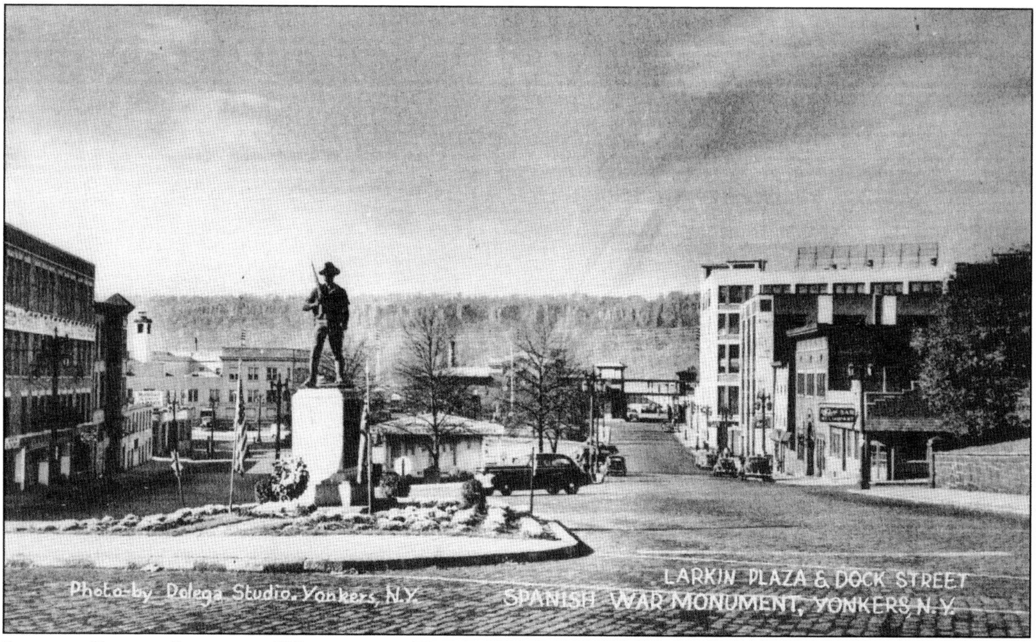

LARKIN PLAZA, LOOKING WEST, WITH *THE HIKER*. In a view looking west down Dock Street, the Spanish-American War memorial statue *The Hiker* takes center stage. The Yonkers gneiss walls of the Manor Hall can be seen on the right. (YHS.)

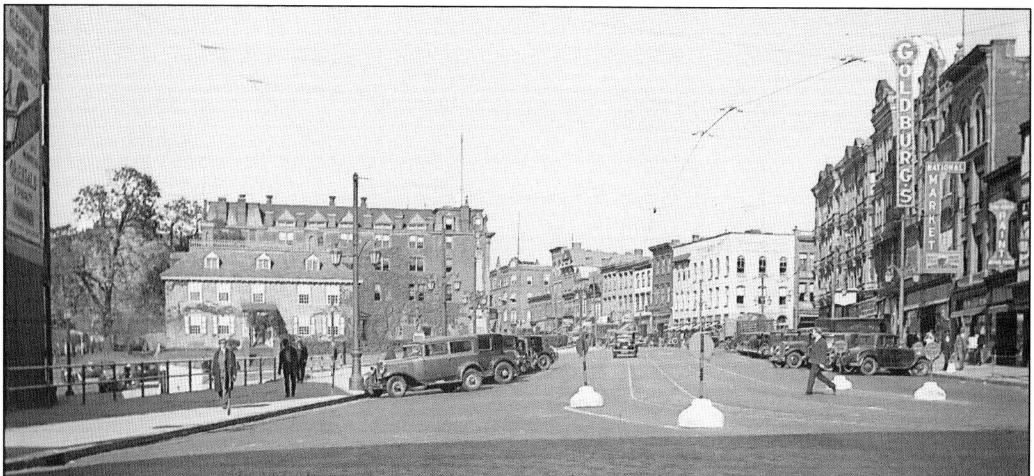

LARKIN PLAZA, LOOKING NORTH. Looking north up Warburton Avenue, one can see the Manor Hall with the Civil War Soldiers and Sailors Monument and the Warburton Theatre. Most of the buildings on the right still stand today. (YHS.)

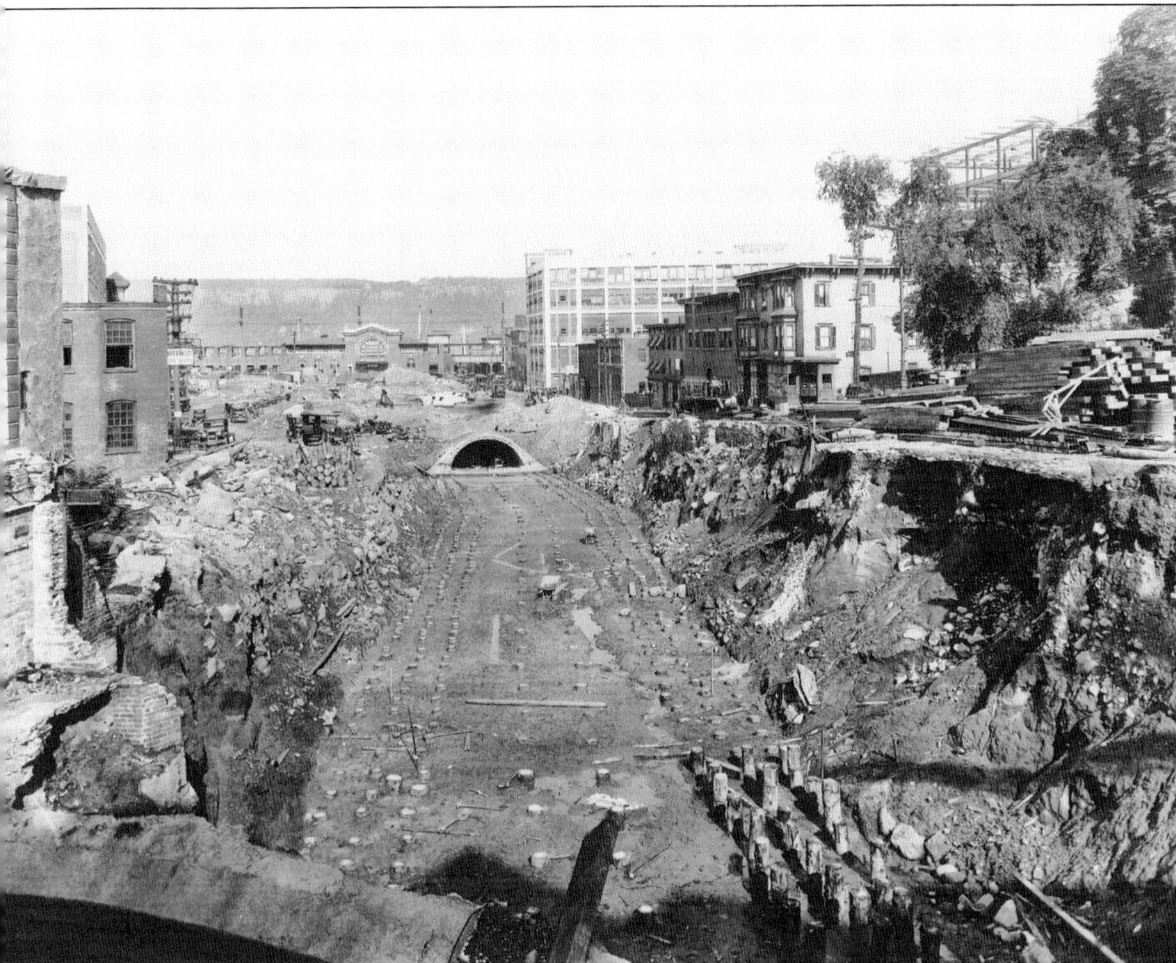

LARKIN PLAZA FLUME. A long view of the cleared plaza with the beginning of the placement of the flume is seen here. The river had been diverted until the flume was completely installed. (YHS.)

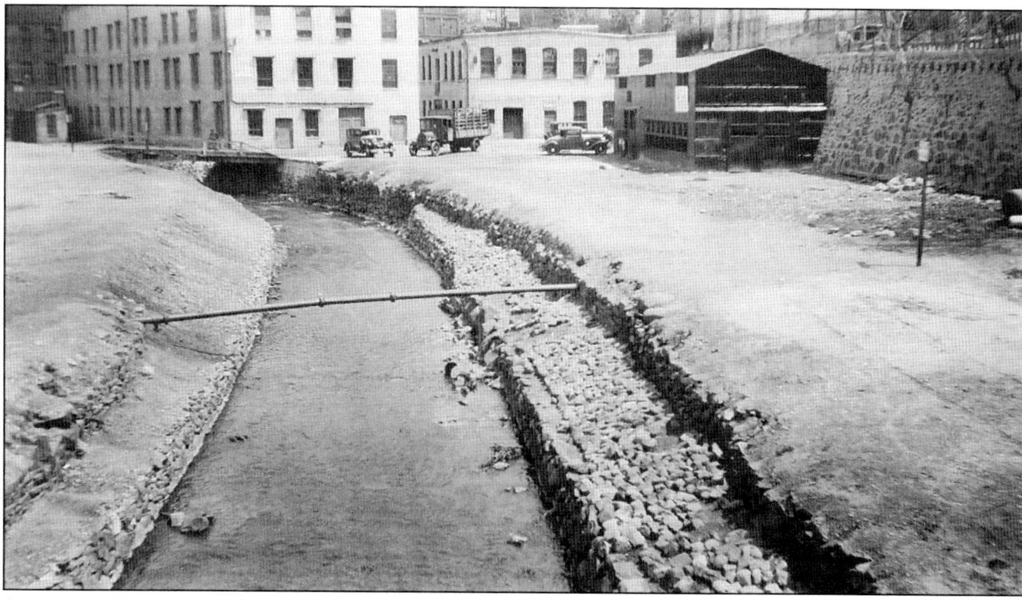

SAW MILL RIVER BEHIND THE FIREHOUSE. The Saw Mill River was also channeled into concrete troughs further up its length. This view is of the river behind the Yonkers Fire Department Headquarters Building on New School Street. (COY Planning.)

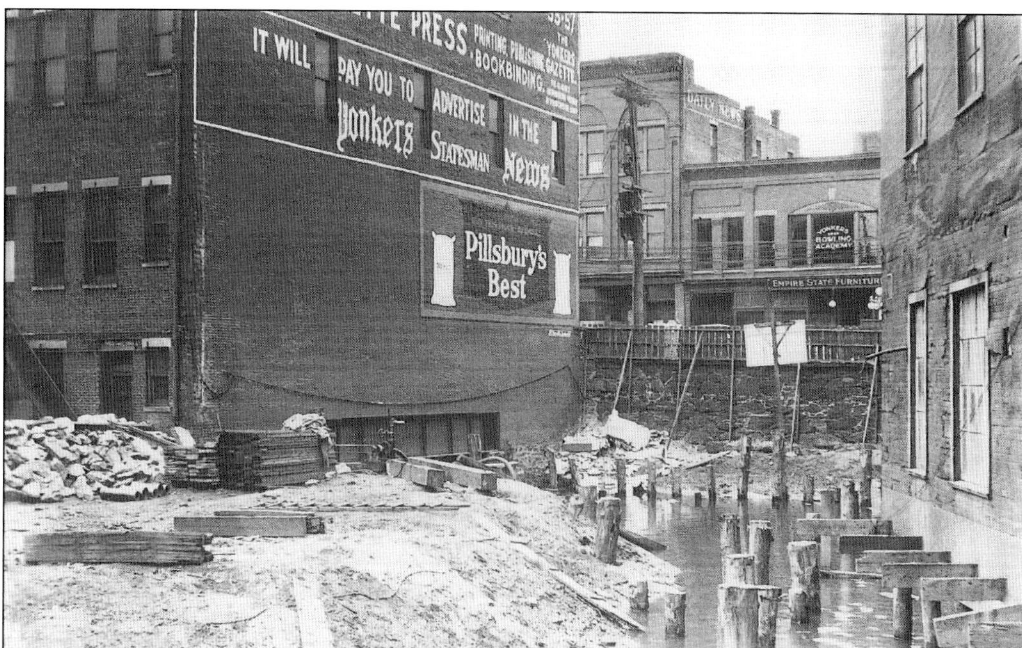

GAZETTE BUILDING ON MAIN STREET. The diverted river ran closer to Main Street. Look past the Gazette Building to see the buildings on Main. Interestingly, when the Gazette was being refurbished prior to its adaptive reuse as a restaurant, the Pillsbury Flour sign was still there and a glimpse of the running water of the river from openings in the basement could be seen. (YHS.)

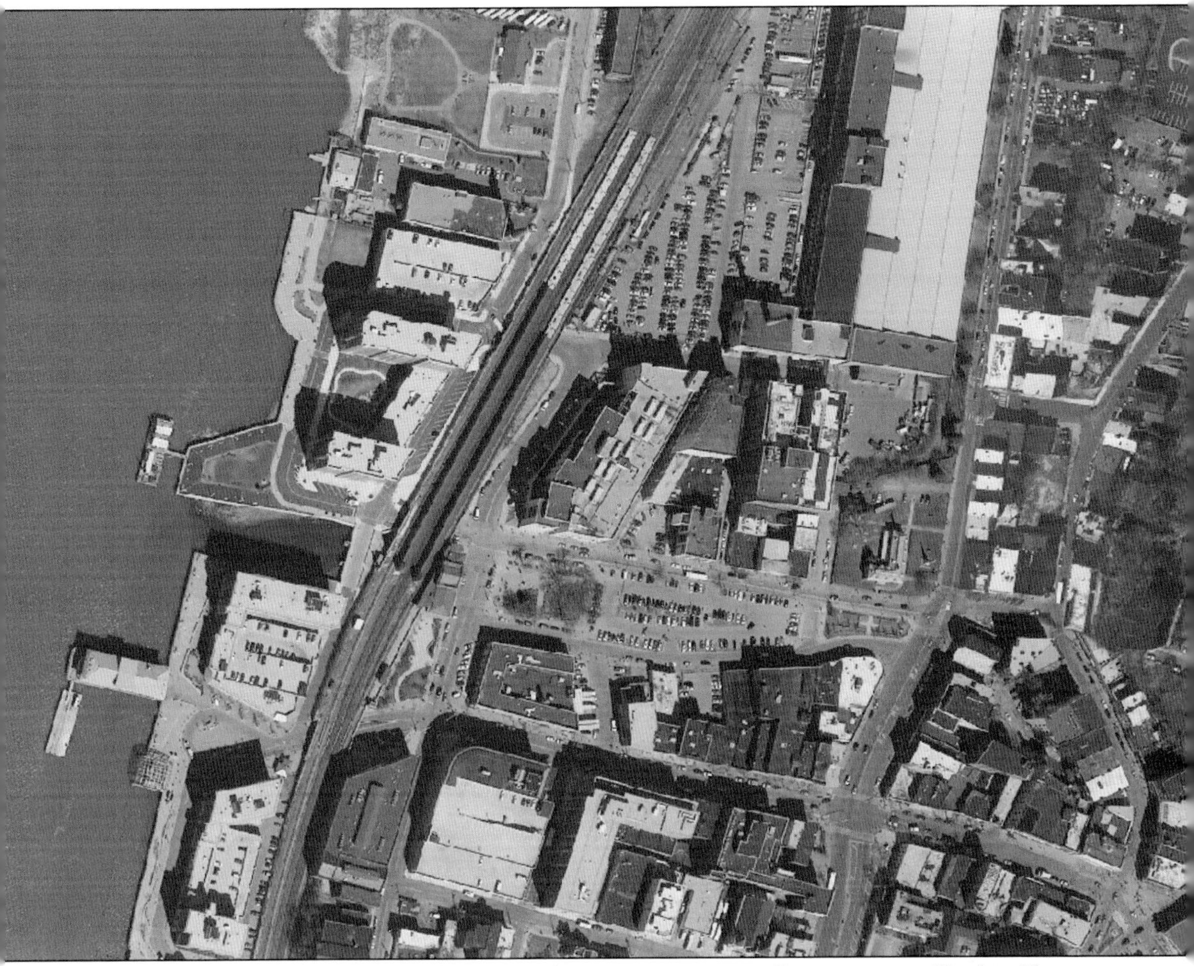

WATERFRONT AERIAL. This aerial, taken around 2010, gives an overall perspective of Larkin Plaza, the pier, and the waterfront. The large grayish buildings in the top center comprise the old Otis factory complex, now called iPark-on-Hudson. Note the location of the Yonkers Recreation Pier jutting out into the Hudson River; directly beneath the pier to its south is the amphitheater, utilized by the Yonkers Downtown/Waterfront Business Improvement District as a concert venue during summer months. Just to the north is the Science Barge, a self-sustaining, green-energy hydroponic farm. Note the parking lot to the right (east) of the pier and train tracks; it no longer exists, having been torn out to reveal the Saw Mill River that flows beneath it. The buildings to the south are slated for demolition to clear the property for a development project. (COY Planning.)

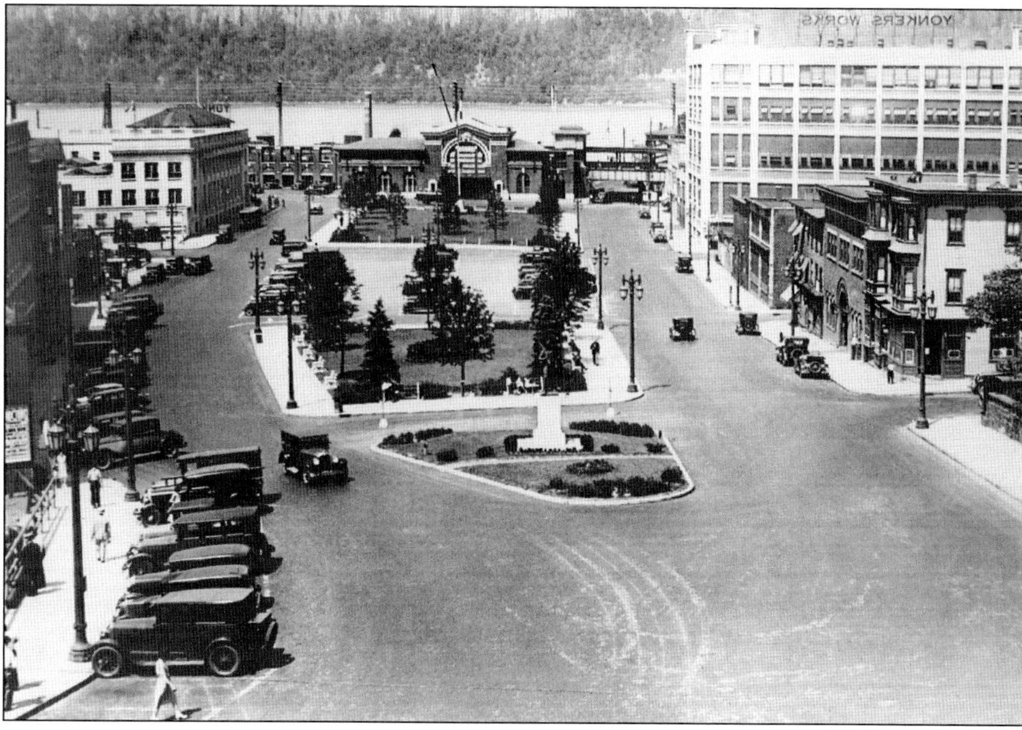

LARKIN PARK AND PLAZA. The so-called Wedge took on many different configurations over the decades. Taken in the early 1930s, this image shows the Otis Elevator Building to the right and the Main Yonkers Post Office on the left. The post office building, built in the late 1920s, remains basically unchanged, with the exception of small changes to the loading dock and was added to the National Register of Historic Places in 1989. (Flynn.)

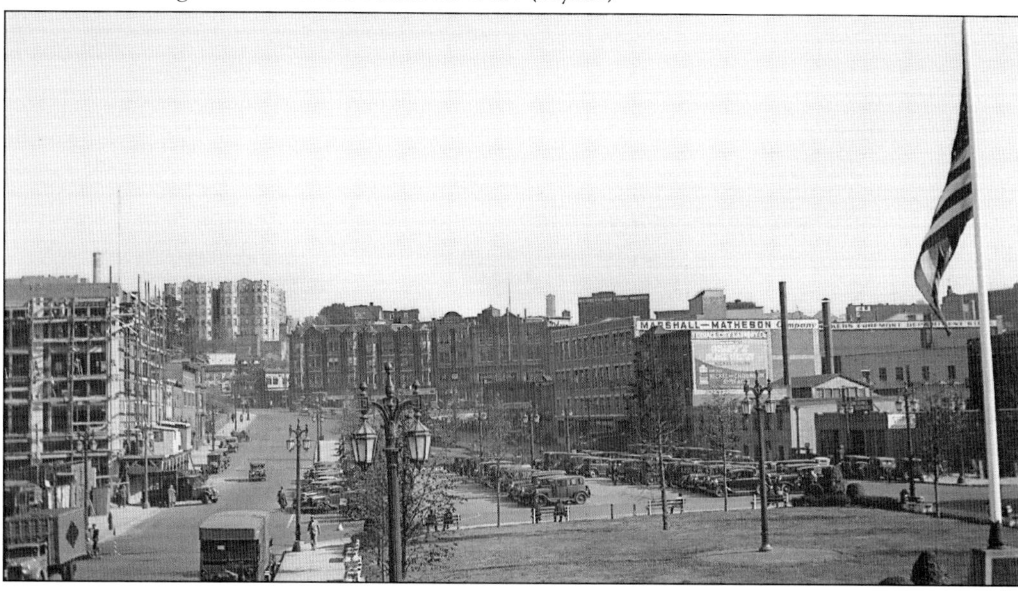

LARKIN PLAZA, LOOKING EAST. Larkin Plaza (in this view looking east, taken at approximately the same year) continues to evolve. The building under construction with scaffolding on the left would become the home of the daily Yonkers newspaper, the *Herald Statesman*. (COY Planning.)

LARKIN PLAZA, 1940s. Note that many of the parklike features of Larkin Plaza have been given over to parking in this photograph from the late 1940s. The demand for parking near train stations and other mass transportation modes continues to increase. (COY Planning.)

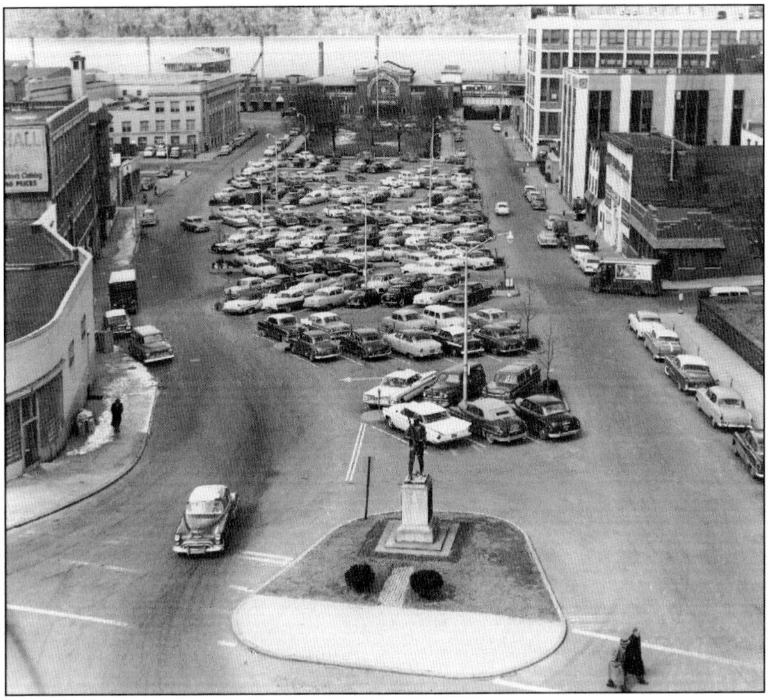

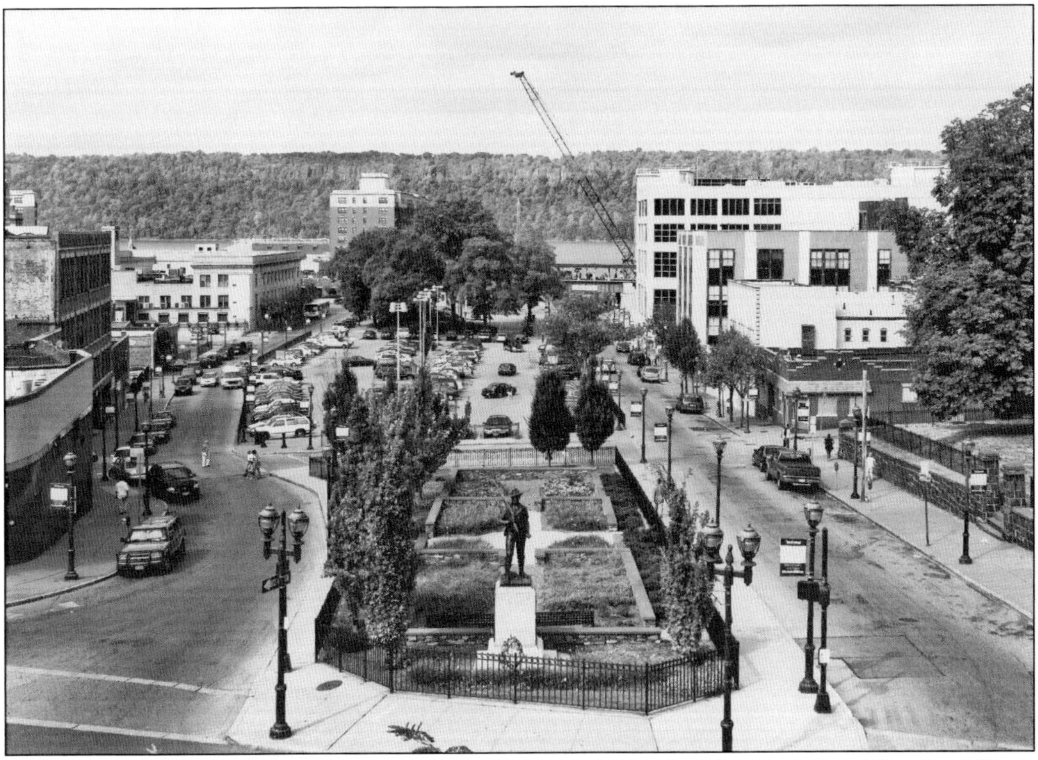

LARKIN PLAZA, 2003. Note that many second stories of the buildings on the right along Dock Street have been lost to fires and other causes. The parking lot has been reconfigured yet again, but now more park has been added to the eastern end. (Joan Jennings.)

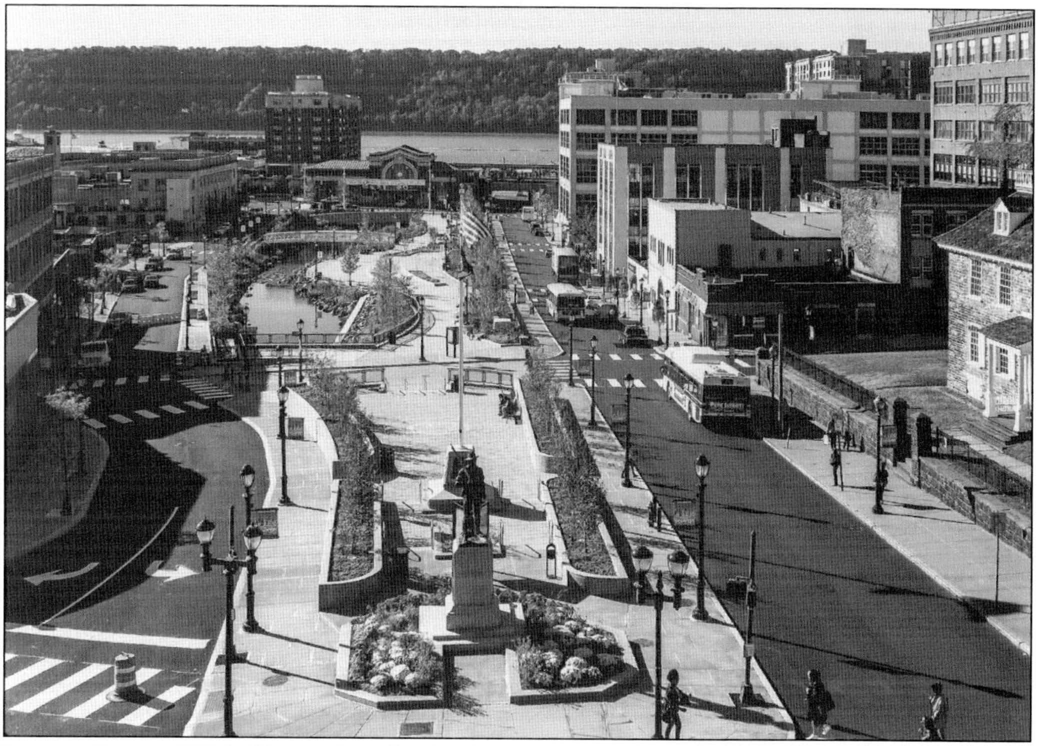

LARKIN PLAZA, 2012. The parking lot has been torn up, the concrete pavement removed, and the river opened (daylighted) in one of the most ambitious projects to return an area to its natural state. (Jim Pinto.)

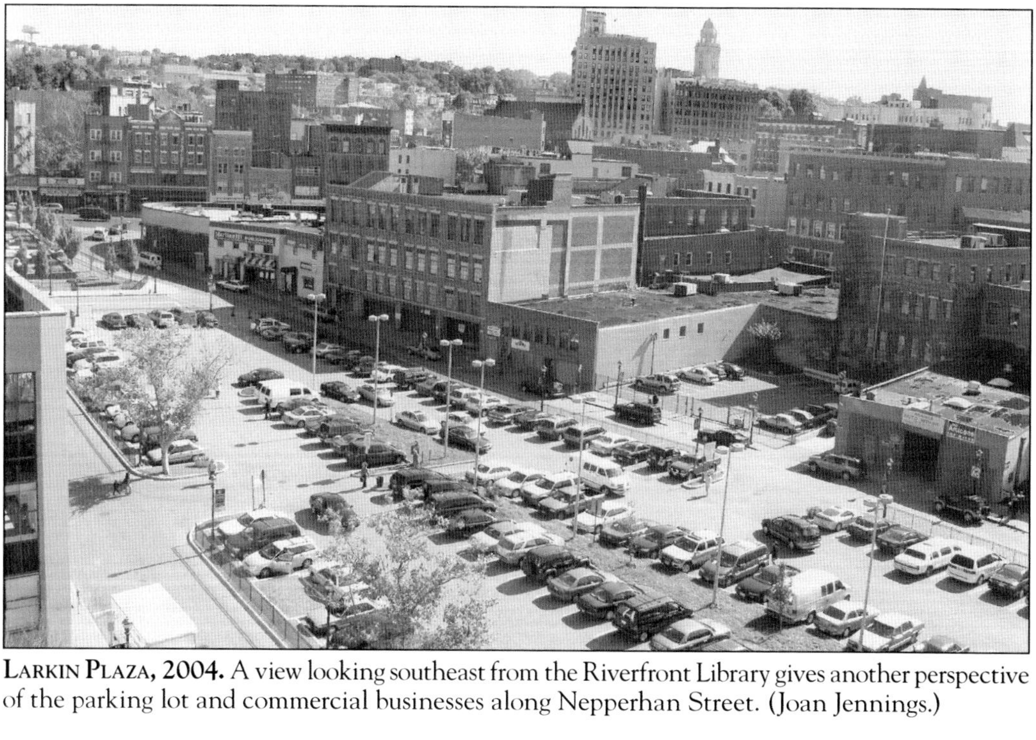

LARKIN PLAZA, 2004. A view looking southeast from the Riverfront Library gives another perspective of the parking lot and commercial businesses along Nepperhan Street. (Joan Jennings.)

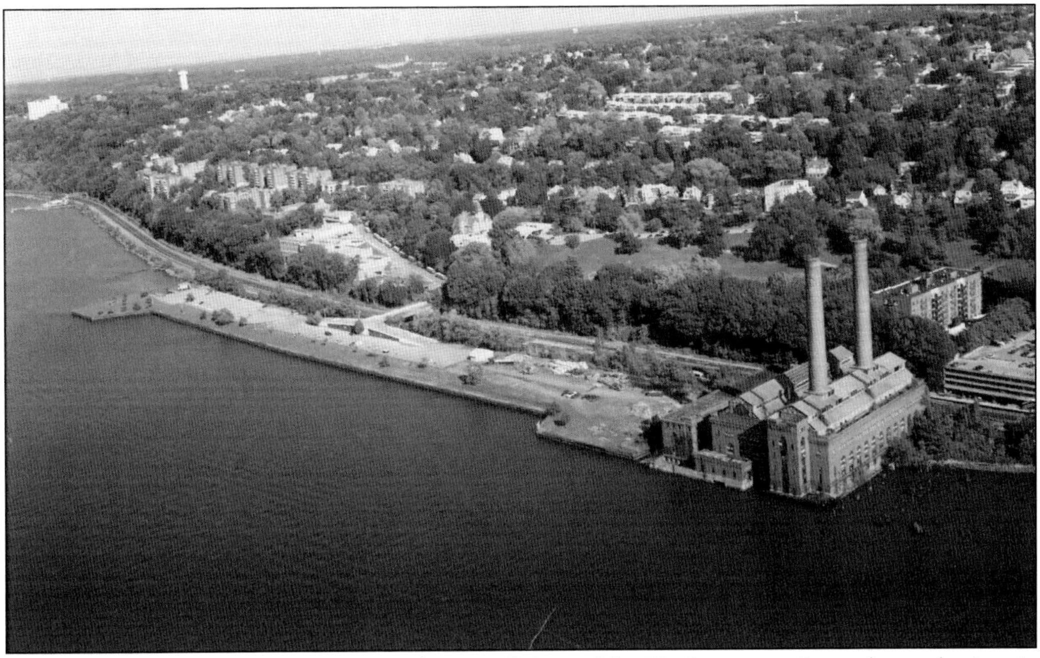

John F. Kennedy Marina Aerial. This aerial shot of the Yonkers waterfront shows the iconic Glenwood Power Plant with its two large brick smokestacks. A marina named for late Pres. John F. Kennedy has a boat ramp. Directly to the east of the marina is the former Glenview Mansion and its modern annex comprising the Hudson River Museum. (YHS.)

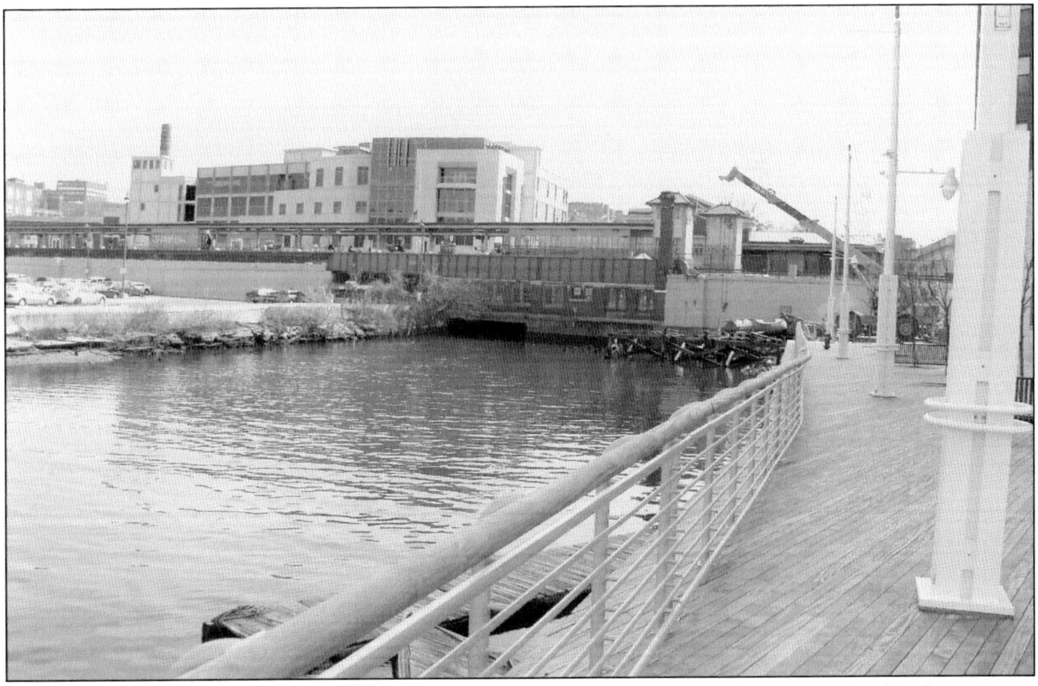

Saw Mill Outflow into the Hudson. The Saw Mill River outflow into the Hudson River travels under the main Yonkers Train Station. The new Riverfront Library is in the center, and a boardwalk has been built. (Joan Jennings.)

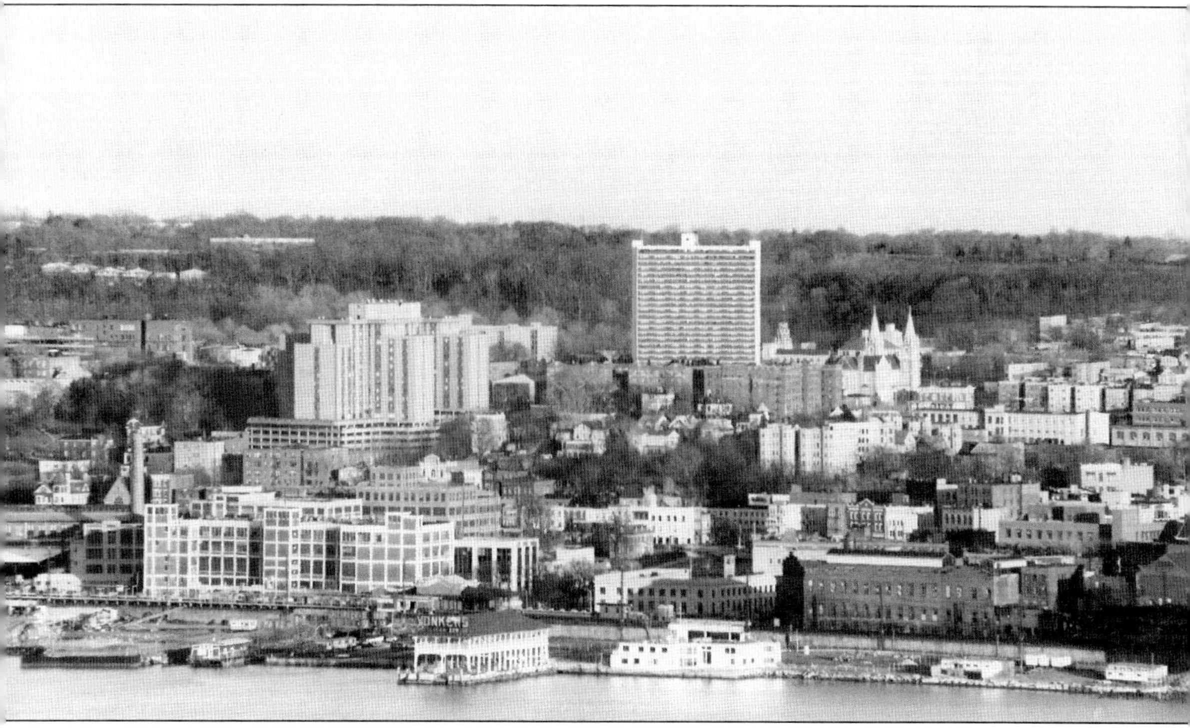

YONKERS PANORAMA TAKEN FROM THE PALISADES. This shot taken from the Palisades shows the Yonkers waterfront in the 1970s prior to the extensive development. Note the open pier, the remaining small industrial buildings on the riverfront, two high-rise apartment buildings, and the distinctive spires of St. Casimir's Church. (COY Planning.)

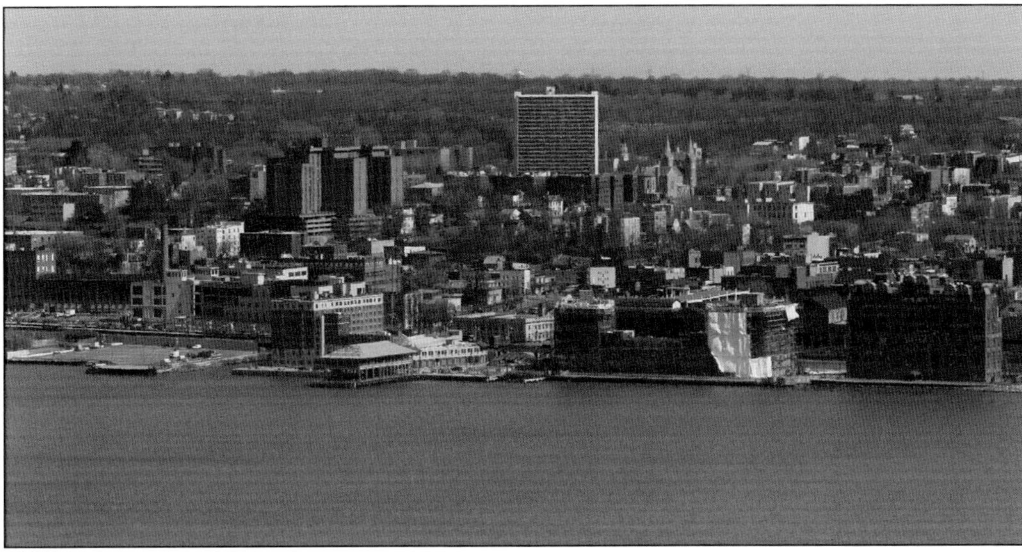

YONKERS FROM THE PALISADES, 2003. Looking east across the Hudson River, this view shows the new market-rate housing under construction on the waterfront. An old power station, adaptively reused as loft apartments, can be seen in the lower right. An Otis Elevator building, newly renovated, now houses the Riverfront Library and the headquarters for the Yonkers Board of Education. (Joan Jennings.)

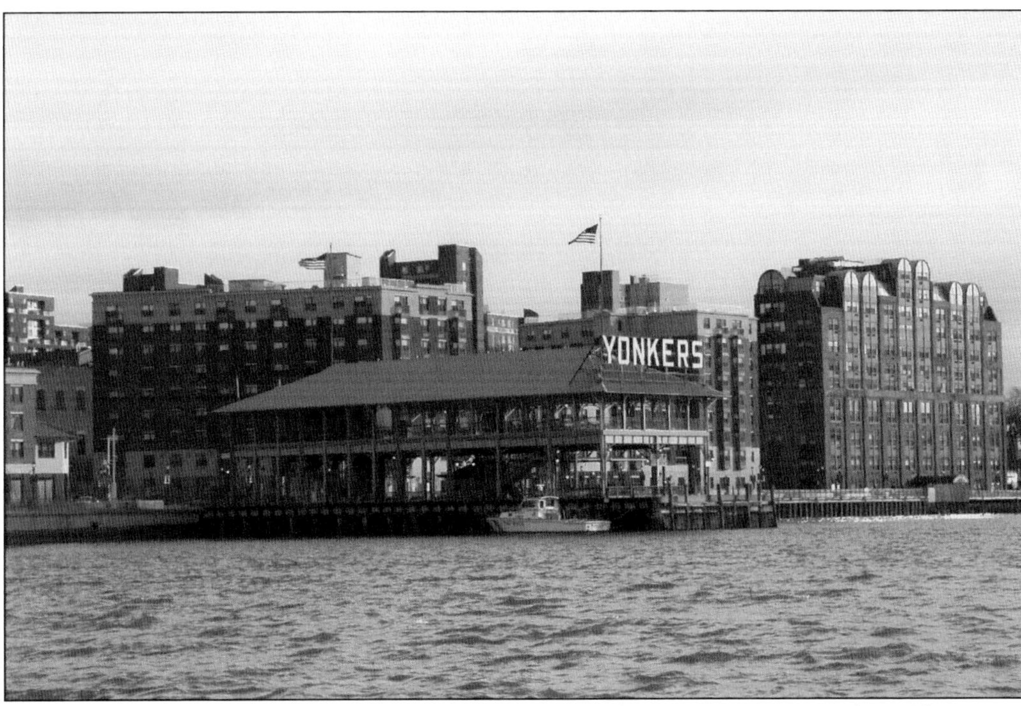

YONKERS PIER AND WATERFRONT. The new market-rate housing is now complete. This image, taken from the Hudson River with a view looking south, shows the historic Yonkers sign and a Yonkers fireboat docked at the pier. (Joan Jennings.)

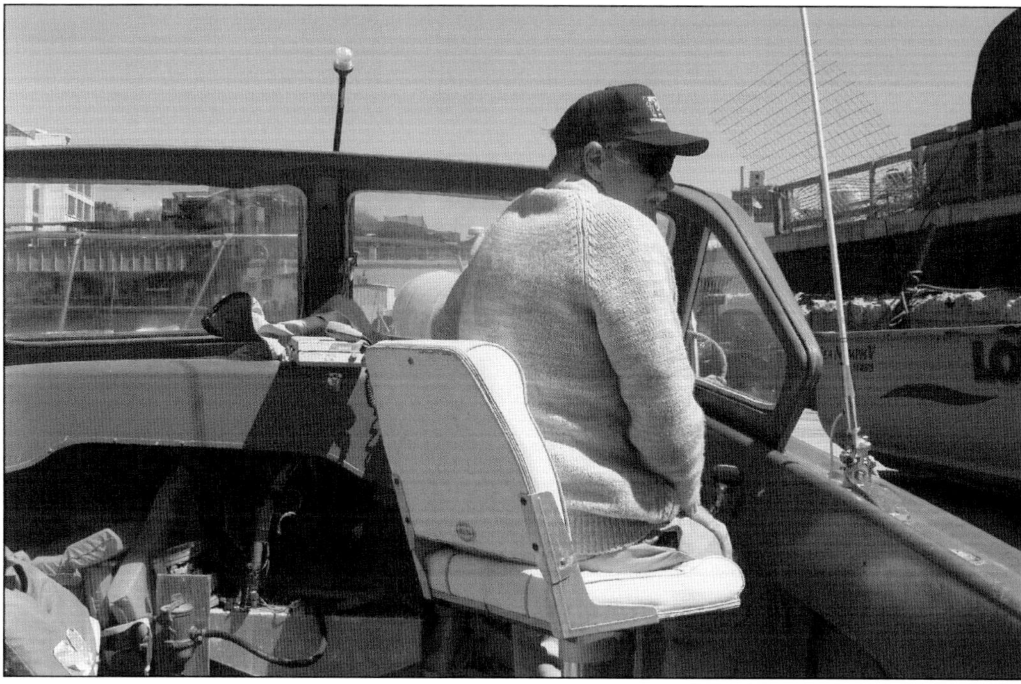

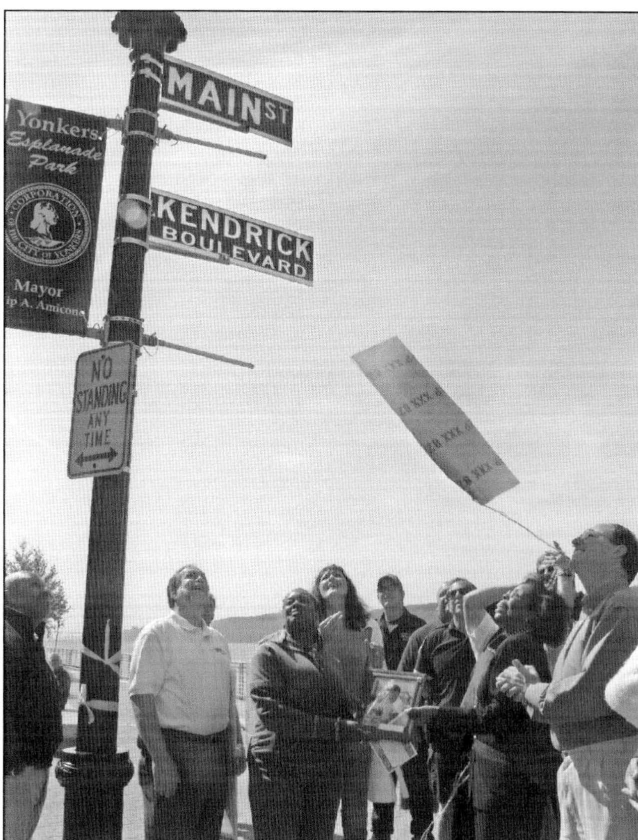

FRANK KENDRICK IN BOAT. Frank Kendrick and his wife, Kay, lived on the Yonkers waterfront from 1952, and they were the Yonkers Volunteer Life Saving Corps. On September 11, 2002, Frank dove into the frigid and choppy Hudson River to rescue a woman and he himself drowned. He is considered a hero of the Yonkers waterfront. (Kay Kendrick.)

KENDRICK BOULEVARD UNVEILING. Yonkers city officials unveil the commemorative sign naming the street Frank Kendrick Boulevard in Frank's honor during Yonkers Riverfest in September 2006. (Joan Jennings.)

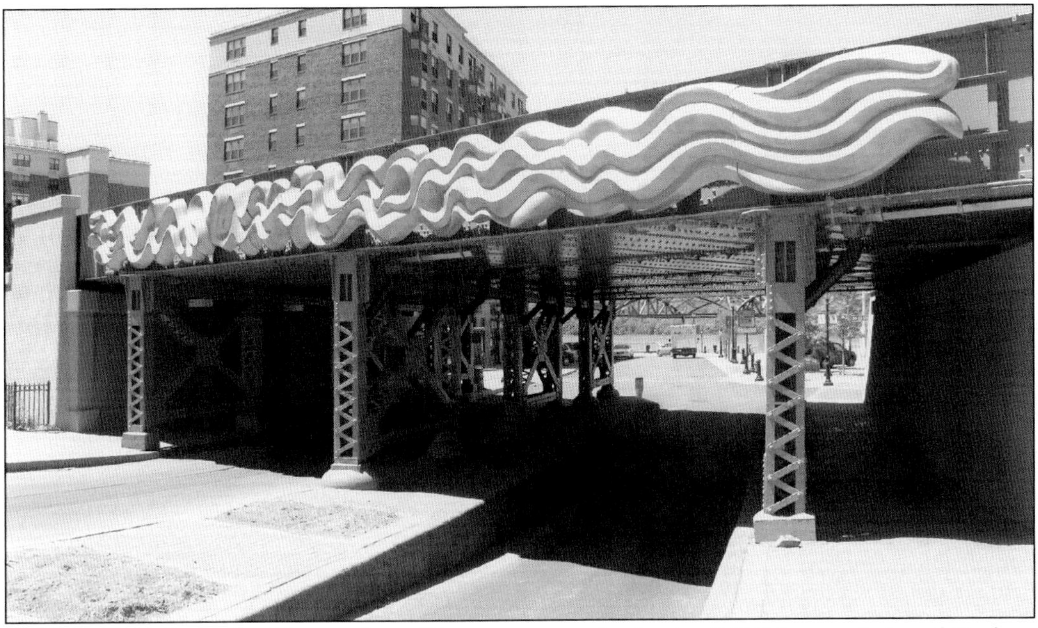

Muhheakantuck. The Metropolitan Transportation Authority (MTA) commissioned Yonkers sculptor Barbara Segal to design and install her cast aluminum interpretation of the river. It is titled *Muhheakantuck*, the Native American designation for the Hudson River, which means "river that flows both ways," a tidal feature characteristic of estuaries like the Hudson. (Joan Jennings.)

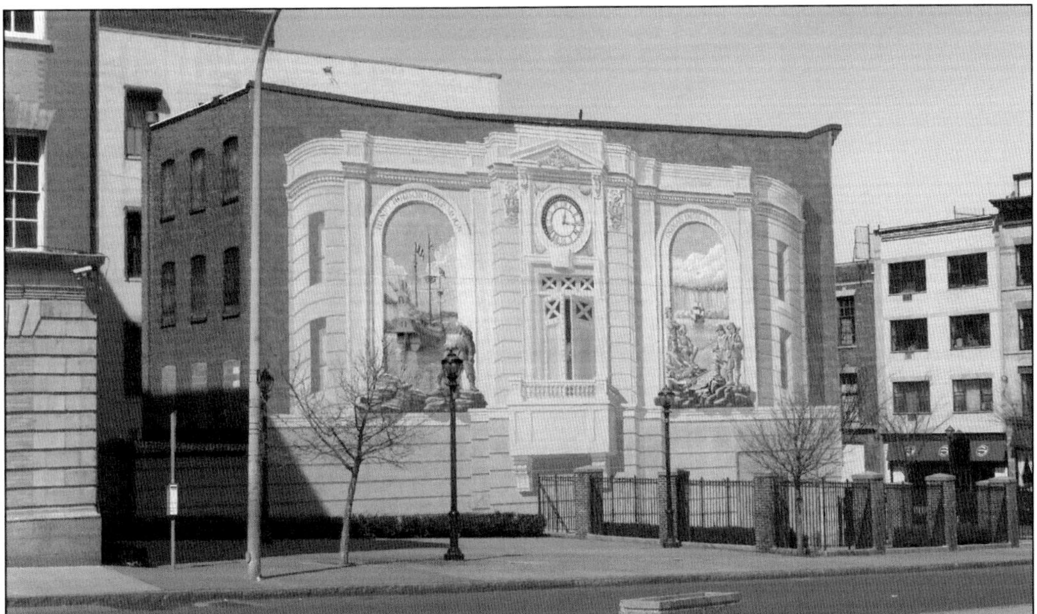

Gateway to the Hudson River. In 1995, Yonkers muralist Richard Haas, famous for his trompe l'oeil ("fool the eye") murals, painted this extensive series of panels representing various early scenes from Yonkers history. The man in a dinner jacket peeking through the door is purportedly Yonkers Prohibition-era bootlegger "Dutch" Schultz. (Joan Jennings.)

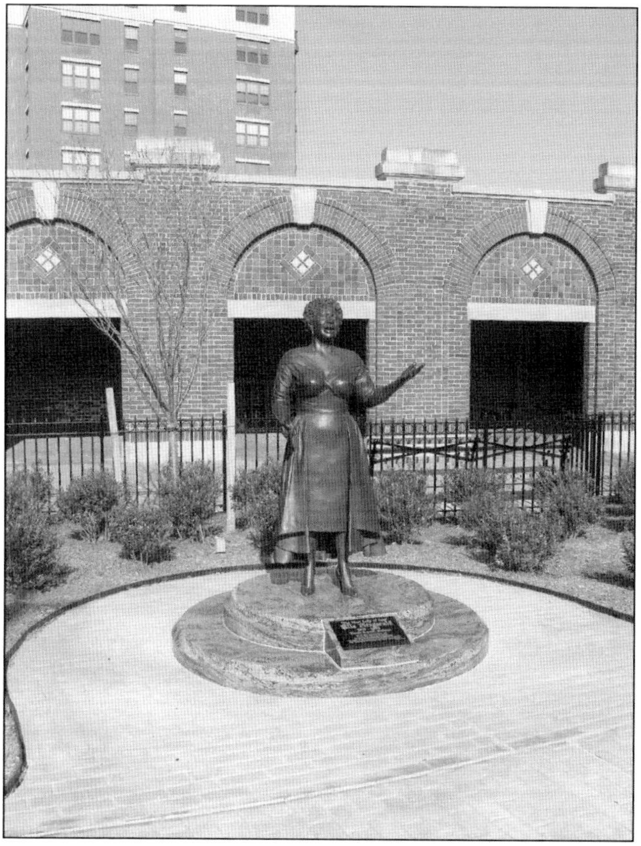

"The First Lady of Jazz" Ella Fitzgerald. Famous jazz singer Ella Fitzgerald spent much of her childhood in Yonkers, attending School 10, which was located at Riverdale Avenue and Prospect Street. Yonkers sculptor Vinnie Bagwell created this large bronze statue, which stands in Tobin Plaza adjacent to the Yonkers Train Station. (Joan Jennings.)

Gold Star Mothers. The Gold Star Mother designation was created during World War II to recognize the sacrifice of mothers who had lost a child in combat. Placed near the train that carried so many youths to war, the bronze figure of a woman is seated holding a folded American flag, as if waiting for a child who was never to return, and flanked by two carved granite slabs. (Joan Jennings.)

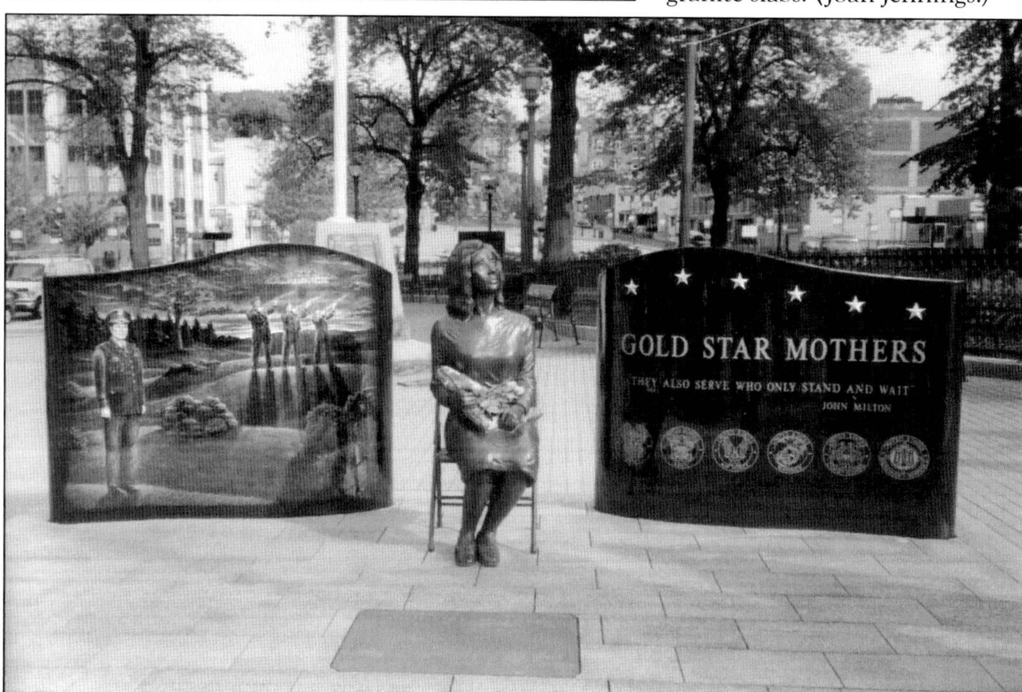

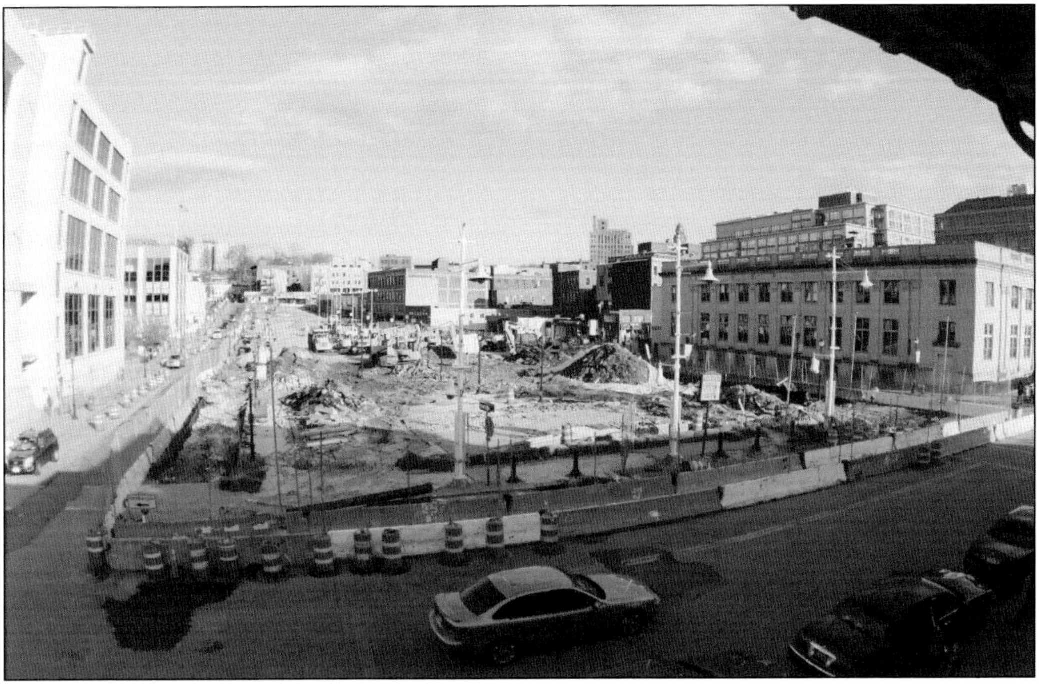

Opening the Flume, Looking East from Train Station. In 2010, work to tear up the concrete parking lot in Larkin Plaza was started. This image was taken from the vantage of the platform of the main Yonkers Train Station. (Jim Pinto.)

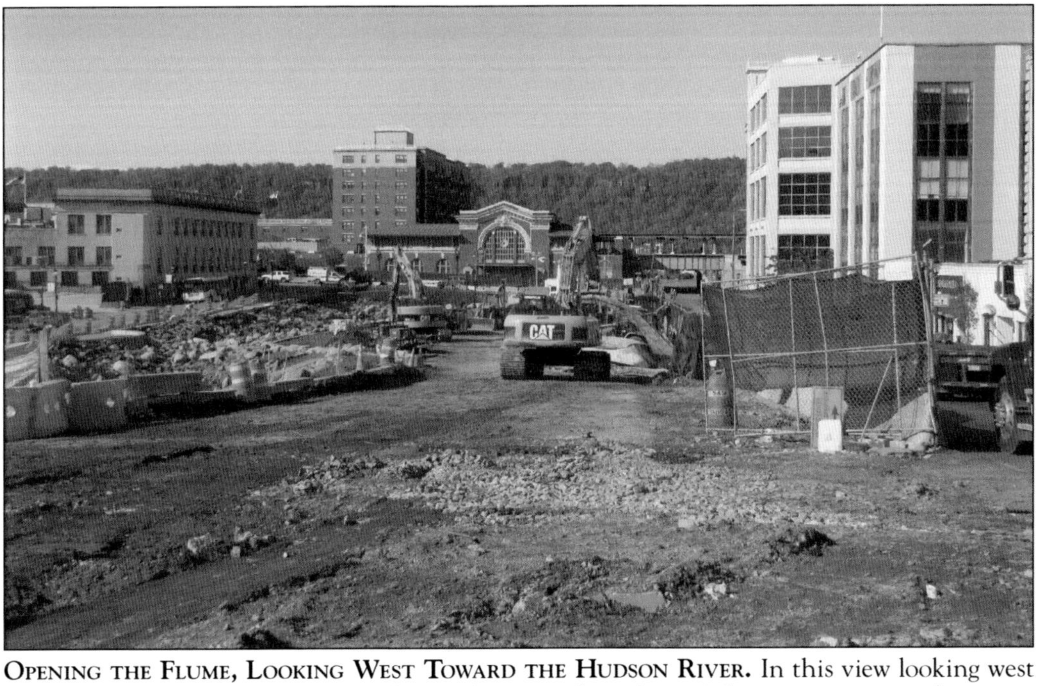

Opening the Flume, Looking West Toward the Hudson River. In this view looking west toward the Hudson River, the Riverfront Library on the right and the train station in the center can both be seen. Soon, the bulldozers would unearth the flume installed by the Army Corps of Engineers in the early 1920s and remove it. (Jim Pinto.)

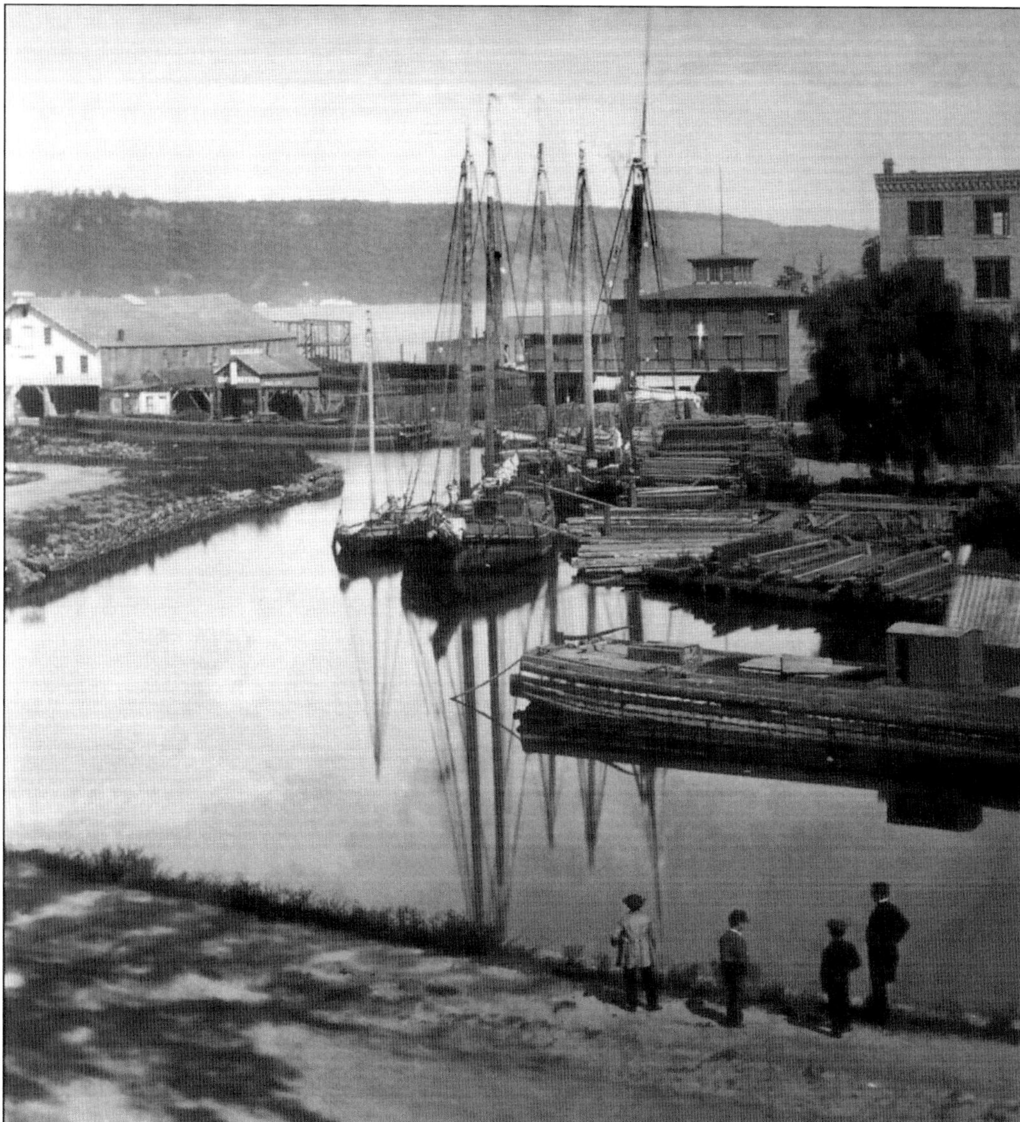

STEREO. Stereo photographs, taken with cameras with two lenses positioned much like two human eyes, created two almost identical images, which would become three-dimensional when viewed in a stereopticon. These images were immensely popular souvenirs, and stereopticons were the iPads of the Victorian era. William England toured the United States in 1859, taking stereos printed using an albumin emulsion, which were later hand-tinted. He published a book called *An American Journey*, which shows his photographs. This single image (to show more detail) from one of his stereos is one of the earliest photographs of the Saw Mill River and clearly shows the functioning sawmills that gave the river its name. (FPMH.)

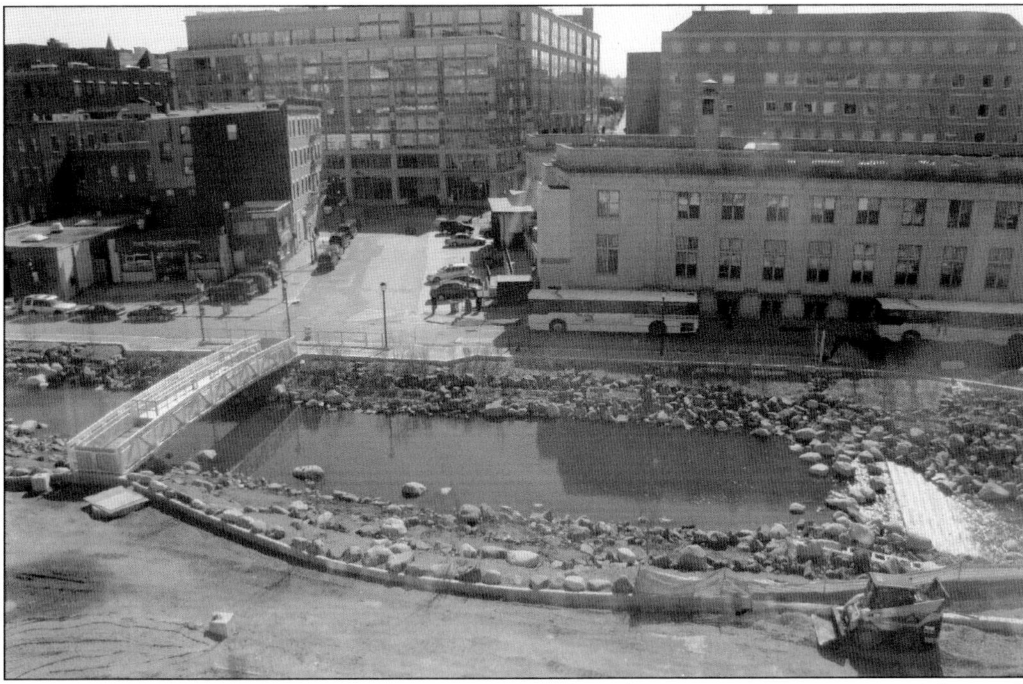

VAN DER DONCK PARK, LOOKING SOUTH. The river breathes again as construction of the newly engineered Van der Donck Park takes shape. Note the bridge to facilitate crossing the river from Market Street to Dock Street and the library and the small waterfall that contains a fish ladder to assist the American eel's migration up the river after spawning in the Sargasso Sea. (Joan Jennings.)

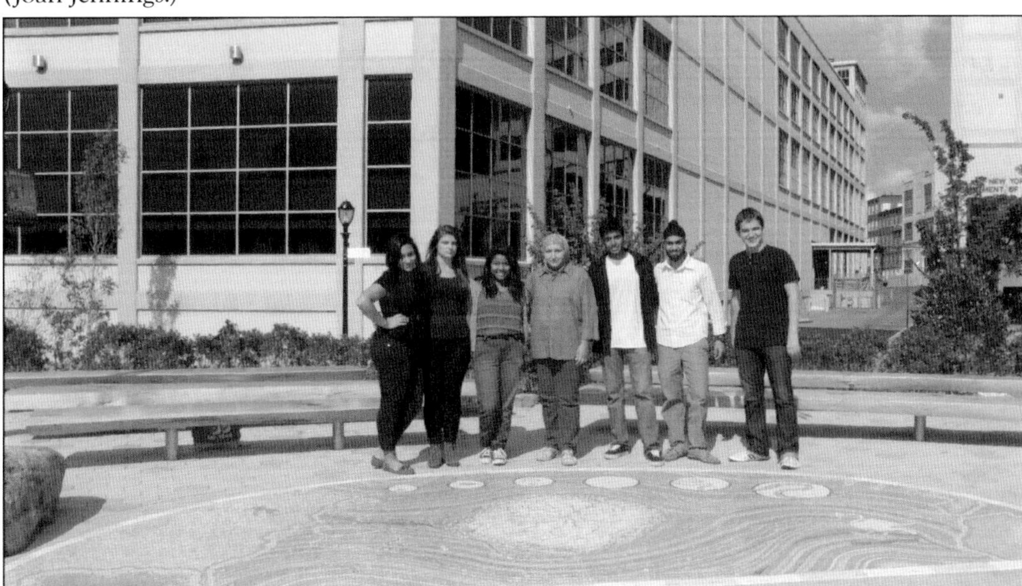

AMERICAN EEL MIGRATION MOSAIC. Yonkers mosaic artist Haifa Bint-Kadi and Yonkers high school interns installed an elaborate mosaic in the new park showing the migration patterns of the American eel, which is the only fish that grows up in freshwater and spawns in salt water. (Haifa Bint-Kadi.)

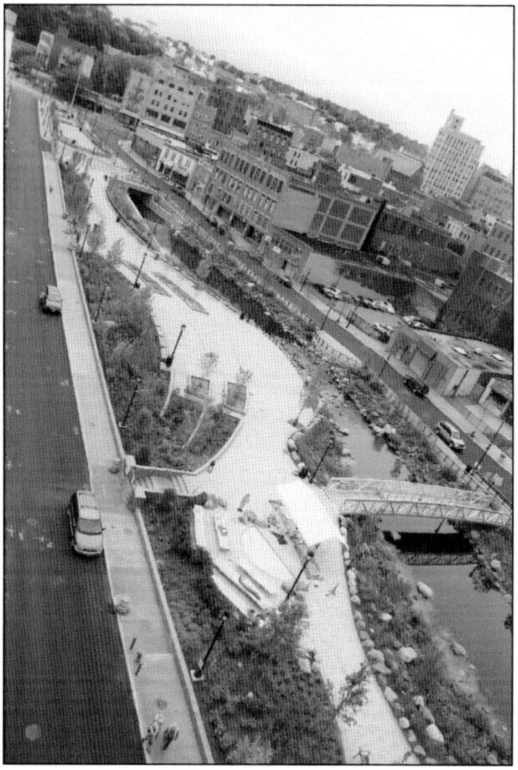

VAN DER DONCK PARK, LOOKING SOUTHEAST. During the final construction phase of Van der Donck Park, the finishing touches were put in place. The Friends of Philipse Manor Hall, the Yonkers Historical Society, and Groundwork Hudson Valley, in concert with the City of Yonkers Planning Department, created educational panels to explain the different facets that came into play in bringing this small but historically important part of Yonkers to the point where it is now. (Susan Thaler.)

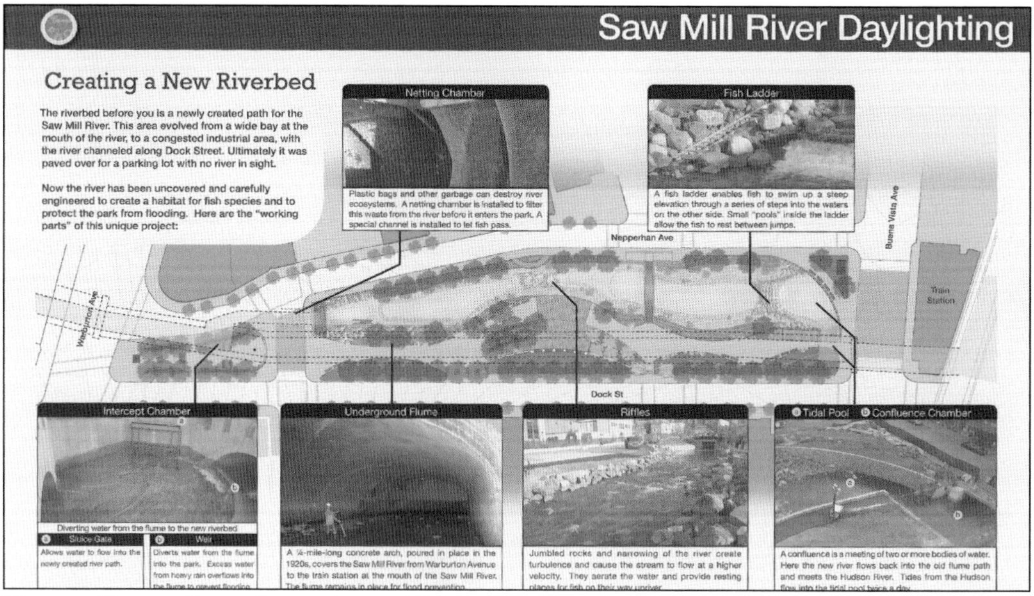

VAN DER DONCK PARK COMES ALIVE. This informational plaque details the engineering features in the new Van der Donck Park: showing a man standing in the river as it comes through the flume, netting chambers to capture trash, the fish ladder to facilitate the migration of native species, and a rendering of the park. Yonkers has come full circle—from its early Dutch roots with the first sawmill built by Adriaen Van der Donck to the state-of-the-art Van der Donck Park. (Groundwork Hudson Valley.)

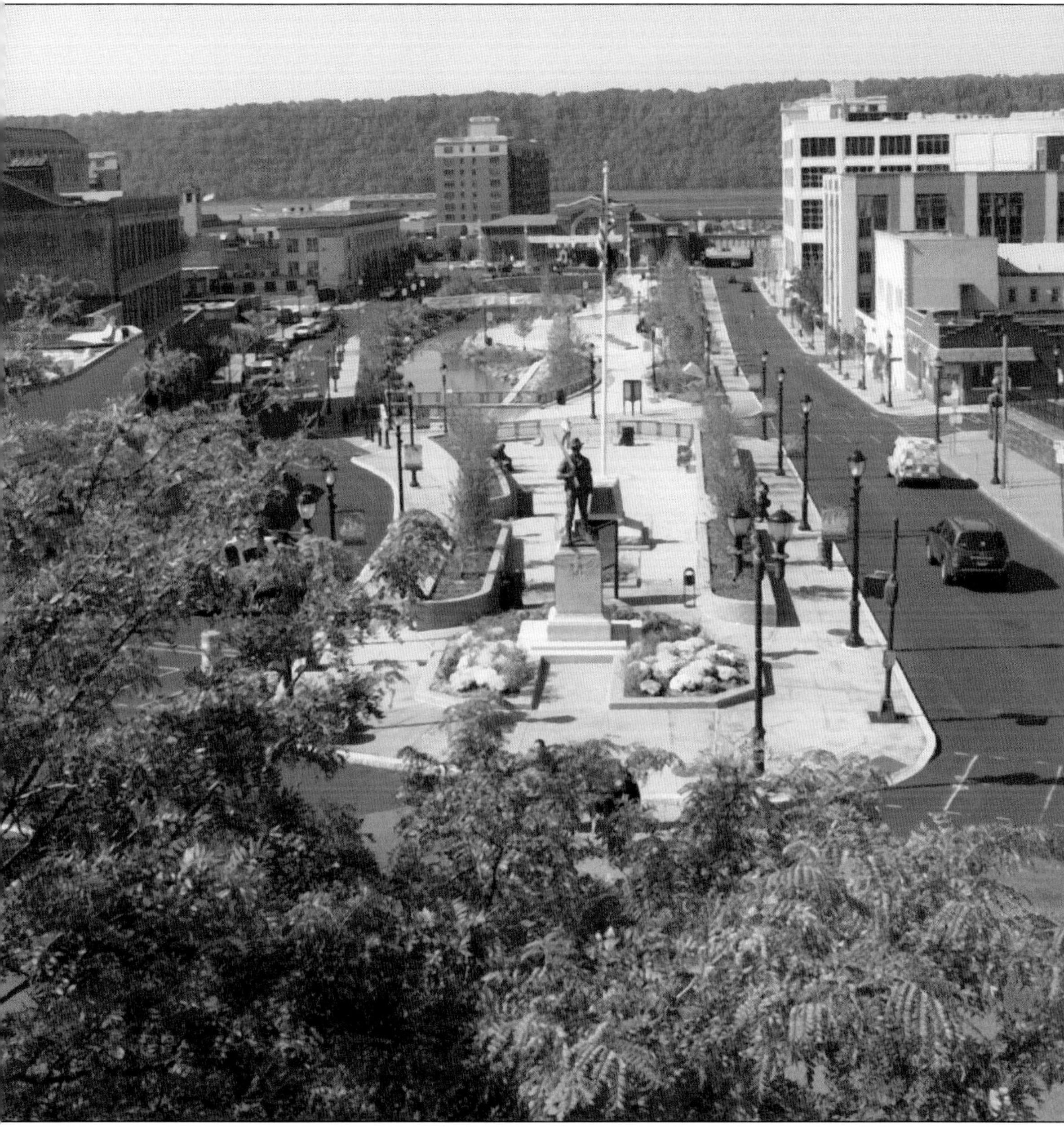

VAN DER DONCK PARK, LOOKING WEST. The more things change, the more they remain the same. Looking west from Warburton Avenue toward the Hudson River over the newly daylighted Saw Mill River, the view basically is closest to that of the one from the early 20th century. The parking lot is gone and was replaced by the Saw Mill River, open to the air as it was 100 years ago in 1912, except that the river is now totally contained in Van der Donck Park rather than running under the buildings bordering on Main Street. Engineering was done for flood control, netting chambers to trap debris and trash were installed, and educational panels and kiosks were installed around the river to explain the history, the industrial past, the ecology, and how what the view looks at was built. From Van der Donck to Van der Donck Park—400 years in the making. (Jim Pinto.)